MANINTHEMIDDLE

*A Year's Travels and
Adventures at or Near
The Equator*

RICHARD WARD

RolyPoly Press

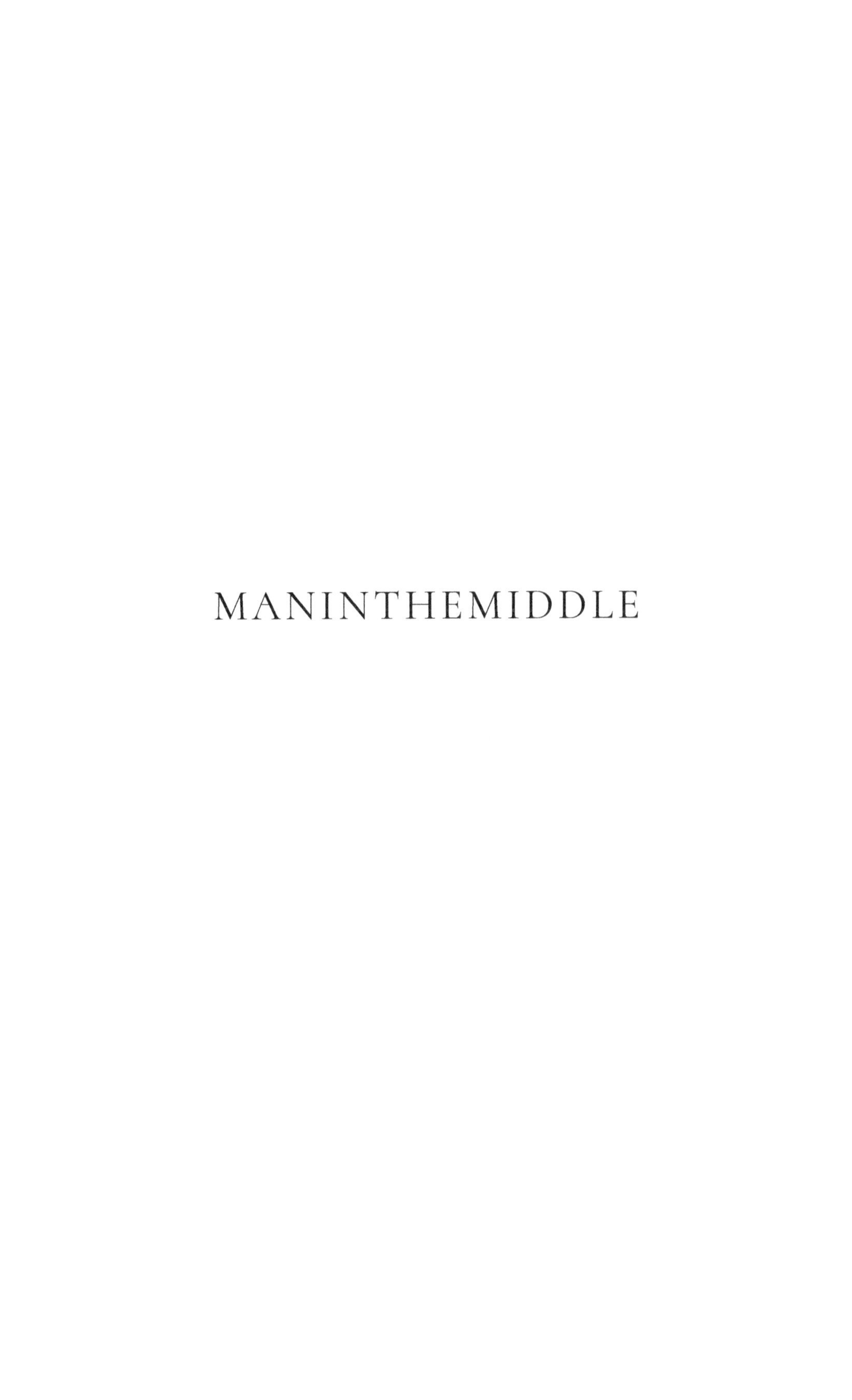

MANINTHEMIDDLE

Contents

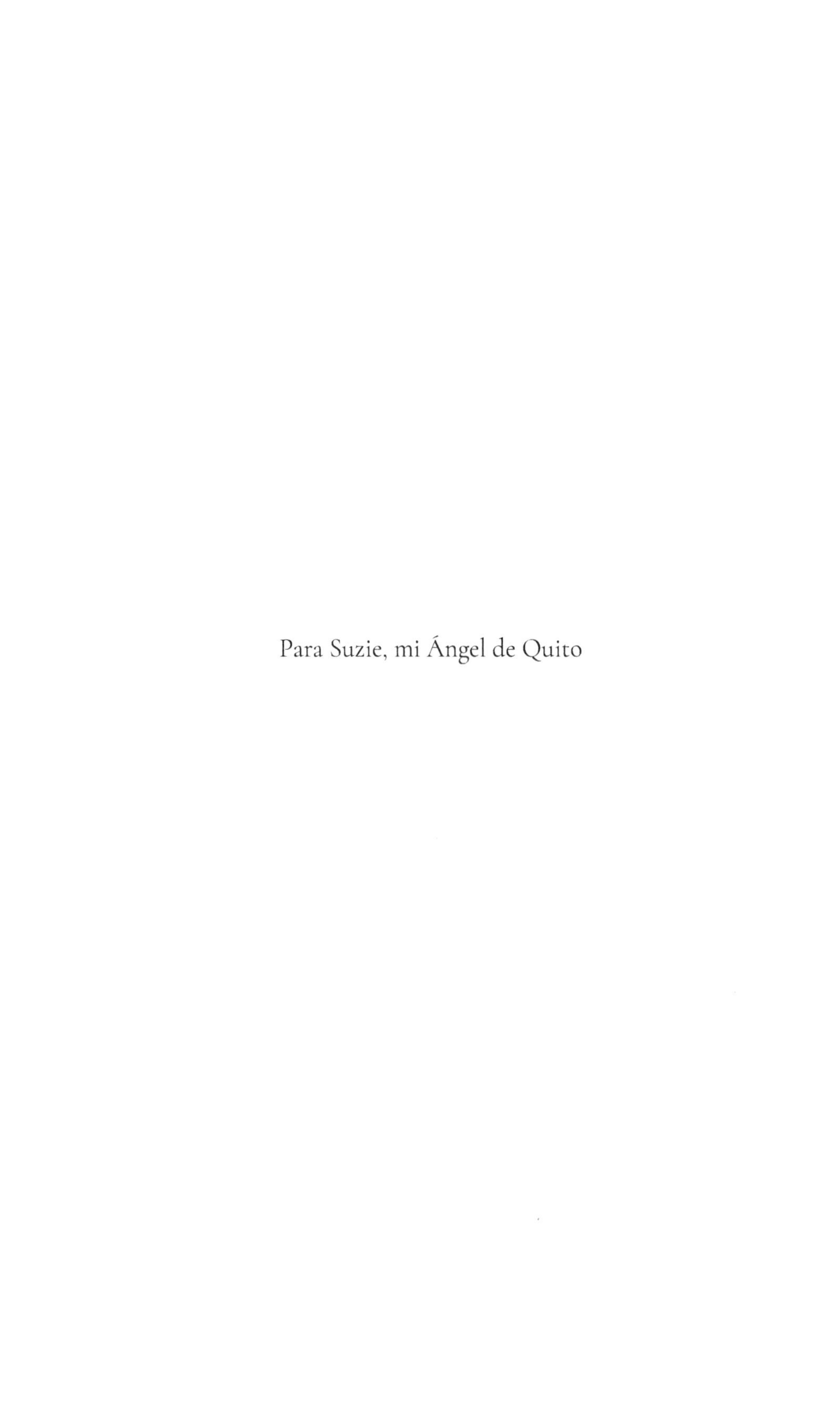

Para Suzie, mi Ángel de Quito

NOTE

MANINTHEMIDDLE is an account of my first trip to Ecuador from July 28, 2011 to August 7, 2012, originally posted as a blog on Word-Press.com. It is informal in style with casual regard to niceties of punctuation and none to capitalization. I typed almost everything in lower case, blithely allowing my Word program to decide when to capitalize. Eccentricities and irritations notwithstanding, the ordering of words in this document tends to be rational and, if expressing a larger concept or experience, more or less holds together as not to be (hopefully) overly confusing to the reader. The dash, in lieu of the tyrannical period, is used throughout, functioning as narrative lubricant. I decided to do little editing as the spontaneity and ephemerality of moment and novelty of experience is best expressed, in this case, *alfresco*.

*Awake! For Morning in the Bowl of Night
Has flung the Stone that puts the Stars to Flight:
And Lo! the Hunter of the East has caught
The Sultan's Turret in a Noose of Light.*

—Rubáiyát of Omar Khayyám

Pichincha

7/30/11

i'm at an internet cafe at la plaza de la independencia (plaza grande), a very impressive affair where the presidential palace (palacio de carondelet) is located—i am fine, if a bit culture-shocked, very tired after arriving two days ago but slept nine hours the first night in my new apartment and felt better—tossed and turned last night but feel ok—today is my first solo expedition through the busy, colorful streets of the old city which transport you back a couple of hundred years—very few gringos in this part of the city—my apartment is in an old building with a courtyard in the middle—the walls facing the courtyard are all windows so everybody can see everybody else's business—it feels like the set of the movie rear window—i have met most of my neighbors except the peruvian woman who lives on the second floor—there is a woman, mariana, who will do my laundry (hand wash) for $2 per dozen items (Ecuador's currency is US dollars) and they will dry on the clothesline in the courtyard, which will take forever in this climate—though it is "summer" it is very wet—lots of rain last night—susana, my ecuador connection, has been an angel and has helped immensely—we went to see traditional ecuadorian dances last night—during the day had lunch at a museum restaurant with a dramatic view of pichincha, the active volcano that overlooks the city at a height of about 12,000 ft—in a while i will shop for food at a local market with my frac-

1

tured spanish—yesterday bought a small two-burner gas stove for $20—need to get a gas canister—my knee is still recovering from my fall at the rio chama a couple of weeks ago but is a bit better—hopefully mending soon—i should be hooked up to the internet at my apartment within a week or so—walking around alone is quite a terrific experience—the few people i've asked for directions have been very friendly—(later)—finally met the Peruvian woman, emma, who invited me for a frenetic ride in the rain around the city in a borrowed car (hers was stolen a week ago) with her cackling friend sylvia—emma is a small, dark, energetic woman of about 45, from cusco, a long-distance runner who has competed in the new york, boston and Miami marathons—sylvia owns a tortilla factory called Toltec and sells to various stores and hotels in Ecuador—sylvia's a little older than emma—she grew up in rio de Janeiro and is more demonstrative than what I am beginning to understand as the typical Ecuadorian character—emma's looking for a new place to live—we drove to a large apartment complex at the north end of town called alta vista with dramatic views overlooking a huge barranca shrouded in early evening clouds—the place reminded me of san Francisco at altitude—the president, correa, lives up here—we passed the gates to his compound—emma wants to live up here too—emma works for a german corporation and is resolutely on the go—she dresses fashionably and wears designer jewelry—then went to a generic café of the sort you might see in any US city, nice enough, with several fire places (quito gets chilly and damp in a hurry and we were cold) where we drank a sort of Ecuadorian mulled wine and snacked on a plate of ordinary good things, but the great attraction of this place is that it is in itchimbia, where I had been the day before with Susana, and we sat overlooking the lighted city, the three plazas near my apartment, santo domingo, san francisco and independencia, brightly lit, with pichincha as silent backdrop, communicating as best we could with our bad spanish and english—

Otavalo

7/31/11

off with Susana on an hour and a half taxi ride to otavalo, the famous indigenous market, about 100 km (driving) north of quito—we ride with bob, an air force lifer, one of these American characters graham greene so loved to skewer—perfectly likeable old guy who loves Ecuador and is spending six weeks in otavalo—bob speaks in abrupt enthusiastic bursts, like afterburners—his parents, also lifers, are buried, at their request, under a flight path near some military base—also in the cab is a computer guy from Toronto and his Ecuadorian wife—she's lived in Toronto for 25 years, speaks with a Canadian accent and works for the Wrigley corporation—I tell her the Wrigley corporation is responsible for three-quarters of my cavities—the two of them are on a whirlwind dash around the country, his first time here—exhausted, they nod off periodically—the ride is through mountainous terrain that reminds me a bit of new mexico—the closer we get to otavalo the more beautiful the landscape becomes—in fact it is stunning, farm plots climbing the green sides of the mountains in typical Andean fashion, deep blue sky, clouds covering the summits, indigenous people everywhere in traditional garb, their children and dogs—Ecuador is the rose growing capital of the world and this is where much of it happens—we pass mile after mile of greenhouses—susana and I have lunch at a fancy place called puertolago, next to a large lake, san

Pablo, which caters to the tourist crowd, more locro (heavy and delicious Ecuadorian soup filled with good things, typical for lunch, *almuerzo*) and my new favorite, jugo de guanabana—imbabura sits brooding over the lake, half covered in clouds—we get another cab and arrive at the market at the tail end and it's also Sunday, which is the slow day, and there are few customers, but the venders are still there with their beautifully colored weavings, really wonderful—I buy a pullover for ten dollars that Susana bargained down (customary) from twelve—I want to buy more things, rugs, weavings, fabulous swinging chairs, colorful, comfortable pantalones—otavalo is old and a bit forlorn and clearly there is much poverty, as there is all over Ecuador—the market is a jewel in its midst—it's too late to find a cab back and too expensive anyway so we cram into a bus for four dollars apiece and wind our way slowly through the mountains in the rain and darkening skies—I think of buses plummeting over the side, down thousand-foot ravines, the river rushing at the bottom—adios motherfucker—about six months ago I read of a bus crashing somewhere in Ecuador, killing 36 people—maybe a hospital bed and and IVs *would* be better—I've blustered a lot lately about going out in style—second thoughts there—meanwhile a wide screen at the front of the bus is playing "unknown," with liam neeson getting the shit kicked out of him in every imaginable way—we buy bags of delicious bizcochos for a dollar apiece from an indigenous woman—I eat two and save the rest for breakfast—

Two resident devils

two resident devils—first, la ducha electrica—the electric shower-head—la ducha electrica is a thing I knew nothing about, absolutamente nada, until I discovered fortuitously via email from maria Elena just what the hell this frightening contraption is—the first couple of showers I took were hot/cold dribbling affairs, frustrating enough, but what freaked me was the slight electric shock I received when sticking my finger in the flow coming out of the little outlet at the side of the showerhead to which the tube for the handheld showerhead is supposed to be connected —wtf?!—was I to meet an absurd thomas merton-like fate, electrocuted my second day in quito?—as the water coming out of the main showerhead transmitted no discernible electric current I decided to risk a quick shower, very quick, mind you, as if alacrity minimized the danger, a rationalization more sensible people would instantly reject—next day, same thing, the little shock from the little flow but no incapacitating, death-dealing voltage from the main stream—another very quick shower—but I was pushing my luck, I knew it, and decided to take no more showers until I got to the bottom of this mystery—that's when maria elena's email arrived asking if I had una ducha electrica—eureka!—online in an instant to discover that la ducha electrica is used all over south America, a seemingly insane contraption combining electricity and water, much like an electric tea kettle, a nice continuous and inexpensive flow of hot water with few reports of electrocution—nice—susana told me to connect the tube and not to stick my finger up there any more—I will be a good boy and not stick my finger up there any more—I've had two shock-free showers since but the trick is to adjust the stream just right for the best hot water, a constant mid-shower tinkering, not too bad, if a weak flow, but in my mid-sixties I'm used to a weak flow—the other resident devil is my 15 liter propane gas cylinder, a fat blue toad squatting in my hallway/kitchen feeding the little two-burner stove that boils my water and will be cooking simple meals as I'll soon quit the extravagant practice of eating dinner out all the time—the stove, the full cylinder, the regulator, the plastic hose, cost about $65—the gas should last three to four months—it makes a cute little ffft! every time you open the valve—if I learned to live with the threat of nuclear war I can learn to live with this—

Mario, San Roque and Cafelibro

8/3

wandering in the direction of plaza independencia, randomly turning down different streets, getting a feel for things, I discover casa del alabado, a converted 17th century colonial house with a beautiful collection of Ecuadorian pre-colombian artifacts—the guide is a young man, Christian, who speaks in Spanish—I think I get the gist of it—a couple of guys from mexico are in the group—the artifacts are exquisite and of the highest order—outside afterwards I meet an Ecuadorian man, Mario, and his friend hugo, from france—mario is about fifty, hugo older—mario lived in new york city for many years with his American wife near union square and speaks good English—hugo speaks german, French and Spanish but no English—his father was german, which made for problems growing up in france—hugo is dressed almost shabbily and smiles as if it's all a big joke, another one who's chosen to wander down side streets—Mario comes across as an intellectual and speaks rapidly and forcefully—he used to teach electronic engineering at politecnica (where I'll soon be teaching english) and now works as a part-time consultant for a Chinese oil company—I get mario's email address and we agree to get together—later Susana takes me to kind of a warehouse/market in san roque, kind of a rough neighborhood, where people sell cheap furniture—dozens of "stalls" where you haggle with merchants over prices—men rush by carrying impossible loads, huge stuffed chairs, stacks of stools, etc—I buy a cheap little wood table to put in a section of the apartment that will be my study and dining area—the table and delivery cost $22—a tough-looking character drives us and the table to my apartment in a fairly new Toyota pickup—once there he demands a tip and Susana gives him a dollar—after a few more errands susana takes me to a club that has tango lessons every Wednesday night—this is cafelibro—cafelibro is a warm and hip place and I like it very much—not a whiff of techno except for people using their little electronic toys, their little cell phones, but not even much of that—it could be new york or san Francisco in the 50s—great vibes and lots of fun—the food is good too—cafelibro has different shows almost every night, from belly dancing to poetry readings, plus ongoing art exhibits—I like it because there are people of all ages here, not just the young—it's near where I'll be working and I can see myself hanging out here a little bit—

Toothless in Quito

8/5

meeting at cec (centro de educacion continua, a branch of epn, escuela politecnica nacional) for new teachers in the linguistics department—I'm the only male and by far the oldest in the group, smiling tightly because of my missing tooth (lateral incisor, lost earlier this year in a drunken fall at Pamplona)—I am everyone's toothless old pappy—our presenter is Andres, the chief coordinator of the program—he studied in Minnesota and is extremely fluent, very good, says funny things—but the funniest thing is the grading system, which would cause Stephen hawking to sit up in his wheelchair—andres says we will only retain 10% of what he tells us and he is wrong—5% would be generous—anyway I take the usual copious, confusing notes that I will hardly ever refer to and decide I will learn as I go along, making many mistakes, which is what I do anyway in all things, as my resourceful and resilient offspring will be the first to tell you—the building where I will teach is called araucaria, a kind of tall skinny tree—there is one growing right next to it, hence the name—the rooms are small—I expect to have about 15 students in each of my two classes—the curriculum is contained in a big book and you are expected to follow it faithfully—there are four tests in each eight-week grading cycle and they are all based on material in the book—I am a little nervous about all this but less than I would be if facing the prospect of walking into a class of ninth-graders at highland high school—after the meeting it's back to plaza (de la) independencia on one of the moving sardine cans referred to as 'el trole' to meet up with Mario at palacio arzobispal, a grand edifice containing a quaint little mall with eateries and such, with a central courtyard where Mario has coffee and I jugo de guanabana—mario has strong opinions on all things, perhaps too strong—interacting with him is like dodging a hail of bullets and finding space to fire back—he is a 'realist' (perhaps working for a Chinese oil company has something to do with it) with idealist leanings—a kind of slightly glib pragmatic socialist—a strong supporter and acquaintance of correa, he comes from money and, judging from a few of his comments, is likely a racist— should we meet again, and I hope we will, I will press him if an untoward comment arises—he has knowledge of herbs and healing and once had an ayahuasca 'experience' that lasted three days—he tells me should I take ayahuasca, which is a possibility, that I do it in absolutely correct circumstance, with a shaman, etc, and go into it with the right frame of mind—listening to him reinforces what I already feel about the ceremony—mario is an interesting cat and filled with a lot of anger about social issues—he is highly critical of US policies and culture, which of course resonates with me—allowing my romanticism to wander I see Mario as a certain latin American stereotype, upper class dropout, leftist intellectual, subversive—this of course all for the screenplay I will be writing later—we walk around the plaza and his demeanor softens, both of ours do, as we talk enthusiastically about the music and art we love—he shows me the interior of the centro cultural metropolitano, an old Jesuit college with a long and tumultuous history—it is very beautiful and has been remodeled with contemporary elements that fit the old structure handsomely—I had visited the exhibition hall a few days earlier to see photographs of famous mountain landscapes—mario takes me up to the roof and we look out over the city—across the street is a church with beautiful Moorish tiles on its cupolas—la virgen de quito watches over us—then we walk to santo domingo plaza, near where I live, and bid each other goodbye, agreeing to meet again—

Independencia!

8/6

street sounds in the old city are wonderful—the lively *cascada* of background Spanish, honking horns, clanging trolleys, rumbling engines, indigenous street vendors hawking their wares, *mandarinas! paragaus! loteria!* sidewalk musicians, the harsh whistles of la policia, cumbia and latin pop emanating from small stores, police, ambulance, fire truck sirens, empanadas and other things sizzling in deep fat in small funky sidewalk eateries—ecuador's independence day is august 10 but the official celebration this year is today, Saturday, the 6th, with many of the city's neighborhoods and plazas shut down for music, dancing, exhibitions, etc—around noon I decide to check out the festivities and record some sounds with my little digital recorder—I am fairly giddy with the treasures I'm recording but later find out, techno-bumbler, that I've lost everything except 30 seconds of a screaming super-amped punk band at san Francisco plaza—as I wander around, the animated crowds, a great colorful pinball machine, bumps me where it will, but my favorite street on this occasion is sucre, a pedestrian thoroughfare with humble shops and restaurants and today two old blind sidewalk musicians, a woman playing accordion and singing traditional songs, and a man playing guitar holding a maraca with his strumming hand and singing so softly you have be very near to hear his heartbreakingly beautiful voice—I feel I am in a very privileged, precious place listening to them, especially the old man, and these are some of the sounds that I lost—maybe I'll see them again—of course I put money in their baskets, standard policy with good street performers and musicians, but absolutely for these wonderful people whose spirits I futilely attempted to capture with my little electronic device—in a different part of the city there is a street performer whom I have seen twice who rigs an instant tightrope across the street in front of cars at red lights and walks quickly across à la a young Philippe petit—he also juggles bowling pins—still on sucre I go into a little place that I'd checked out previously and have a good almuerzo for $2.25—the place is really small and has tiny chairs—sitting at the table with me is a young colombian girl, lade, and we converse—she is very kind with my bad Spanish—she tells me she's been in quito for four months and lives by herself, working every day at a shoe store—she has no friends here—she says people are much nicer in medellin than in quito—lade is 19—when she gets up to leave I see she is about six months pregnant—for some reason even after sopa and jugo de guayaba (the nutritional benefits of which almost miraculous) I'm still thirsty and go the fruteria next door for some jugo de toronja (grapefruit) served in a plastic glass for 85 cents—the place is colorful and crazy busy and reminds me of coney island—maybe what I love about the old city is that it transports me to a different time, maybe my childhood, new york in the fifties—I wander over in the direction of independencia on Garcia Moreno and watch a wedding procession of upper class people as jostling crowds gawk through the iron fence surrounding the church, La Compañía de Jesús, some taking pictures—on Garcia Moreno there is a young handsome well-built man with a ponytail selling those little membrane bird whistles you put in your mouth—he is a confident natural performer and expert at making all kinds of remarkable sounds—people laugh at his routines—around five I meet Susana in front of the santo domingo church at the plaza—there are many old churches in quito, all very impressive if you're into those kinds of things, which I am not—give me ten seconds in the rain forest or an old man singing and playing guitar on sucre with his basket and meager collection of tarnished coins—susana is there with one of the many people she helps (i'm definitely one), garaze, a young basque woman just arrived for an internship at eugenio espejo, the largest public hospital in quito, and very much jet-lagged—several minutes later susana's friend noemy arrives in a rush of breathless energy that will be her signature trait for the rest of the evening and presumably for all eternity—we amble off in the direction of a neighborhood called san sebastion where friends of Susana and noemy are playing in a band—on the way we meet up with another friend, Marcia—in the company of four spanish-speaking women I stumble along and strain to catch a little of their excited talk—noemy asks me how I'm doing and I respond estoy en un sueno and she and Marcia are concerned that I am tired, which I am, but what I mean to convey is that I feel like I'm in a dream and we finally manage to figure that out—many barrios in the old city are cordoned off with trucks, buses or ropes and each has its own celebration—at san sebastion there is a lighted bandstand with the usual speakers and paraphernalia—dozens of people line the streets, indigenous people in traditional dress and ordinary quitaños and on the sidewalk near the intersection is a uniformed brass band out of the 19th century or a fellini film that I think is some kind of nostalgic touch for the celebration but is in fact of a type common all over Ecuador—they are a motley bunch, somewhat dusty and raggedy, ranging from the old to the very young—the boy playing the symbols is about 8 or 9—I am of course immediately captivated, but not so much as when they suddenly begin playing a traditional dance tune in a lively almost military fashion and with noemy's urging Marcia, garaze, Susana and I begin dancing in the intersection while noemy takes pictures and everyone else watches in amusement, especially, I am certain, the old gringo who is very self-conscious and more deeply into his dream but the hell with it and I plunge in, giving a little bit of the funk and brio (not too much) the occasion demands—when I glance at the crowd I see that people are openly smiling at me and Susana says it's because I can dance, that most gringos are stiff—not the people I run with of course but the stereotype is inescapable and this time works to my benefit—a gnarled little drunk with a bandage on his hand shuffles into our circle smoking a cigarette and moving his hips lasciviously—he seems harmless enough but then comes up and flips me off with both fingers—I'm taken aback for a second, then give a wide smile and he turns abruptly and leaves—maybe it's the missing tooth—people smile at me, apparently approving of the way I'm conducting myself—quien sabe—this little man's routine will repeat itself throughout the evening—another drunk blissfully twirls in and around us, eyes closed, arms outstretched, as if flying—the band plays on and I'm getting a little tired, my knee is hurting, I'm at 2,900 meters, and I've only been here ten days and still getting my legs—there is a lull and the mc comes over to our group with his microphone, voice booming throughout san sebastion, and interviews each of us—me llamo Ricardo, I say, my voice echoing—soy de los estados unidos, en el estado de Nuevo mexico! viva Ecuador! and the crowd goes wild—then Susana's and noemy's musician friends file onto the bandstand and start warming up and I'm a little leery of the electronics after the charming brass band but they launch into a high energy cumbia that has a couple dozen people including our group instantly dancing like mad, totally spontaneous, it's the music that has the power—now this is cool and I'm into it, no longer in the middle of the intersection with people staring but in the collective with its revivifying energy and I look over and next to me are two small old indigenous women in their colorful clothes boogying like mad and I think oh my god, where the hell am I, anyway?—is this really happening?—the little man gyrates up with his cigarette and flips me off again and I give him another big smile—all kinds of little kids dancing like crazy—a woman close by crouched down breast feeding her baby—susana is with four children all holding hands dancing in a circle and I join in, clockwise, counterclockwise, back and forth, all of us smiling and into it—there is a lull and I feel a tapping on my leg—a little girl in a yellow sweater wants me to pick her up to dance, a summons from god, and off we go twirling around and around and i think jesus Christ if my knee gives out and I fall with this little girl I'll be spending the rest of my life in purgatory so there's no chance of this happening, as if I'm the sole defender of the crazy human race itself—but damn I'm fuckin tired and at last the music stops and there are a couple of traditional dances from neighborhood groups in their colorful costumes, the thread, revealed, very much unbroken—by now I'm almost stagger-ing—we head over to la ronda, an utterly packed charming narrow street closed to vehicles with lively little eateries and clubs and we have a ten o'clock dinner of good food and drink—poor jet-lagged but game garaze is on the verge of collapse and Susana and noemy pull off the seemingly impossible and find a cab in the middle of the madness and we take garaze and Marcia home—I'm somewhere be-tween exhaustion and catatonia—by now it's well after eleven and Susana and noemy want to go to a disco so I say why not and a short ride later we're in la armonia, a dark cave back in the eight-ies with an mc, thumping music, twirling lights, cigarette smoke, vodka and cranberry juice, human bodies crushed together mov-ing up and down on the dance floor, fog machine, two big screens with crazy lights and music videos from the nineties, it looks like, I don't know, and at first I'm thinking goddamn I don't want to be here but then I'm on the dance floor with Susana and noemy and I get some energy and I'm into it again, the gringo standing out like a sore thumb and people are sneaking glances at me and though I'm in maximum energy-conserving mode I can still move with some rhythm so it's ok, I'm having fun, it's ecuador's inde-pendence celebration and, well, holy shit, look at this—people keep piling in and the place is jammed, full of cigarette smoke and en-ergy and somewhere in the middle of all this noemy has the screen tech project in the middle of all the random images of dancing, jungles, beaches, blinged-out pimps and Ecuadorian esoterica: *bi-*

envenido a Richard de los estados unidos!—there is a twenty minute performance by a local pop singer, a stocky guy in a jump suit, then more dancing and then the highlight of the evening for many, including Susana, an extended performance by shalo, an Ecuadorian pop singer who is something of a cross between tom jones and mick jagger, full of energy and just enough cute sexiness to give grandma a thrill and a pretty damned good voice too—it's touching to see half the club singing along with him, his songs obviously very popular—women vie to give him napkins for his sweaty brow and after a swipe they're thrown theatrically all over the floor (the napkins, not the women)—he slings the microphone cord around like a lion tamer's whip and zeroes in on different women for long smoldering looks—the guy's an undeniable pro and i like him—he's good—shalo—I am so tired the twirling lights look like cats jumping off the walls—mercifully, Susana and noemy decide it's time to go—

El Panecillo

8/7

today a drive to el panecillo with Susana and garaze—I am not hung over but fuzzy-headed and have a headache—despite the fun my new situation is stressful and I'm feeling it—the traffic in quito is terrible and there is pollution, especially driving through the horrible tunnels and doubly so if you get behind one of the buses spewing noxious diesel fumes—it is Sunday and I was going to take it easy after the festivities but Susana calls and asks if I want to go to el panecillo, the great hill overlooking quito upon which stands la virgen de quito, a huge structure a little like the statue of liberty though smaller and younger and implying a sterner injunction, happily ignored by the majority—la virgen is especially striking at night when bathed in light—though not exactly chipper I accept the invitation because, to paraphrase zorba, the one unforgivable sin is to pass up an opportunity to experience something new, and off we go in susana's son's car which she drives expertly in the lunatic traffic, up the steep hill to see the virgin and the city over which she presides—it is windy up there with many people, couples, families enjoying their day off, kids flying kites, *las cometas*, remnants of which cling to the electric wires, plastic refuse that does little for the scenery except remind you of the inescapable ugliness of our age—there is a lot of refuse on the ground too and but for the impressive virgin and the panoramic view there is little to recommend—in the distance, though shrouded by clouds, are the great volcanoes, cotopaxi, chimborazo, cayambe, antisana, awe-inspiring even if I can't see them—a reverent goodbye to la virgen and off to a restaurant where we sit outside on a balcony eating *ceviche* (cold soup with stuff, often shrimp), fish, *chifles* (fried green banana chips) and the best *ahí* (Ecuadorian salsa, not too picante) I've had to date—garaze keeps glancing at two slightly scruffy smart-looking twenty-something males sitting next to us—they in turn are clearly listening to our conversation, susana's clear espanol de quito, garaze's rapid espanol de basque and my halting espanol de gringo estupido, a curious mix to be sure—we drop garaze off at her new apartment and go to the slick supermarket *supermaxi* in the biggest, fanciest mall in quito, *el jardin*, quite on a par with anything back in the states—here the fretful tourist is reassured all is right in the world—*supermaxi* is ranked by lonely planet as #321 of 332 things to see in quito, a comforting endorsement for culture-shocked gringos—*el jardin* is right there with it I'm sure—I, happy consumer, buy an aluminum steamer for my vegetables, and Susana, everyone's guardian angel, drives me home where I will take three aspirins and steam some broccoli and potatoes for dinner—

Everyday stuff; el palo; groundhog day on Ecovia

8/8

my apartment, which is on the first floor of a two-story building about 200 years old, is very agreeable—it's shaped like a staple, the long part being the kitchen/hallway lined with windows on one side overlooking a courtyard—the bedroom and bathroom are on one of the perpendicular sides and are set apart and quite private—it's taken a while to get used to the windows as anyone can see me shuffling about the little kitchen area but I'm very boring and everyone's lost interest and besides they are all very discreet and civilized and hardly anyone's in the courtyard anyway—having said this you can be sure they have me pretty well studied and should my habits deviate in peculiar ways there will be something to talk about—my little "study" and dining area is in a nook next to some windows and is private except for a view from emma's apartment on the second floor but she's moving so fast all the time undoubtedly everything's a blur—clop-clop she goes with her high heels—out the door early in the morning for a five kilometer run (not in heels) and then rushing back to dress for work and clop-clop out the door again—much of the time she's gone on business trips, flying all over Ecuador for her german corporation doing what I don't know—her English is worse than my Spanish so the few times we've interacted communication has been minimal—emma is on planet fast-forward; I am on planet pause, possibly rewind—the other people who live here, also on the first floor, are doctor perez, a pediatrician, his wife, mother and two teenage daughters—I've only seen doctor perez twice—his mother is mariana, the woman who hand washes my laundry for $2 per load—she is the matriarch and commands much respect—her granddaughters clean emma's apartment—after mariana does the laundry it is hung in the courtyard to dry, which can take a while in this climate—it rains frequently in the afternoons and this is the dry season—during the rainy season I'll probably be hanging stuff inside—I have no refrigerator so the food I buy is relatively non-perishable and calculated to last for a week until I go shopping again at santa maria, a small supermarket, part of a chain, about a ten minute walk from my place, down rocafuerte, across santo domingo plaza and onto Bolivar, up a little hill—santa maria is a nice store, well stocked with excellent things—it is small and colorful, probably similar to a good barrio market in Spanish harlem or anywhere else in latin America—some of the products are a little different from what I'm used to and it's taken a while to scope things out, but the range of my purchases keeps expanding—on my first visit I walked up and down the cleaning supplies aisle three times before finding dish soap, *lavavajillas*, which is solid and sold in little plastic tubs—mostly I get fruit, papaya, guineos (bananas), grapefruit, apples, limes, mandarinas (tangerines), tomate de arbole, granadilla y guayaba—I am eating more fruit than I ever have—probably enough vitamin c in my system to ward off colds for the next decade—I also buy vegetables, broccoli, peas, spinach, green beans, potatoes, carrots, onions, garlic, all good quality though probably not organic—cheese and butter last for a couple of weeks in the coolness of my apartment—bread lasts a long time—I go shopping on Tuesdays when there is a 20% discount on fruits and vegetables and also buy a small amount of meat that I cook that night after work—people mostly ignore me but I still get a little nervous at the checkout stand with shoppers on line watching the gringo—I stuff as much as I can in my backpack and carry the rest in the yellow santa maria plastic bags like any other quiteño—my purchases, including a decent bottle of *vino tinto*, cost about 25 to 30 dollars a week—of course this doesn't include the chocolate addiction that costs another six dollars—I've discovered a couple of sources that sell good Ecuadorian dark chocolate for three dollars per bar—speaking of bar, a word must be said about *el palo*, the stick that is propped against the main door at night to prevent *los malos* from breaking into the compound, stealing everything in sight and carrying away the doctor's daughters—susana thinks this is overkill but mariana deems it necessary and what mariana says is law—rocafuerte is a charming street during the day but can be dangerous at night—there's a lot of poverty in quito, which leads to lots of crime, and this is not a fancy neighborhood—the problem with *el palo* is that when I go out at night I sometimes forget to tell mariana, hence the possibility, returning, of being barred from entrance, the stout member lodged firmly against the door leaving me at the mercy of *los terrores de la noche*—this has not yet happened and I do have keys for an alternate entrance, so it isn't an automatic worst-case scenario, but it's a tricky deal because when I tell mariana I'm going out I'm faced with the dilemma of putting the stick in place or not when I return—when mariana's not here I leave a note that says, "regresaré esta noche mas tarde–por favor no poner el palo en la puerta–gracias–richard"—I had to look some of that up—today I went to the general teachers' meeting, held in a different epn building—yesterday Susana showed me how to take the bus, the *ecovia*, which seemed fairly straightforward at the time, and indeed, getting there wasn't a problem, though I missed my stop and had to walk an extra ten minutes—the meeting was a generic affair, new teachers introduced, classes assigned (I'm getting high schoolers—shit!)—materials distributed, class list, clumsy old grammar book, a couple of dry erase markers—talked to a tall grim-looking gringa who frightened me with tales of mayhem against gringos, rip-offs, assaults, how one time she was drugged in broad daylight with some kind of aerosol roofie, waking up fours hours later with everything stolen, luckily, she says, not her kidneys—I think this woman is crazy and vow to give her wide berth but it's unsettling because stories of robberies are legion—even the Ecuadorian consul in phoenix told me to be careful—a little shaken, high-schoolers, aerosol roofies, missing kidneys, headache returning, I get on the bus and think I'm going in the right direction but everyone gets out at some terminal and now I'm lost because I don't know anything about this place so I ask which is the right bus and think I understand but get on what seems like the bus I took in the morning because it stops at the same place, near epn, so I get on a bus going in the opposite direction and it takes me to the terminal again where everybody gets off and I go through the same routine and end up back near epn where I get off because I think if I keep going I'll end up on the outskirts of quito after dark and I want my kidneys—it's groundhog day, I'm going around in circles, so I say the hell with it and get a taxi, which is fine because they are cheap—the traffic is nuts as always but I am delivered safe and sound to my apartment—I am bewildered though because I still don't know what happened on those buses, but some day maybe I'll figure it out—

A good first day; el trole deflowering

8/9

first day of classes and I am happily surprised to find my students attending university, not high school—there are also several professionals—I have two classes, two hours each, from two to six pm—the usual routine, introductions, some words about new mexico and its culture—they seem very decent and not as shy as I anticipated—their spoken English is fair—some are much better than others—I'm teaching grammar and the book is god-awful and I see right away I'm going to have to ad lib to make things interesting, but at the same time I'm expected to cover a unit per week for the bi-weekly exams—these students are here for the certificate, they need to pass the exams, and while they may be moderately entertained by my diversions I'm responsible for covering the material—still, I'm bothered by the book, with its emphasis on US popular culture, reality tv shows, outdated slang, information technology, consumerism and the like—the classes are mostly female—the majority of the students, especially the males, are studying some kind of engineering, mechanical, electrical, computer, environmental—a few are in medicine, with one doctor, mayra, who works in a psychiatric hospital—sofia is a counselor in a psychiatric clinic, works part-time as a coach in a program for handicapped athletes, and at the same time is getting her master's degree in sports psychology—paola has a degree in biology but is really interested in independent journalism—Javier, who is quite fluent, is getting his undergraduate degree in physics—carlos is studying electrical engineering—his hero is jim Morrison—he's seen the oliver stone film and has most of the albums—gladys is a seamstress whose goal is to design and make clothes—sandy is a cook and wants to get into the tourist industry—milagros is studying corporate psychology—several are parents—veronica is a mother of two and is studying to be an English teacher—mayra, the doctor, has a young boy—monica, who is by far the most fluent and speaks with a curious accent that sounds almost Russian, has two children and wants to teach english—this is what you would call a refreshing change—no thugs, gangsters, wise guys, personality disorders, drug dealers, sly classroom texting, slackers or attitudes—they are polite, respectful and seem eager to learn—not that I have anything against my former students, but I like this—I am self-conscious about my tooth and slightly inhibited—I've decided not to use my $450 state-of-the art false tooth because it's uncomfortable and causes me to speak with a faint impediment something like a lisp that's probably noticeable only to me—this is a sharp bunch and I'm sure they see the missing tooth right away—the headache that has been plaguing me the last couple of days returns halfway through the first class and stays the rest of the day—a throbbing at the base of my skull that is probably stress—quito is more than I bargained for with its crowds, pollution, crime and not least the strain of my own ignorance of the language—couple this with all the elements, small and large, of adjusting to a completely new culture, living situation and job, plus being virtually the only gringo in my neighborhood and on the workaday trolley and bus rides cheek-to-jowl with ordinary quiteños who are mostly polite and don't stare but are certainly aware of me (some checking out my pockets and backpack) and it is not surprising I'm a little stressed—I get a little pissed off at this but I need to cut myself some slack—I am human after all—I'm also extremely fortunate that I have a wonderful friend here, Susana, whose kindness has helped me immeasurably—she got me the job, the apartment, and guides me patiently through the pitfalls and confusions of my new life—I will have more to say about this extraordinary person later—anyway it's been a good first day and I think this will probably work—i like the students and though learning grammar is about as fascinating as getting teeth cleaned I'll try to make it as interesting as possible—the day ends with one of the small dramas that occur regularly here—riding home in the cattle car known as "el trole" I feel a probing finger in my back pocket and turn around to see a stone-faced middle-aged indigenous woman staring straight ahead like some guard in front of the president's palace—I give her a hard look and she returns a quick non-committal glance—clever gringo, I have put my wallet in my front pocket—the touch of her finger in my back pocket, on my ass, is a violation, but at the same time strangely, even thrillingly, intimate—I have survived my first pickpocket attempt, a virgin no more—I am happy—

Not quite the middle; a vow to return

today is the holiday officially celebrating ecuador's independence—it's Friday and there's no work and friends susana and noemy take me to la mitad del mundo, the designated equatorial line that's actually a little off but who cares—it's a festive occasion and families are here for the nice weather and music—I get the obligatory picture taken straddling the hemispheres but of course it's not really the equator—it's less noteworthy than my greatest feat, pissing in four states at one time, sadly unrecorded for posterity—those were the days when such things actually counted for something—the coda, a few minutes later, was an actual Texas tourist and his kids puzzling over the wet spot on the ground and the guy, let's call him rick perry, touching my piss and then smelling his finger—I recall him ushering his kids away and looking evilly at me and my disgusting friends—I'm a sap because I felt a little sorry for the guy and to this day take no pleasure in his hapless probing, but am still justifiably proud of the awesome scope of my micturition—that such a thing is a high point in my life speaks volumes but I'm beyond the point of worrying about it—at least I didn't order a drone strike my third day on the job blowing 22 pakistanis including four children to a fine pink frappe (now who would that be?) or help orchestrate the total destruction of a once developed country, kill a million people, righteously oversee the torture of human beings and celebrate it in a book tour—no, I'll take bunyanesque pissing any day and when I think more on it I'm goddamned proud—now, you wanna know how the great salt lake got filled?—there's a nice little museum at mitad del mundo with a scale model of quito and a dimmer switch to simulate sunset and nighttime with thousands of twinkling lights and then a couple minutes later sunrise with all the quaint sounds I love so much here, crowing roosters, church bells, the cries of street vendors, which you'd think straight out of another century but are very much a part of modern life, at least in the old city, where I live—when I first moved here there was a rooster crowing every morning but I haven't heard him for a while so I imagine he's gone the way of the pressure cooker like most things resembling meat tend to do in less refined and comfortable quarters, which would be most of the world and certainly much of quito—I can't say living here is an eyeopener because you don't have to experience something to know it exists, but you'd better damn-well keep your eyes open if you want to keep your detachable parts and maybe some non-detachable ones as well—anyway, after mitad del mundo we go to a modest incan ruin, rumicucho, once a fortress, surrounded by impressive mountains and valleys—up here you try to imagine what it must have been like—what you get is mostly silence and wind and a few noises from the rustic dwellings below, a rooster destined for the pressure cooker, the faint braying of a donkey, an odd screaking sound that may be a bird or some rusting part moving in the wind—the ruins are vaguely interesting but the real mystery is the vast and overwhelming landscape—driving back to quito the sky is clear enough that we can see antisana, the snow-capped volcano SE of quito and a few minutes later the extraordinary cotopaxi, the same height but more dramatic than kilimanjaro, illuminated by the pinkish light of the setting sun—it is unusual to see these volcanoes from quito as they are normally obscured by clouds—noemy wants to go to a favorite eatery near her neighborhood for *morocho y empanadas* and Susana with her expert driving maneuvers us into a ridiculous parking space on the ridiculously crowded and jumping street, la jota, that reminds me of *blade runner* without the futuristics and gloom and we squeeze into the tiny open-front restaurant and find some benches facing the wall and stuff ourselves with delicious hot *morocho*, a spicy milk with corn, and two huge *empanadas*, one filled with chicken, the other with cheese—this is a very popular, busy place and people are seriously into the good food, vacant seats snapped up like chum in a feeding frenzy—for me this is something of a revelation and the high point of the day with the possible exception of cotopaxi—like macarthur I shall return—tomorrow, mindo—

Mindo

as London burns I happily turn my attention to mindo—mindo is a town a couple hours northwest of quito located in the middle of a cloud forest that's home to one of the largest varieties of plant and bird species in the world—noemy picks me up at eight in her old pickup and we get Susana—I have already learned that ecuador's mountain roads and daredevil drivers are the stuff of high anxiety, if not nightmares, and am reassured when I realize noemy's pickup couldn't beat an anaconda in a drag race—of course an engine with the compression ratio of a new year's balloon from 1974 presents its own problems, primarily to other drivers who pile up behind us like irritable and dangerous consumers on line at walmart waiting for the latest upgrade on whatever the fuck those things are—I am amazed at the chances they take, passing uphill, around blind curves, recklessly cutting each other off to avoid head-on collisions—but the landscape soon turns magnificent as we putter along, steep green mountains and deep valleys at the bottom of which are different sorts of rivers and streams, anyplace, if you choose to get out and explore, a mysterious paradise—*what is out there?—would I dare?—why not?*—poisonous snakes, pumas maybe—*what else?*—your own fears—safer out there than this highway or Anthony burgess's London with its droogs and desperados and the relentless police state coming down—I see in my mind's eye the breathtakingly ignorant david Cameron waving his little stick, making gassy, impotent noises, the whole deal unhinged, all the more reason to stop the truck and get out, plunge into the forest—but we'll go on to mindo, the tourist stop, civilized, bird watching, hotels, restaurants, a sweet little butterfly farm, a *mariposario*, all this very nice and still Ecuador, so not *too* developed—in mindo I am pleased when a gringo daddy at the *mariposario* sternly (and loudly) commands his little girl to take her hand out of the fountain because the water is *very dirty* (we are not in boulder any more, darling!)—there are lots of the brilliant metallic blue butterflies, *morpho peleides*, I've read about that are so common in the rain forest, plates of mushed banana to load your finger for friendly lepidopteran encounters and things to buy at the gift store—I dab a little banana on the top of my cap and get a visit from a *morpho peleides* to the delight of the little girl who's hand is already disfigured from the pestilent water—out of there—the butterflies fill me with nameless dread—susana has booked two rooms at *selva virgen*, an eco-lodge in Puerto quito, about a half hour west of mindo—it is a nice place built in the sixties, looks like, in the middle of this beautiful forest—susana insists upon this being her treat, in spite of my protestations—I have a room of my own, clean and agreeable, overlooking a small courtyard with a fountain—we get lunch, almuerzo tipico, and then go for a walk on a trail behind the hotel—the variety of plant species is remarkable, extremely dense—one of my heroes is the great ethnobotanist, Richard schultes, who explored the amazon in the forties and identified thousands of plant species for western science (of course he had the common sense and humility to understand the natives knew far more than he did) and though I've never been especially interested in wild plants I can understand his passion—there are so many different species you could literally spend weeks studying a square meter anywhere—there are cultivated areas next to this trail, with palm trees for palm oil, mandarinas (tangerines) and papayas, and also, growing wild, trees with greenish fruit the size of soccer balls, about which noemy and Susana haven't a clue—my favorite thing is the groves of huge bamboo trees, some individuals nearly the diameter my thigh and all of beautiful green, yellowish color—again I want to take off on my own to explore the wilder parts but am inhibited from doing so by the obligation to stay with my hosts, who watch me anxiously lest I wander even a meter off the trail—I'm sure there are snakes, possibly poisonous, but Susana and noemy don't know—back at the hotel we go swimming and at dusk there's a chocolate-making demonstration and noemy insists I take a turn grinding the roasted cacao beans for a photo-op, a request with which I dutifully comply because my friends are having fun watching me experience these new things and I want to make them happy because they are so good to me—the cacao grounds are mixed with sugar and cream creating a sublime slightly gritty paste that we sample slathered on slices of banana—after dinner there is a night walk on a forest trail led by a hotel employee, a small rough man with a dirty cap and polo shirt and attended by about twenty hotel guests, mostly families with children—five of the parents hold diesel-fueled torches, the sweet thick smoke transporting me to quito's tunnels and an instant bad mood—more fucking pollution!—but within minutes everything changes—though we are not more than several hundred meters from the hotel, in the darkness with the thick growth all around us, light and shadow from the yellow flames playing off the trees and foliage, the impression is of being deep in the forest—everyone speaks quietly—the trail is difficult, in spots muddy, steep and challenging, with large rocks and fallen tree limbs—my bad knee doesn't help matters and the light from the torches is marginal and deceptive—we walk next to a stream which the meandering trail crosses several times on crude narrow wooden bridges—though the shallow water is only a few feet below a fall here could mean a sprained ankle or worse—as for my knee I don't even want to think about it—those in the lead shout "bridge!" and the word is passed down the line—sometimes instead of "bridge!" it is "tree!" or "rock!" of course in Spanish, ordinary words taking on more than ordinary significance—this on a hotel outing—I wonder if someone will yell "*culebra!*"—at one point a man falls on one of the bridges and everyone stops in concern—he gets up slowly and seems all right—I say to Susana this is not Disneyland and she laughs—no, definitely not Disneyland—more like an episode of *survivor* or *lost*, with the now quite serious group picking their way along the trail speaking in hushed tones with occasional bursts of nervous laughter—but in spite of the hazards it is wonderful—instead of irritation the torch fumes fill me with imaginings of 19th century jungle excursions, the yellow flames bathing everything in a mysterious and protective glow, shadows dancing like spirits—there are sounds too, trilling frogs, crickets, an occasional night bird—after a bridge crossing I'm next to the guide and ask him, *hay culebras aqui?* and he replies, *si—venenosas?* I ask—*si*, he says, *venenosas*—I suspected as much and say nothing to Susana or noemy but tell them a hotel-group activity like this would be unthinkable in the US because of litigious concerns—and there it all is, isn't it, in a very sad nutshell—whatever we have become I want nothing to do with it—the walk ends and I'm sad—the magic is gone—but i'm exhilarated also because it won't be too long before I'll be in the amazon in much wilder circumstances—it's about ten and we return to our rooms and I read some of chris hedges' *empire of illusion* and though he is our old testament prophet and speaks words of fire and damnation I soon fall asleep but awaken later to partying and what sounds like a soccer game that lasts until three or four in the morning, the situation made worse because the window of my room is screen, not glass—with maybe three hours sleep I meet noemy and Susana for breakfast and then we go to a waterfall not too far away, an idyllic spot but for the tourists, including us of course, and hang out for a bit—the water is cool but tolerable and I've borrowed noemy's extra pair of orange spandex bottoms because I've forgotten my bathing suit at the hotel—I've had a run of forgetfulness lately—tired, my knee unsteady on the slippery rocks, wearing orange spandex trunks, I'm not in the best of moods—but it's hard to forget where I am and this helps—assuming one is not

in a hospital bed or being tortured in a prison camp, why shouldn't
this help anywhere?—remembering where you are—driving back to
quito we are again blessed with clear skies and glimpses of antisana
and cotopaxi and this time, for extra measure, cayambe—

Stay on the sunny side

8/19

it's Friday and I've been teaching for two weeks, doing my best to work around this dreadful book with its dated cultural references, more irritating and misleading than quaint—the vocabulary contains words like *window shopping, refund, shopaholic* and *go over,* as in *how did the interview go over?*—I want *prolix, diaphanous, tintinnabu-late* (teen-teen-nah-boo-lah-tay) and *class warfare,* but let's face it, the words in the book are more useful to today's consumers, or maybe consumers ten years ago since there doesn't appear to be a whole lot of consuming going on now, or job interviews for that matter—I'm happy to see the decrease in consumption but not the suffering of ordinary people—my students are a bright bunch and understand very well the workings of this barbaric system, pessimistic about the future but wanting like all young people decent lives for themselves and their children—anyway I'm making up my own vocabulary lists that have more to do with a different world but blast it, one of the supervisors, lucy, an attractive and intelligent Czech-american, sits in on my class today and later in her office informs me that I'm going too slowly, not covering the material properly, that the exams will be strictly covering the material in the book and while there's nothing wrong with my vocabulary words they should really be *supplemental,* if there's time *left over,* and *perhaps I might like some pointers in making the classroom experience more fun and interesting?*—I've always been a spoiled, cranky and rebellious teacher, hiding in the classroom, doing my part to bring the pillars of the temple crashing down and these words from my supervisor sting, more so because I know she's right—what's worked in the alternative settings I've taught in won't work here—there's an established curriculum that needs to be followed and I'm doing the students a disservice by going off on my own—damn her!—I feel like a ten-year-old called to the principal's office, my ego bruised, the smug fellow politely corrected—but there's nothing to say as this is strictly a language course that has been developed by the cec staff and I'm in no position to carry out my little revolutionary battles—but what nags at me is that this, in its way, is a microcosm of what's happening with the US educational system with bush's 'no child left behind' and his successor carrying the baton with his 'race to the top,' running the next leg of the neo-liberal relay designed to destroy public education in the US, top-down dictates from a corporate class that require everyone in the system, from administrators to lowly teachers and students, to conform to a standardized imperative demanding conformist, mechanical learning at the expense of real critical analysis and creativity—with the stakes so high everyone caves and goes along, even if the quality (symbolized by this awful grammar book I must teach) is terrible—we all lose except for the publishing companies that crank out standardized tests in a billion dollar industry and the private educational firms that take over for "failing schools"—as if there were jobs out there for these hapless products of the brave new world of public education, not to mention college graduates chained with crippling debt in a grotesquely skewed economy with no prospects of anything resembling "hope and change"—I thank her for her suggestions and leave her office embarrassed and chagrined, now thinking about the bus ride home on ecovia—the day before, coming home from work, *el trole* was far the worst it's ever been, so fucking crowded I literally had the breath squeezed out of me—I'm not agoraphobic but I don't like crowds and with my fears of thieves and pickpockets that are apparently everywhere in quito I follow susana's advice and decide to take the same bus, ecovia, that ran me in bewildering, déjà vu circles ten days earlier—before class we'd gone together and she'd showed me where to get on, near the school, and said I should get off at the terminus, *la marin*, which I will recognize because everybody gets off and what's more it's the same place I boarded the bus for the teachers' meeting, no problem—ecovia is preferable, Susana says, because it's less crowded than the trolley and it's simply a matter of getting off and walking up *montufar*, a bit of a hike, but one that leads directly to my street, *rocafuerte*—this same morning before class I'd also tried to get my *censo*, the Ecuadorian green card, at the immigration office but arrived at the wrong time and will have to return and so i have all my valuable documents with me in my little red REI backpack, passport, visa, certificate of employment, rental agreement, electric bill, etc as I board the bus in the darkness, going home at a later than usual hour because of the meeting with lucy—at first the bus is crowded, but not as bad as the trolley, though filled with sketchier clientele—it's not been such a good day, missing out on the *censo*, the mild rebuke from lucy, still uncertain of my fellow quiteños' intentions, very much in the grip of two psychic left feet and no doubt in manner and vibe communicating this to all and sundry—so much for susana's lesser crowds as before long I'm stuck in the usual toothpick jar, unable to move, backpack gripped in security mode in front of me with my left hand, holding the bar with my right, wallet in my front right pocket—all very uncomfortable and no idea where the fuck I am in the dark and can't see out the windows anyway because of the people—but two things going for me: one, I'll know when to get out as it's the last stop and everybody exits, and two, my wallet is safely tucked into my front pocket where no pickpocket dare venture and if the clumsy attempt by the Indian woman ten days earlier is any indication I'll know immediately and initiate appropriate countermeasures, whatever the fuck that might be, some kind of verbal ruckus—*no toque mi bolsillo, puta!*—which might get me stabbed—so these are the conditions and this woman, in her thirties, dark, not bad-looking, gypsy-looking, wearing a heavy red sweater, moves her way next to me and *leans in* real friendly and I think, well, my belongings are safely tucked away and one could do worse than have an exotic woman leaning into you on a crowded bus and I sort of give her a little smile in the dark—isn't it nice that this woman finds me agreeable—much nicer than the usual hair-sniffing rigor mortis contact—we go along like this for a few stops and then suddenly she gets off, but before leaving looks up at me with those dark pools of mystery she has for eyes and says, "perdon, *monsieur*"—*monsieur?*—but I've felt nothing and *surely*...I pat my front pocket, pat it again, pat it a third time...believe me, I have felt not a thing, not a tickle, not a movement, not a vibration—now I'm in some kind of dream—perhaps my wallet is in my backpack, which, though clutched tightly with my left hand, I check to see if still there—more people get on in the dark, pushing, jostling, crowding, everybody talking in low conspiratorial whispers about what's just happened to the gringo—I casually pat my thigh again, trying to remember what was in the wallet, a throwaway—outdated cards, maybe five dollars—no loss—the woman a wraith, a demon—*a gypsy*—the bus comes to a stop and most people get out but some remain so I know it's not the terminus, *la marin*—the next stop everybody gets out and I follow—right away I see it's the wrong place, completely alien, vast milling crowds, cacophony, huge growling buses everywhere, metallic whales spouting diesel fumes, swirling lights, a carnival—I keep patting my thigh, as if my wallet has taken temporary leave and will soon return—I ask a man where *montufar* is and he points in the direction from which I've come, way back—this is obviously a bad part of town, it is night, there are crowds and I'm carrying all my important documents in my backpack—I've heard passports fetch $15,000 or more on the black market—it's also said people will slice the straps of your backpack and run off with it, especially nice red gringo REI backpacks like the one I'm carrying—at least I know the general direction to walk, puffing out my chest and looking like I know exactly where the fuck I am and what I'm doing—just another commuter on the way home to the wife and kids—calm and casual—inside the little man in fetal position sucking his thumb—some seriously ugly mother-fuckers around these parts—the one thing in my favor is everyone's surprised to see me here, as if I'm an apparition—kind of catches them off guard—and I'm moving—not too fast, but moving—everywhere motion, noise, activity, shouting, pushing—i try the old trick of becoming invisible but i don't think it's working—i walk past two women having a violent argument that spills out onto the street with a dozen onlookers shouting, egging them on—a bottle smashes not too far from me—then I'm on this little railed-off walkway with room only for one-way pedestrian traffic—if the bad guys come I'm fucked—off with the pack and over the side—I make it past there and ask a nice couple, salt of the earth types, where *montufar* is and they can't agree on the exact directions but I'm getting closer—I thank them profusely—a little less alien now, slightly better neighborhood—I can't find *montufar* but then I'm on *guayaquil* which leads to santo domingo plaza and I can breathe a little easier—wondering if I still have my keys I put my hand in my pocket and–what's this?–my fingers go right through my pants wiggling around stupidly in the night like some little puppet show for children—I look down and see a clean slice down the side of my pants—this so shocks me that I become light-headed and I'm in some realm I've never been before—this simply cannot be—but it is—as if I see for the first time a green moon that's been there all along—*the woman has sliced my pants on the outside and the pocket on the inside with a razor and has carefully lifted my wallet through the two openings, chuckling to herself, exiting with a "perdon, monsieur" and I never felt a thing*—I am amazed, awed, flabbergasted, stunned—touched by pure genius for the first time in my life—that such a thing exists in this world—I think more about my wallet and realize there was no money at all—for her sublime efforts the woman got nothing but a cheap billfold and some photocopied documents—I can see her spitting and disgustedly throwing the worthless thing on the ground—*fucking gringos! my genius wasted on such a cheap fool!*—as for myself I feel like one of kubrick's hominids touching the monolith for the first time, only it was the monolith that touched me—then I'm through the arch of santo domingo and on *rocafuerte*, dazed, depressed by the perfidy of quiteños and mankind in general and I pass a panadería I've walked by many times without entering—I am suddenly aware of an enormous thirst and I walk into the brightly-lit open front store to be greeted by a pretty and smiling young woman surrounded by freshly baked goods, croissants, cookies, bread, and a large cooler filled with bottled soft drinks and juices—I buy a chocolate croissant for the morning and two bottles of *nectar de mango* and drink one right on the spot—the brand is *sunny*, pronounced like the people the Shiites are having problems with and few things have ever tasted so good or given such succor to my soul—and now I am amazed again—the friendly smiling woman, the warm brightly-lit bakery, the sweet nectar—this is quito—and perhaps life—much darkness and trouble, but not without its marvelous sunny moments—

Leroy or Fauntleroy?

now quito has me very uptight—I feel like the new kid under attack from the bullies for his lunch money—everywhere I go I'm checking people out—susana suggests I take a cab home from work and the idea is appealing—she knows someone in a taxi company and perhaps a deal can be made for a driver to pick me up at cec each night and deliver my pathetic gringo ass to my doorstep for 40 bucks a month—either that or move closer to cec, which is in a safer part of town—I don't want to move—in spite of the hazards of my neighborhood I'm seduced by its charms and I love my apartment—no, I don't want to move—this means make a deal with the cab driver or get back on the trolley and suck it up—but fuck ecovia—I never want to get on one of those fucking buses again, especially heading in the direction of *la marin*—I'd rather walk past a yard of snarling rottweilers on the way to work every day—if I can take an alternate route I will—taxi or trolley?—taking a taxi will be a capitulation—the bad-ass mama in my head tells me to get my behind back on the trolley (Leroy!) and stand up to the bullies—but how nice it would be for little lord Fauntleroy to step into a shiny yellow cab every night and be whisked home safe and sound!—no fuss, no muss!—what's 40 bucks a month compared to being ripped off every two weeks, which is the rate it's been happening—sure, only one successful attempt, but 50% is not a winning ratio—my wallet stolen once a month—or my kidneys—on the bright side I guess my kidneys couldn't be stolen once a month—even if I'm carrying five or ten bucks it adds up, and the psychic strain is ridiculous—yes, I'll take the cab—maybe not—I don't know—in any case susana's gone for the week and won't be able to talk to her taxi friend—I'll take the trolley this week and see what happens—which will it be, bad-ass Leroy, or little lord Fauntleroy?

Weegee in Quito; street sounds; Bolívar approaches

8/21

it's a nice day, a Sunday, so I decide to take a walk around the neighborhood up to plaza independencia—I always like walking around these old streets, especially on weekends when everyone's out enjoying themselves—but now after my bad experiences I'm not the kind and gentle soul I was stepping off the plane three weeks ago—I'm a wised-up motherfucker is who I am, developing an attitude I can feel swimming around inside me like an ugly little alien hatchling—fuck with me and I'm all over your face, motherfucker—ain't no cocksucker gonna steal my shit without a fight—that's right!—but everyone I look at is after my shit and I can't fight the whole fucking city now, can I?—and smart people say it's useless to resist, especially if the bad guys have any kind of hardware, which makes sense—but there's a difference in the way i'm carrying myself, from the expression on my face, to the way I walk, to the cast of my chest and shoulders—don't fuck with me is what it all adds up to—but quito has me freaked—last week I had dinner with Mario and afterward walking to catch a cab we passed a teenager lying in the gutter, his face badly beaten, a cop standing over him—that same week riding in susana's son's car i saw a very inanimate young man stretched out on the sidewalk with

43

a bunch of other young men standing around as if looking at a sack of spilled groceries—the day before my romany adventure on ecovia, riding home on *el trole*, I saw a man in a dark suit stone dead on the sidewalk in a large pool of blood, more curious onlookers standing around, straight out of a weegee photo—now let's put this in perspective—if I were in new york I'd think nothing of it, or very little—this stuff happens all the time—quito's a city of two million—let's get a grip here—but since I'm a foreigner and stick out like a neon sandwich board it adds another dimension—in new york nobody takes a second look but here is a different story—bad case of the woolies, no question—but here's the thing—I've got my little digital recorder along for a second try having figured it out and I'm on *sucre* standing next to the blind man playing his guitar and singing his sweet songs while people walk along paying me no mind whatsoever, thoroughly involved in their Sunday lives, families, old people, kids, all sorts, and 99% of them are just fine and decent as they could be—they don't even want my money—and they are as charmed by the blind musician as I, if a bit blasé, and many stop to listen and put coins in his bowl, some aware of the recorder in my hand, some not—then I have almuerzo at the same place I talked to the girl from Medellín and the waitress is friendly and the food good, topped off with a dollop of strawberry ice cream for dessert—I walk to plaza independencia, rougher attitude tempered with sweet music and lunch and I'm in the middle of the plaza when the sky opens up for fifteen minutes and I offer two teenage boys shelter under my umbrella for a while before they go running off across the street to *palacio arzobispal*—my pant legs and shoes are soaked but it's fine and everyone's excited by the sudden storm and taking it in good humor—just a few minutes earlier the plaza was filled with hundreds of people and now it's empty and virtually flooded, the water gushing from the *canales* and downspouts of surrounding grand *edificios*—the storm subsides with grumbling thunder the cannons of bolivar's approaching army, a touch of blue behind the breaking clouds to the north—the rain stops—people

cautiously return to the plaza—I buy some good Ecuadorian chocolate and head for home—

Getting back on

today's the day I get back on the horse and I'm a little nervous
about it but there are other things on the agenda like getting my
censo at immigration and reviewing material in class for tomorrow's first exam—first thing in the morning I get my papers in order
and take a taxi to immigration, which is across the street from the
mall, el jardin—standing on line i meet a Korean guy, chung, and
we talk about life in quito—I tell him about the incident on ecovia
and he says a week ago a woman bumped into him on the bus,
sliced open his jacket and took his wallet, which would seem incredible if not for my similar experience—he quickly realized what
had happened and chased the woman down, making a big fuss until a cop came—the woman had passed the wallet off to a partner and the cop made her call him on her cell phone and the guy
came back—chung got his wallet and the two perps got hauled
off—we have a good laugh over this and I feel a little better since
I'm not the only one in quito being targeted—I also realize, and
chung, a veteran of ten years in quito, agrees, that the gypsy on
ecovia might have had an accomplice—maybe while she was leaning into me someone else was slicing my pocket—chung's a young-
looking 60, stocky, with a great flat Korean face and a full head of
black hair—he's here to stand in line for his friend, an acupunc-
turist, who arrives shortly—chung relates my story in Korean and

they laugh—chung seems to be one of these guys whose been into a lot of things, getting by on his wits and good nature—at present he's managing the business side of the acupuncture clinic he and his friend have just opened—he's also been involved with language schools in seoul and encourages me to consider teaching there after quito because I can make good money—I tell him it's something to consider—we agree to have dinner soon and he gives me his business card: *Centro Medico, Acupuntura Coreana, Dr. Dong J. Ahn, A.D., Dr. Chung Y. Lee, Ph.D, Administrador*—inside at the official's desk I am chagrined to learn that a mere copy of my passport is not sufficient, something I obviously should have known (and had known three days before) but typical of the many instances of brain malfunction these days and I take a taxi back to my apartment and return with my stiff new state-of-the-art-electronic-chip-passport—while waiting for my number to be called I talk with a pretty blond german tourist who'd had her backpack cut open a few days earlier, not realizing her money and passport had been stolen until after returning to her hostel—she shows me her stitched-up backpack, a bulky yellow and black affair—I've seen these tourists with their big backpacks shuffling down the sidewalks looking wide-eyed and a bit lost—they might as well have fluorescent orange bullseyes painted on their backs—though obviously I also stick out, compared to them I feel like an undercover agent—the *censo* costs four dollars and I take it next door and for fifty cents get it laminated—eventually I will get a color copy for the obvious contingency—the *censo*, apparently, is the indispensable ID, with more clout than a passport copy or even the original—back at my apartment I have a grilled cheese sandwich, some *chifles* and a bottle of *sunny* nectar de durazno and then take the trolley to work—at one pm the trolley is not bad—in class we review the units for tomorrow's exam, touching on all the important points, including the depressing vocabulary words—classes end and I head down veintimilla (famous general) to 10 de agosto (ecuador's independence day) for the santa clara station—I am still undecided about the taxi/trolley question and this week will probably determine the outcome—the ride home, while very crowded, is not bad—nobody seems to pay me much notice—I have a new 80 cent wallet in my front pocket—in it are ten dollars and the *censo*—I am carrying my compact umbrella in my right hand, which dangles casually covering my wallet pocket—I grip the bar with my left hand—this will be my MO, my defensive posture, from here on—no backpack unless absolutely necessary, and it will be a cheap one I will soon buy—at the santo domingo *parada* I shoulder my way through the passengers (*"permiso, por favor, permiso"*), get out, hustle across rocafuerte, a dangerous crossing because of the traffic, walk through the arch and merge with the stream of people heading home—I'm still paranoid and jumpy, on the lookout, but again I seem to be of no special interest to anyone—I stop at my new haven, my oasis, the panaderia, and buy a croissant (*un cacho*), some chocolate-tipped cookies and two bottles of *sunny* nectar de mango—the same young woman still there, still pretty and smiling—we have a short conversation and I am happy to hear that she took a few English classes two years ago at cec and she is happy to hear that I teach there—her name is Mercedes—I leave with my bundle—this time of day it is getting dark but the street is busy with ordinary folk and kids and everything is well lit—open front restaurants with barbecue grills right on the sidewalk cooking plantains, pork and chicken—other funky little eateries serving up their own dishes—I'm looking over my shoulder down alleys for goblins and trolls—some day, if I survive, I'd like to eat in one of these little places—

The question decided

8/28

astonishingly I have survived a week on the trolley with pants and kidneys intact—I am touched by the concern for my safety voiced by friends and loved ones and the impassioned response to the Leroy/Fauntleroy debate, the majority coming down on the side of, surprisingly, Fauntleroy—surprisingly because it's not my choice, having been raised on the mean streets of east side midtown manhattan where just walking out the door one faced the harrowing specter of being run over by a fashion model—much sound and heartfelt advice was offered too, from carrying an air horn to memorizing the old testament backwards and reciting it loudly whenever feeling threatened—concerning Leroy/fauntleroy some suggested a mixture of the two, a direction towards which I am naturally inclined—it's the fine art of combining don't fuck with me and after you, sir, madam, with a respectful bow and tip of the cap—the trolley was generally less crowded than I'd braced myself for, though still packed, and, as usual, few paid any attention to me except for discreet looks, probably resulting in brief offhand speculation and subsequent lack of interest, from my point of view a happy response—I am keenly aware of my fellow passengers while pretending not to be, all the while holding my umbrella hand over my right front pocket and gripping the bar with the other—to say my antennae have been fine tuned and extended several millimeters would be an understatement—what I am discovering with this more careful and subtle inspection is that the majority of trolley riders are quiet, gentle and boring, just like me, fauntleroys, suffering with patience and, if possible, good humor, the discomforts and indignities of the ride home on this awful conveyance—by the end of the week the taxi/trolley question has been settled—I can survive on the trolley, if not ennobled at least a little stronger and smarter—smart enough, anyway, not to get on ecovia and head in the direction of la marin—I've been following hurricane Irene on the web and communicating with my son in Brooklyn via skype and email—he's been looking forward to some excitement, having never experienced a full blown hurricane—I can understand but am not so excited, having lived through several as a kid—I keep skyping him Saturday night but not much is happening—by Sunday morning the worst is over and he's a little disappointed—curiously, so am I, wanting him, and myself, vicariously, to experience a little of a hurricane's monstrous force—but not too much—a big widow-rattling blow, a few candle-lit hours without electricity, but no bitch Katrina—as services and infrastructure continue to crumble in the united states natural disasters are a much more serious business than they should be, as anyone from new Orleans can tell you—

Good night and good luck

8/31

a US friend is in quito for three weeks, staying nearby with a male friend of hers—their plan is to do some charitable work for poor children—yesterday she came to say hello and we walked around my neighborhood a little bit—this friend, let's call her teravinda, is a well-built middle-aged woman with tinted blond hair—teravinda lived in quito more than 20 years ago and loved its charm and the friendliness of its inhabitants—in those days, she relates, one could walk around freely at night even as a young woman from the US, even a little *borracha*, and feel no fear—life was good, life was free from *los terrores de la noche*—It's nice to see a familiar face in quito but as we walk around I sense that she is a little uptight—even though teravinda speaks fluent Spanish and knows quito, or knew it 20 years ago, something is very different, something, even, very wrong—again, it's fine to see teravinda—she's a good person—but accompanying her on rocafuerte I feel a bit uncomfortable myself—a woman with blond hair in Ecuador stands out, especially a *gringa*, and if the coloration is not clearly natural there is a sense, fair or not, that some sort of statement is implied—for teravinda, being somewhat large does not help matters—men stare unabashedly, and women, well, who knows what the women feel, but they are obviously not friendly—I'm a little ashamed but I find myself not so subtly burdened by her presence—fully absorbed in the process of finding my own logistical and psychic way around this new territory and culture I'm reverted to half-stumbling uncertainty, reminded, through her, of my own alien stature—a simple matter of crossing the street—actually not so simple—becomes twice as difficult with this revenant shocked at the changes she's experiencing, stumbling and uncertain herself—we go shopping for my week's groceries at santa maria and return to my apartment and then because it's late I must leave for work—from the trolley station I see teravinda, a blond beacon in the middle of santo domingo plaza, clutching her handbag and walking hesitantly in the direction of her apartment—when I return to my apartment after work I check my email and am astonished by a message from teravinda saying she's been robbed by a man with "a long knife" near her apartment and how she doesn't feel safe anywhere in quito, that it's changed so much, and that she thinks she's "out of here"—just as I was beginning to settle down about quito I am alarmed again—this is fucking ridiculous—but I can't resist a rueful shake of my head like some old *veterano*—I had a bad feeling the moment I laid eyes on teravinda—from her stature, to her tinted blond hair, to her halting uncomfortable manner, she had all the trappings of a mark, which is why I felt uneasy walking with her—poor teravinda—expecting the quito of 20 years ago she walked into a completely different, disorienting, darker situation—she probably should have known better but it's hard to close the curtain on nice memories grown idyllic over time—this explains her extreme reaction of wanting to get out of the country immediately—like waking from a nice erotic dream to the reality that your home has been foreclosed and you've got two weeks to vacate—who the hell needs this reality—back to sleep—a couple of days go by and I get a call from teravinda and she's calmed down a little—the guy robbed both her and her friend in front of their apartment in broad daylight ballsy as can be, and when she put up a fuss he pulled out his long knife by way of indicating this was his day job—she and her friend are not going to leave Ecuador immediately but instead quit the horrors of quito and head for the coast for some beach time, which sounds like a good idea—she asks if I want to hang out that afternoon but I have a prior commitment that I can't break—for some reason this makes her a little snippy—I ask her to email me while on the coast so I know where she is and how she's doing and she responds by saying I'll know exactly where she'll be, *at the beach*—a few moments later our conversation is finished—que te vaya bien y buena suerte, teravinda—

Mi ángel de Quito; Cotopaxi

9/3

I am blessed to have a guardian angel in quito and her name is Susana hidalgo—I got to know Susana via email and skype while still in Albuquerque, having been introduced to her by my friend, dale alverson, who, ceaselessly bugged by my inquiries about Ecuador, put us in touch—dale is a doctor and university of new mexico professor who has worked with rural clinics here and this is how he got to know Susana, who is a translator—it's difficult to get the measure of a person through email and skype but conversing with Susana many months left me with a favorable impression and also the feeling that she welcomed my visit—susana, through different turns in her own history, has gotten to know a Belgian diplomat who owns the house on rocafuerte, where I live, and manages the apartments while he's away on various diplomatic postings—he is now in Jerusalem—thus was I able to rent my apartment, for the very agreeable price of $100 per month plus the usual etceteras and, in addition, largely through susana's good offices, I was hired at cec—it is fair to say that without Susana (and dale, a crucial cog in the machinery of my present explorations—all praise!) I would probably never have come to Ecuador—from setting up the essential conditions for my survival—job, apartment, telephone—to meeting me at the airport, to guiding me around the city, to procuring a prescription for my blood pressure medication, to showing me some of the wonders (with her spirited and enterprising friend, noemy) of Ecuador, to patiently helping me with my spanish, to being a good friend and enthusiastic aficionado of dancing and Ecuadorian music, to being steadfastly and genuinely concerned for my health and well-being, susana has been *mi angel de quito*—Saturday Susana has arranged for a trip via tourist van to the great cotopaxi, one of the highest active volcanoes in the world, 39 feet higher than Kilimanjaro and somewhat similar in appearance though I think more impressive—cotopaxi is about an hour-and-a-half south of quito in the cotopaxi national park and about 20 minutes north of the delightfully named city of latacunga—our driver is a heavyset guy of about 45, businesslike but not unfriendly, with a big mustache and bulky sweater—we're accompanied by a young couple from Colombia and their ridiculously cute and precocious five-year-old daughter who sings little songs and peppers her parents with questions—arriving at the park, at the gateway to the road leading to the volcano, we run into some problems because of my status as foreigner which are eventually ironed out in some incomprehensible fashion though the deciding factor seems to be the seven dollars I give to another guide who will travel with us part of the way—he is a good rustic character of about 35 whom I like immediately—he lives nearby and knows a lot about the area, though he has never been to the top because, he says, there is too much lightning—it is chilly and I have bought a gray alpaca scarf for five dollars from one of the indigenous vendors in the parking lot—cotopaxi is about five miles away and its snow-capped summit is periodically visible through the clouds—we travel along a rough dirt road, getting closer, and stop at a little tourist place with museum, bathrooms and food stand and I get a cup of coca tea, a pastry and a small bag of coca leaves—after the pastry and tea I take two leaves in the side of my mouth and begin to chew—right away I feel the slight numbness that is characteristic of chewing coca, though for full effect one is supposed to take it with burnt limestone or burnt quinoa stalks—chewing coca is good for preventing altitude sickness and since we'll be above 15,000 feet I figure why not, though I really don't know how potent it'll be without the additive—soon we are in the middle of the vast, flat expanse at the foot of cotopaxi, in this, the dry season, something of a lunar landscape and very windy—we stop at a small lake, Limpiopungo Lagoon, facing another volcano, Rumiñahui, cotopaxi at our backs—the wind blows my cap onto the mud flats and I race after it before it skips into the lake—this is a special cap (allen harbor—marine service inc.) given to me by my brother years ago and I refuse to let it get away—it is covered with limpiopungo mud as are my hiking boots—people are amused at the image of me loping across the mud chasing my cap—from there we begin the winding rugged journey up the slope of cotopaxi to the parking lot at 4,600 meters—it is a jolting, somewhat alarming ride but I have complete faith in our driver who expertly maneuvers past obstacles and around curves, some of which overlook considerable drops—it is windy and the summit is covered with clouds—at the gritty and muddy parking lot there are perhaps two dozen vehicles and a couple of tour buses—the wind howls, the ascent looming ahead, its higher reaches lost in the clouds—we are at snow line, several hundred meters below the first base camp, which is used for hikes to the summit—it's really blowing a gale up here and it's cold—susana stays in the van while I try out my knee and endurance, carefully walking higher, not as high as some of the others who attempt to get to the base camp, but high enough to give myself a little test—the knee isn't too bad and I'm reassured by my condition—if I had to I could reach the camp, but there's no sense pushing it—maybe in a few months I can get to the top—turning around I look at an immense and forbidding landscape, the wind almost blowing me over—the wind, aridity and great expanse of mountainous volcanic forms partly covered with clouds gives me a feeling of being in Patagonia—beyond this overwhelming landscape is the bottom, the end of the earth—there is nothing inviting here,

nothing friendly—you are firmly in your very small and vulnerable place—it is exhilarating, alien, as wild as anything I've seen—I'm
over 15,000 feet high, about a thousand feet higher than Wetterhorn
in the rockies which I climbed over three decades ago—of course
we've driven up here but I don't feel too bad walking around, and
this is where the ascent would begin—I really want to get to the
top some day—at the parking lot there's a group of young men who
take off down the slope on their mountain bikes, careening and flying like crazed penguins on wheels—it is almost beyond comprehension how they survive, but they do, and we pass them several
times on the ride back—would I undertake a slow-motion trudge to
the summit of cotopaxi? perhaps—a suicidal dash down its slopes
on a mountain bike?—never in a million years—it's late in the afternoon and lunch is part of the deal so we're transported to lat-
acunga, a charming little city with narrow streets crammed with
Saturday market-goers—unfortunately lunch is less than charming
as we're herded into a fast food chicken place at a table beneath a tv
set playing a very silly sitcom from Guatemala—the tv show is better than the food, which should give you an idea how bad the meal
was—but still I am pleased—I have walked on the slopes of the great
cotopaxi—

A too-anxious parent?

9/8

my intrepid son is off to India for a month, having left yesterday, his birthday—he was supposed to call me, anxious parent, via skype or send email signifying well-being, but long after his scheduled arrival in Mumbai there is no message, and I am freaked—mumbai is one crazy city of 21 million and for a first-timer plunked in its midst it can be a tad disorienting, to say the least—still in the throes of my own quito struggles I am perhaps overly worried, but that's what parents do, and I absolutely cannot sleep and keep trying his cell phone, to no avail—I feel doubly cut off and helpless with both of us being in strange places—finally i reach him at 2 pm quito time—never has the sound of his irritated voice sounded so wonderful—happily now I can sleep—this new age electronic communication has its benefits, I suppose, but has it raised our level of anxiety and dependence as well?—we need instant assurances and gratification for everything and if we don't get it there's hell to pay—what did people do before skype and email?—

Valle de Los Chillos

9/11

i go with Susana and noemy to valle de los chillos which is a kind of suburb of quito or actually more like a separate city of about one million—los chillos is warmer than quito and gets more rain—some parts of los chillos are urban but others have a distinctly rural feeling—we have lunch at a marvelous, colorful open-air restaurant and eat a type of delicious pulled pork dish (hornado) with Ecuadorian corn on the cob—much larger kernels than its US counterpart, a little tougher and not as sweet, but very good—much less hybridization here—after lunch for some quiet digestion we visit the grounds of lovely catholic retreat built by germans a hundred years ago but there's a marching band practicing in the valley below and the feeling is more like Saturday morning before a high school football game—there's a small church here straight out of brothers grimm—I like valle de los chillos and especially want to return to that restaurant—back in quito that evening we go to a multiplex for my first Ecuadorian movie experience and Susana, thinking I don't want to sit through an Ecuadorian movie, buys tickets for "crazy stupid love," the sort of movie I rarely see and despite my inward groans I am pleasantly surprised by a most charming production that the audience also enjoys—

A Sunday surprise

9/12

the perils of Fauntleroy receding, I'm feeling more comfortable walking the streets of quito—as in any urban setting with potential for misfortune you keep your eyes open and go about your business as naturally as possible with a straight back and peace and goodwill in your heart—I think of teravinda and wonder how she's doing on the coast and if I'll ever hear from her again—as today is Sunday I go for a walk and almuerzo and am delighted to come across an afro-ecuadorian dance festival in santo domingo plaza—afro-ecuadorians comprise roughly four per cent of the population and most live on the coast in the province of esmeraldas, at least part of the initial population having ditched a foundering slave ship off the coast in the mid 16th century—quito has a modest afro-ecuadorian population mostly relegated to the slums of the northern and southern extremities—racism is a big issue here just as in the US though light-skinned ecuadorians have no problem rooting like crazy for their mostly black futbol team—I am familiar with the dynamics of racism in the US in its subtle and overt manifestations but really haven't much of a clue here except to understand that it exists with its own cultural lineaments and peculiarities—my sense is that the afro-ecuadorian culture of esmeraldas is closer to its African roots than that of its afro-american counterpart in the US, possibly even in gullah communities, but this is supposition—trying to pin down "culture" with its diverse embodiments is a hazardous undertaking for the armchair anthropologist—a trip to esmeraldas is on my agenda—the crowd in santo domingo plaza is lively and riveted by the performers from the coast—there are a lot of afro-ecuadorians, many of them youths in full hip-hop regalia, some feigning indifference to the dancers but, one senses, inwardly as engaged as everyone else—how could you not be?—behind the dancers is a bandstand where different bands play their infectious, rhythmic music, with lots of drums and marimba—the dancers are young, beautiful, brilliantly costumed and irresistible—some are highly skilled and elicit much admiration and heartfelt response from the crowd—it's a warm afternoon and the mostly female dancers are sweating and working hard and you can't help but feel that we aren't too far from the mother continent itself, not too much of a stretch to imagine that this is not really Ecuador (since when did Ecuador become ordinary?!) but rather Nigeria, Ghana or Senegal—but this is the wonder of Ecuador—a six-hour trip to the coast, or anywhere else for that matter, or simply staying right where you are, if you are open, will transport you to a place that kindles something deeper than what you are accustomed to—a nod to my friend larry who will claim that he experiences the same thing every day in new Orleans—if he will only ditch his bluetooth—

Pichincha, from my street, Calle Rocafuerte

Susana

La ducha electrica

Fat Boy

Exhibition hall, Centro Cultural Metropolitano

Gringo sin diente

Some of the music I lost

Quito, circa 1930

La Virgen, from the old city

La Virgen at El Panecillo

Los cometadores

The courtyard and my apartment

Santa Maria

A Tuesday shopping

Nook

El palo

Mariana

Monument, La Mitad del Mundo

From the top of the monument, north and south (not exactly)

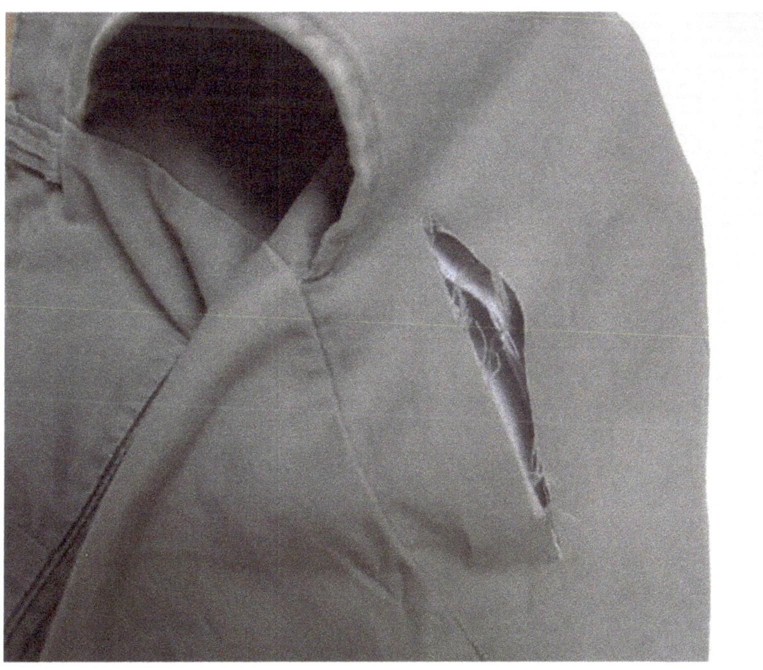

A staggering work of pant-rending genius

Deliver us from evil

Susana at Limpiopungo Lagoon–behind: Rumiñahui

Cotopaxi

A landscape vast and wild

Sunday surprise

A hopeful connection

tonight I have dinner at cafelibro with chris Jarrett, a young man I met in the teachers' lounge at cec through an acquaintance—chris is a fullbright grantee spending a year in the village of rukullakta (kichwa: *ruku*: old; *llakta*: village), near archindona, living with a kichwa family of the napo runa, an Amazonian subset of the larger kichwa group that primarily inhabits the Andean corridor—his goal is to learn kichwa and to document the traditional stories, songs and customs of the napo runa—as chris explains, the kichwa language has two main variants, the sierra, or highland north, and the Amazonian—the Amazonian is divided into two groups, the napo and the puyo—napo runa is kichwa for "people of the napo"—napo is the napo river, runa means "people," or "the people"—this is how I understand it, anyway—corrections, if needed, will be posted subsequently, as I have every intention of developing this connection with chris and his life with these people—perhaps the main reason for coming to Ecuador is to experience the amazon and I am fortunate to have met him—as we have dinner and discuss his project I am struck by his thoughtfulness and dedication, very unusual qualities in someone so young—I don't ask but I figure him to be in his mid-twenties—chris graduated from elon university in north Carolina with a double major in international studies and Spanish—I am a little surprised that he accepts me so openly and encourages a visit, already formulating plans for my stay in rukullakta for a week with his host family—I can't really picture the sort of life he talks about, the physical setting of the village in the rain forest, the family, the village elder and "yachak" (shaman), carlos, "the farm" that we will visit, deeper in the jungle, but I'm excited about it and commit right on the spot—chris speaks fluent Spanish and some kichwa and will act as my guide and interpreter—one of the most important rituals in napo runa society is the early morning custom of drinking guayusa (wahy-YOO-sah) tea with family members as a way of starting the day, which serves to reinforce bonds on a regular basis—it is also a way of passing down knowledge to the younger family members—if I go I will be taking part in this daily ritual, waking up at four in the morning to drink this strange brew gathered around a fire with others in the yachak's lodge—he also mentions the possibility of drinking ayahuasca in a ceremony conducted by carlos—this too sounds interesting—so—it looks like I have a respectable entrée into the amazon without being too much into the typical tourist routine—I will be living with a kichwa family, apparently, and spending a few days deeper in the jungle in more primitive conditions—I will also see the fair trade operation of harvesting and marketing guayusa tea under the Runa brand, a fledging enterprise employing local growers as a way of helping the economy in an eco-friendly, sustainable manner—chris is interested in the development of indigenous economies using these types of models—the end of the first teaching cycle is October 4th and I would leave for rukullakta some time after that—I will make some kind of monetary contribution that we will discuss later—all this sounds very good—

In the company of women

9/19

a weekend in ambato and Baños with Susana, noemy, and three of
their female friends plus one of the friends' five-year-old daughter
and another's dog, all packed into noemy's tardigrade pickup, even
more sluggish with the extra human and canine cargo—this five-to-
one adult female-to-male ratio causes a little ambivalence—nothing
wrong with hanging out with attractive women but when they get
going on one of their high-decibel, high-speed, cackling palavers in
Spanish I have about as much comprehension as a deaf and dumb
anthropologist plunked down in 16ᵗʰ century mato grosso in the
middle of some female hazing ritual—the best I can do is grin, stare
off stupidly and good-naturedly into some middle ground, strain
to pick up a few words and hope that what I don't understand is
not too much about me—of course it isn't but in situations like this
a small amount of latent paranoia is stirred—silly fellow—it's as if
I'm a very large fly on the wall that only understands about 20%
of what's being said—not understanding a language is never pleasant, akin to being invisible in some circumstances and overly visible
in others, but as some panglossian souls aver, it's all good, and ambato and Baños are beautiful places and these are really good people—noemy picks me up Saturday morning with Susana and their
friend, Isabel, a woman who works for ecuadorian public television—next we pick up monica and her dog, junior, a friendly lit-

77

tle poodle/terrior mix, and it's off to ambato to get Alicia and her daughter Allison for Saturday night and Sunday in Baños—the occasion for this trip is Alicia's birthday and after a very good restaurant lunch of *fritada* washed down with vintage mountain dew we return to Alicia's casita for a small birthday celebration—alicia, a single mother, has a clean home reminding me of northern new mexico with the sort of humble poverty that is so much healthier than its urban counterpart—the house is part of a small compound where family members live—outside is a cement basin for hand washing clothes, *una lavandería*, and several green garden plots and small irrigation ditches trickling with clear water while white pullets scratch at the dark earth—there is a small grove of *tomate de árbol* next to alicia's house—I pick a few of the fruits and alicia makes juice in her blender—ambato is about 115 kilometers south of quito, located in the province of tungurahua—tungurahua is the name of a currently active volcano of about 5,000 meters near ambato that spews smoke and ash in varying amounts according to its mood—this particular day it's feeling peaceful—it's also capped with snow, a bit unusual, making for a handsome sight—the massive volcanoes cotopaxi and chimborazo are also fairly close but we can't see them this afternoon for the clouds, though coming home Sunday we do—leaving ambato we arrive in the colorful tourist town of Baños about 45 minutes later and secure hotel rooms for the evening at the *flor de oriente*, noemy talking the clerk into letting junior stay in their room—noemy could talk a fire eater into drinking kerosene—we have dinner in a busy restaurant and walk down streets full of tourists past restaurants and bars going like crazy—Saturday night and Baños is jumping—we go to a waterfall next to La Piscina de la Virgen, a series of thermal baths—noemy, who enjoys her camera, photographs the waterfall at least two dozen times—then we're in a funky bar listening to a duo playing traditional songs with speakers big enough for a sports stadium and I suffer again through one of my great peeves with this era, idiotic overamplification, sitting at the table with my right hand covering my right ear and sipping bad wine with my left—the players are full of yeats' passionate intensity and I yearn for my hotel room—the next morning I walk around a bit and then we go in noemy's pickup to a big waterfall and everybody gets soaking wet and screams and it's all fun—this waterfall is powerful medicine—walking back to the parking lot we pass a guy who takes your picture with a big boa constrictor for two dollars and noemy wants me to do it—I demur because it's just too fucking hokey but noemy has a knack for getting her way and plunks down two dollars and kind of pushes me into the snake, insinuating that maybe I'm just a little scared—ridiculous, I'm not afraid—the guy puts the snake around my neck, it's a good 35 pounds, and the serpent weaves its head around and looks at me and I'm very calm indeed—the guy then plops a feather bonnet on me that slips down over my forehead and what can I do but immerse myself in the festivities and grin like a fool, everyone having a good laugh at my expense—I see that my friends are emboldened by the boa's passivity and want to get their picture taken also—what I thought was a jungle photo-op strictly for tourists has its appeal for the locals, who aren't quite as brave and blasé as I've imagined, though only Isabel and noemy get their pictures taken—I've suddenly developed a real fondness for boa constrictors—on the way home we see the volcanoes and noemy jumps out and takes a hundred photos—I have a headache coming on and close my eyes, sleeping off and on as the women laugh and talk all the way to quito—

An afternoon with Mario; morocho Visigoths

9/24

today, Saturday, I meet Mario at santo domingo plaza—we walk to plaza de la independencia and have some pilsener, a good Ecuadorian beer, in the courtyard at palacio de arzobispal—I get a kick out of talking with Mario though I do most of the listening which is fine because he is intelligent and a font of knowledge about Ecuador, speaking rapidly and forcefully, punctuating his oracular pronouncements with bursts of manic laughter and sometimes spittle—mario is an interesting mix of cynicism and leftist sympathies who despises US policies toward latin America—he wants me to read Eduardo galeano's *Las venas abiertas de América Latina*, which I would like very much to do but must find an English translation—sad to say I am slacking on my Spanish—no excuse for this, just laziness—I know just enough to get around and to order food—there is an interesting thing developing in the US called "occupy wall street," a kind of fledgling, low-level version of the arab spring—a couple thousand people showed up to protest last weekend and there is a permanent contingent of several hundred hearty spirits camped in zucotti park, in new york city, now known as liberty park—there are supposed to be large demonstrations today—mario is sympathetic towards the movement and correctly

80

identifies the criminal bastards of finance as the source of so many of our ills—of course it is the rotten system that allows these worms to thrive—I have marveled at how much shit US citizens will eat before they get off their asses and do something about it—perhaps this is the beginning of something—of course it's the end of something for troy davis, namely his life, murdered by the state of Georgia last Wednesday—in this Christian nation there is a deeply-rooted, vengeful, old testament side to our national character—according to the latest gallup poll 64% of US citizens support the death penalty—while it may be *the* cardinal sin to take another's life apparently the majority of citizens think it's fine for the state to do so—I've always believed the state should be held to the same moral standards as the individual—otherwise, what's the point of having a moral code?—and what about mr. davis' "brother" in the white house?—here the perceptive reader will recognize a self-serving rhetorical ploy to get me going on the bastard—our nobel peace prize laureate president has from the beginning overseen a vast killing apparatus that continues unabated—he has increased military spending, including for nuclear weapons—he intones somberly of his success in targeted assassinations, including US citizens, without recourse to legal proceedings—he assumes for himself the right to make these decisions—i could go on for paragraphs—all this for the obvious cowardly and bloodthirsty political reasons that show clearly what this man is all about—the only thing that's changed is the person at the helm—the ship of state maintains the same bloody course, bodies and gore strewn in its wake—with the majority supporting state-sanctioned murder and a president eager to make his bones, it's hardly surprising not to hear a peep from the white house about the cold-blooded snuffing of troy davis—as far as the "real world" of politics and international relations is concerned, mario's cynicism is perfectly justified—we share more bitter laughter about the folly and perfidy of the grownups who run the world and then Mario takes me on a fascinating tour of parts of the old city I have not explored (I have not even touched the majority of it) with its wonderful old buildings, many of which have the original stone foundations and walls from the time of the incas—mario knows his stuff—he points out details I probably would never notice, like the bones of cows embedded in some of the floors at the entrances of shops—many of the front doors in the old city are marvelous as well, including the one at my building—one day I will do a little photographic tour—I would also like to photograph the dogs of my street, a breed apart from our beloved pets in the US—coming soon, a post entitled "dogs and doors"—we pass through a neighborhood almost exclusively occupied by indigenous people from various parts of Ecuador, another world, virtually right around the corner from my neighborhood—here vendors are everywhere selling cooked food, vegetables, clothes, funky second-hand items from old eyeglasses to used electronics—a few minutes later we're in the commercial district where people fill the streets in search of bargains and fun and I find, with mario's help, some badly-needed t-shirts, made in Ecuador and of excellent quality—I bid Mario goodbye in santo domingo plaza—an hour later I'm with noemy and Susana and we're back at the great morocho and empanada place stuffing ourselves like Visigoths—at least noemy and I are—I would never dream of putting Susana in such a crude category—

Maybe it's beginning

9/25

as I was hanging out with Mario yesterday new york cops pepper sprayed defenseless women directly in the face while others of the city's finest arrested about a hundred more who were doing no more than peacefully protesting—this is an escalation on the part of authority that hopefully will steel the resolve of demonstrators to come out in greater numbers to protest the profound inequities that plague us—most of the protestors are young and probably don't realize the extent to which the ruling elite in the united states will go to protect their interests—the ruling elite anywhere for that matter—there is no limit to the violent methods they will use up to and including lethal force if the situation gets to the point where they feel their place of obscene privilege is threatened—there are many lessons to be learned all around as this develops—it's going to be a real eye-opener for young people similar to the way my generation's eyes were opened after numerous assassinations, Vietnam, Jackson state, kent state—the way the eyes of the oppressed in the US have been wide open from the start—it's high time for serious action if we're ever going to get from beneath the killing treads of this machine that is bulldozing our world to the edge of extinction—for the first time in as long as I can remember I have a glimmer of hope—it's the new generation of people in their twenties who are waking up and beginning to fight back—I am so proud of them—their actions, one can only hope, speak for the majority—bless them—it's going to be a long struggle with no guarantee of success, but it has to happen, with non-violence and massive numbers capable of bringing this monstrous system to its knees—maybe the revolution is beginning—

More like home

10/3

the rainy season is upon us and I have begun, contrary to logic, to walk home from work instead of taking the trolley—the main reason is that because of the rain, especially in the evenings, twice as many people take the trolley—what was nearly an impossible situation before is utterly ridiculous now—dozens of soaked, musty people anxious to get home fill the station like surly ruminants waiting for the next car and when it arrives, already hopelessly crowded and steaming, windows shut tight and fogged, push their way into the car like a single-minded beast heedless of any poor souls trying to get off who in turn must push their way through the oncoming mass with the sort of intensity and purpose similar to escaping a burning building—no quarter given to these straining souls and there are some who don't make it off and must exit at the next stop or even the one after that—sometimes people get caught in the doors and though I haven't seen anyone seriously injured I can imagine it happening—I've never missed a stop but it is always a concern, the more crowded the trolley and farther away from the door the more intense the worry—on top of this imagine being the only gringo in the crowd, together with the ever-present possibility of being robbed and you have what amounts to a slightly uncomfortable situation—even so, at least before the rainy season, I'd been getting used to it and even taking a certain pride in my developing equanimity, but this evening after waiting forty-five minutes for an opening that never came I said the hell with it, forfeiting my 25 cents, exiting the station and walking home in the rain, protected by my bent five-dollar k-mart umbrella, enjoying the freedom of movement, the not unpleasant cool evening air, the beautiful colors reflected in the streets, the many tiendas and restaurants I'd never noticed before—from the station at santa clara it takes about 40 minutes to get to my apartment on rocafuerte—I walk down 10 de agosto, a typical thoroughfare, for about 20 minutes, to guayaquil, where the old city begins, not at all typical, to plaza santo domingo, through the arc and then to rocafuerte, past my panaderia where I am now a regular customer buying my usual cachos, galletas and *sunny* nectar de mango or sometimes durazno—where in the beginning I was nervous walking on my street in the evening i have now come to love its wonderful funk and vitality, the chattering school children in uniform heading home, working people with their shopping bags, the little storefront restaurants with various foods cooking on grills, smoke and delicious smells drifting into the night air, shady-looking toughs, men and women, hanging out smoking and spitting, the neighborhood characters, some of whom I am beginning to know and say hello to, el departmento de bomberos (fire department) with its bomberos (firemen) I walk past every night, the police precinct and the noticeable police presence, something I do not object to—cops in quito, at least so far in my experience, are not the same as the thugs in Albuquerque or other US cities—I recently asked my students if cops in quito were known for killing people and they looked at me with puzzlement—they were shocked when I told them that 14 people had been killed by the Albuquerque police department in the last 20 months—there are certainly dangers in quito, but law enforcement doesn't appear to be one of them—I've also begun to take home food from one of the little restaurants I've been eyeing for some time, about a block from my apartment, very good *seco de pollo* and *menestras* for $1.50—the owner is a wonderful, wise abuelita who greets me warmly whenever I visit—more and more rocafuerte is beginning to seem like home—

Arrival in Rukullakta

10/9

today I meet chris Jarrett at his hostel in the mariscal district and together we travel by bus to cumbaya, a relatively wealthy suburb of quito, from there taking another bus, very crowded and featuring a christian rap duo part of the way, for five hours descending through mountains and cloud forests finally arriving in archidona, a small town in the mid-northern oriente, the beginning of the amazon basin and near the village of rukullakta, home to about 2,000 napo runa (kichwa: "the people of the napo")—chris has attended two days of meetings for fullbright grantees spending the next year or so in the Andean region and fills me in on some of the stuff he's learned, as well as information about Ecuadorian politics and development issues, the latter occupying the front burner in any serious discussion concerning the future of this beautiful country—Ecuador has the highest deforestation rate and worst environmental record in South America—the magnitude of the challenges facing Ecuador, particularly its indigenous communities, is daunting, especially considering the grimy foothold of the oil industry, but I suppose there's hope even if it seems there's no stopping the petroleum juggernaut, not satisfied until it has torn up and fouled every remaining precious wild space on this planet—certainly the amazon is one of these spaces, though our preservationist arguments sound feeble against those of the hard-headed commanders of progress and profit who have convinced us the world will plunge into darkness and our god-like systems founder on the rocks of chaos and entropy without their product—there is no question they are our masters but like all masters they need the cooperation of the slaves to continue—this is where people like chris come in and, not coincidentally, all people rising up against this twisted program we've bought into for the last many years to the point of insanity and ruin—as I arrive in archidona half of me is in the amazon and the other half is back with the young protestors for whom I've been waiting for the last 20 years—anyway I am here and I have opened myself up, for what I don't know—what little traveling I've done has taught me that experience can be deceptive but something much deeper is also possible—even as a little kid I wanted to go to the amazon, in my imagination some humid, richly verdant, dimly-lit diorama with real snakes, hooting birds and the ever-present threat of curare-tipped arrows—and of course the great river—not knowing anything about the larger issues of cultural and habitat destruction, mineral extraction, farming, cattle ranching and the hundred other evils that beset this vanishing wilderness, the image of a slightly menacing, infinitely mysterious paradise was firmly imprinted at a very young age and has remained—that this paradise seemed slightly menacing made its medicine all the more powerful, but that this medicine has not proved powerful enough against the onslaught of what passes for civilization has been a bitter and tragic reality to swallow—every trip to the library in those days saw me immediately in the section where the jungle books were—I'd check out as many as possible and read them right away and then read them two or three more times—riding the bus to archidona you see the huge tracts of land that remain but it's easy to be deceived—the amazon is still enormous but not compared to what it was and what's left is fast disappearing, though this is difficult to conceptualize—most people probably don't really care about the amazon—most people on the planet today live in cities—even most people in quito, while possibly caring about the amazon, probably don't know much about it—the hubris and ignorance of the modern world, the urban world, at the foot of the amazon, is supreme—we disembark in archidona and chris calls a taxi driver friend, roly, who arrives shortly and drives us to rukullakta—roly is a somewhat comical young guy we will see several mores times in the next week driving around town in his cab like a character in an amazon sitcom—the village is only five minutes away—it has rained and it is late afternoon as we ride down the unpaved road, pulling up in the section of the village where chris's host "family" lives—for one week this will be my family also—the napo runa of rukullakta are divided into clans, or families, each group having its own area in the village—on the left side of the road there's a heated soccer game in progress on a small muddy field, shirts and skins, about a dozen kichwa men covered in mud and sweat playing with a small soccer ball—chris has told me about the seriousness of these games, pitting men from chris' family against challengers from other parts of the village—along a low creaky bamboo fence women sit watching, commenting and laughing in kichwa and Spanish at their sliding and straining kinfolk—chris introduces me to some of the women and they offer their hands in gentle shakes—this is the manner of greeting—very gentle—some barely touch my hand—they ask chris about me in Spanish—children smile shyly—in the twilight on the small muddy field the soccer game continues, mud and bodies flying, much laughter and spirited banter—amazingly there are no serious collisions, testament to the skill of the players—I'm splattered with mud, baptized, and the women look to see my reaction—I smile and so do they—chris's host father, edmundo, is one of the players—he is more reserved than the others, a handsome man with shoulder-length black hair and a headband—chris runs into the house and changes into shorts and sneakers and joins the game, his white skin standing out in the dusk among the darker bodies—he's not bad but the men are lifelong players—their moves and control are second nature—one of the players is a boy, maybe 10 or 11, and very good—the twilight, the small muddy field surrounded by rainforest, the skill and passion of the players, the laughter of the women, leave me in something of a dream—I'm in an unusual place here indeed—finally it's too dark to continue and the men stop, sweating, covered with mud, tired, clearly happy with the game, gathering to drink lemonade prepared by the women—I'm a bit awkward, standing off to the side, but it's okay—chris knows most of the people and interacts with them easily—a lot of joking and laughter—a few of the men acknowledge me—people drift off and we head over to chris's family's cement block house across the road—I am introduced to edmundo, his wife Irene, and their two girls, Jenifer, 14, and sacha, 8—they are a very handsome family—I am directed to the girls' room which is now chris's but while I'm here chris will stay with the whole family in an adjacent room—the house has two bedrooms, a small kitchen with a gas stove and wood table—there is no refrigerator—next to the kitchen is a living room with a stereo system with huge speakers and a television set, its border decorated with the girls' stickers—around back there's a small cement structure housing a toilet and shower—to the side there's a lavanderia fed by a stream—the back yard is the rainforest—for dinner we start, in typical Ecuadorian fashion, with soup, then chicken and rice and a bit of salad, sitting around the wooden kitchen table with chris and the family doing most of the talking in spanish as I throw in a few words, mostly to indicate that I am marginally sentient, a little self-conscious but not too bad and the family is relaxed and very polite, if a bit distant—they obviously like chris very much and it's easy to see why—he is bright and engaging with just the right amount of gentle teasing humor, a most endearing fellow indeed—we've been invited to a birthday party for a young girl and after dinner go to the community building alongside the soccer field and sit in chairs lined up against the wall while festivities unfold—it is the custom when entering a room to shake everyone's hand and this people do, greeting each person with the usual gentle grasp—I meet carlos, the village elder and yachak (shaman), and his wife, maria—they both wear traditional face markings—it is determined that carlos and I are the same age, 64, which creates, at least in my imagination, a sort of connection—the simple, bare, but colorfully painted concrete room with its tin roof is dimly-lit with a couple of light bulbs—edmundo's stereo system is arranged with its huge speakers and I'm distressed to think the music will be blasting but thankfully it is not—there's a table with a birthday cake and large plastic bottles of soda—we are served another dinner and though I'm not in the least hungry out of politeness I finish as much as I can—chris tells me it's not necessary to eat everything but that all drinks should be consumed—the birthday girl is a natural performer and has everyone charmed and laughing—we gather round and sing feliz cumpleaños—cake and soda is served and I am stuffed—I force myself to eat a bit more—the girl's father hangs a square piñata with barbie's image on the side—instead of blind vicious bashing with a stick or baseball bat a plug is pulled and the goodies come streaming out with the usual scrum at its base—the adults have a trick of knocking the candies out of the children's hands, initiating more free-for-alls—some kichwa pop is played on edmundo's stereo and the birthday girl dances—people filter out and the party is over—it's a relatively late bedtime by village standards, around 9:30, since things get going early in the morning for the drinking of guayusa, how early I will soon discover—

Otherworldly awakening; first guayusa; more

barely asleep, a little after midnight, a neighborhood rooster starts in, big, powerful crowing triggering a response from other roosters throughout the village—what is it with these fucking roosters?—they're not supposed to crow in the middle of the goddamn night—one gets going and they all start in—some kind of dumb competition—but why does the first asshole start?—the chorus of idiotic crowing gets the dogs going and the whole village is in an uproar, the villagers, I'm sure, happily snoring right through the whole thing—but I'm not as upset as I'd normally be, say, at my hillbilly neighbors in Albuquerque partying and guffawing or their silly little rooster going off at 6 am—no, the dogs and roosters are going but so are jungle birds, frogs, crickets and cicadas, and so it's fine, really, look where the hell I am, under mosquito netting in the amazon for chrissakes, and soon it dies down except for the forest sounds and I'm asleep—but not for long because only minutes later, it seems, someone's blasting a radio or cd player with some of the wildest, strangest music I've ever heard—it's the beginning of guayusa time, three or four in the morning—one by one more machines come on, some playing wigged-out kichwa techno-cumbia, some playing haunting traditional tunes, otherworldly sounds that open my eyes in wonder—no one's stirring in the house so I stay in bed and try my best to sleep but in a while the lights come on and I know the game's up so I arise and in the dark and chris and I go to carlos's lodge across the road next to the soccer field—the lodge, attached to his home, is of traditional design, circular, dirt floor, wood sides, thatched roof, a choza—carlos's parrot perches on top of the wall in the open space beneath the overhanging roof—several people are sitting on a wood bench along the wall, gathered around a small fire tended by maria, carlos's wife—a blackened kettle full of guayusa tea rests on a grate above the fire, the large deep green leaves floating in the liquid—the ceiling above the fire is blackened with years of smoke—there's a small hanging wooden platform about five feet above the fire used for smoking meat—after quiet greetings all around with the typical soft handshakes chris and I sit and maria dips a *pilche* (PEEL-cheh), a small bowl made from the shell of some kind of fruit, into the kettle and hands it to me, about three-quarters filled with guayusa—she hands another bowl to chris—the tea has a pleasant earthy smell and taste and we drink slowly, listening to the quiet talk, mostly in Spanish, some kichwa—present are carlos, maria, another woman whom I don't know, and max, carlos's godson and chris's kichwa teacher, incongruously dressed in a clean shirt, slacks and dress shoes—chris, gregarious as ever, joins the conversation asking questions of carlos and max who answer willingly and at length—max especially has stories to tell, mostly of the healing properties of local plants and also stories of snakes, especially boa constrictors, whose *manteca* has strong curative powers—the boa is obviously a significant presence in the stories and imagination of the napo runa—we stay for over an hour, drinking more guayusa, and then head back across the road for breakfast—the tea is supposedly very powerful but I feel no more buzz than I get from green tea, with the same clear-headed energy (which I badly need), very agreeable—breakfast is scrambled eggs, fried potatoes, regular tea and toast—max comes over and for an hour gives a kichwa lesson to chris in the living room as I sit in—some kichwa words: flower: *sisa*; river: *mayu*; world (the natural world [spirit]): *pachamama*; leader: *pushak*; poor: *waka*; snail: *churu* (some smiles here because churu has a double meaning: vagina); yuca (manioc): *lumu*; house: *wasi*; fire: *nina*; good morning: *alli-pun-cha*—after max leaves chris and I talk for a while about life in the village and I look at a paper he wrote for one of his classes—the weather turns hot and I'm drowsy—irene's out back washing clothes on the lavanderia—I don't know where edmundo is—sacha and jenifer are at school—time passes, clouds build, edmundo reappears, we have lunch, chicken soup with carrots and yuca, a plate of rice and chicken—after lunch there's a terrific rainstorm with thunder and lightning and everyone takes a nap—I sleep deeply, drugged by the crashing rain on the metal roof, and wake over an hour later, the girls back from school peering in at me and giggling—I feel very much the curiosity but it's fine—having felt this way more or less ever since arriving in Ecuador I'm getting used to it—chris and I go into archidona via village bus (25 cents) and visit the runa tea operation (guayusa) where I meet nick olson, runa's young direc-tor from the US, who takes us on a tour of the small but expand-ing facilities—this is a hopeful enterprise, one manifestation of the drive to create local, eco-friendly, sustainable businesses in the ama-zon—it's a struggle but runa tea seems to be catching on, with dis-tribution in the eastern and central united states—nick speaks of the challenges of coordinating the business, not the least of which getting the local guayusa growers in sync with the necessary produc-tion schedules and business protocols—profound cultural dynam-ics at work here—I can't help but feel that nick, well-meaning as he obviously is, may be a bit eager to fit a square cultural peg into a round hole—I wish them all well—the world inexorably changes and people do what they must to survive—this is as good a solution as any—alas, it must be so—it is impossible to escape the feeling of the amazon under siege—the crushing gears locked in place—maybe it's just me, my problem—I've come to this part of the world to see what remains of something magical and extraordinary, a planetary treasure fast disappearing—are ventures like runa tea simply rear-guard operations or the beginning of something revolutionary and salvational?—we say goodbye to nick—I have borrowed a pair of runa's rubber boots because tomorrow we're going deeper into the jungle for a few days at the family's farm—back in rukullakta it's dusk and chris and i help edmundo and irene plant yuca in a section of the forest behind the houses—the dirt is soft from the rain and we wear our boots—irene has cut about fifty roughly 12-inch sections of yuca stalks that we stick in holes edmundo jabs in the ground with a pointed pole—in three or four months there will be good-sized plants with roots to harvest—yuca is a staple, crucial to survival—the sky grumbles, light rain falls—in the kitchen before dinner we eat *ukuy*, cooked crispy little insects harvested by a shuar healer, Guzman, who will accompany us to the farm tomorrow—they taste a little like popcorn husks—during dinner the lights go out for ten minutes to everyone's delight—edmundo fetches his flashlight—though there is still some reticence to talk very much to each other, the feeling between the family and me is good and I am more comfortable—the girls are openly warm and friendly, always smiling—edmundo, Irene and the girls retire early and chris and I stay up awhile talking about his project and future plans—in a year he will be in graduate school in san Antonio beginning his doctoral studies in environmental anthropology—more and more I am impressed with this young man—tomorrow an hour ride and a hike in the forest to the family farm—

At the farm

trying to get into the three o'clock, four o'clock, five o'clock rhythms of guayusa mornings, mad roosters, village dog serenades, unknown jungle birds with their powerful, evocative calls, but with little success and I sleep poorly but still lie in wonder at the strangeness of everything and curious about the trip to the "farm"—up again before light, shuffling over to the lodge, chris still sleeping, I enter with only maria, carlos and the same woman from yesterday, whom I only know from sight, in attendance—they greet me warmly and I shake their hands gently—I like this greeting—to me it signifies awareness of the dignity and integrity of the other and also a certain reticence, as if acknowledging the contingent nature of the ritual—the custom of shaking hands is an interesting thing, probably originating as a gesture of absence of immediate ill intent—after all, everybody shakes hands, the murderer with the saint, the banker with the homebuyer, the politician and the constituent—harm comes later—we recognize the handshake as an ancient formality while deeper perceptions exist simultaneously—shaking hands with the politician or banker knowing full well they don't have our human interests at heart—in other contexts handshakes can be meaningful—in the end it all comes down to what's in the soul, communicated through action—the women's handshake here is much gentler than the men's, sometimes barely a touch—I forget and squeeze a little too hard, cringing inside—body language and expressions are indecipherable—I wonder what they think—much deserved and understandable skepticism, no doubt—understanding emerges with time and even then we can never be certain—I'd like to think they recognize me as a good guy but the cultural divide will always exist, a gap that I cannot measure—a lot of it has to do with language—not only is my Spanish weak, my kichwa is nonexistent—but underneath it all I hold to the understanding that we're all human and this guides my behavior—I am respectful and attentive, searching for nuance and cues, careful to do or say nothing that offends—not that I am capable of saying very much—smiling, appropriate eye contact, intuitively monitoring my body language and gestures, discreet observation of theirs, all these things come into play—I am the non-threatening other, slowly picking up manners and customs—humor is always a big thing—I look to see what makes them laugh, trying to understand as much as I can—chris is obviously an indispensable help—there is much kidding and teasing and sex is an open topic of humor—as outsiders we are subjects of amusement and chris tells me that this can wear a little thin but he tries to keep it in perspective—it's a kind of hazing and a bit of a test—I don't think there's anything malicious about it—I think, but am not certain, there may similarities between kichwa humor and native humor in the US—this is only a feeling and as with so much else I may be wrong—next time around as an anthropologist I'll get into this—after breakfast, getting ready to go to the farm, I meet Jamie, a young guy from the US, maybe 18, a big strong-looking dude with funky clothes, tie-dyed t-shirt, scruffy facial hair and one of those piercing stares that makes you a little uptight—I can see chris is slightly uncomfortable too—the amazon attracts all kinds of characters who come for all kinds of reasons, witness yours truly, and I hope jamie's of the harmless variety—it could be he's self-conscious or insecure and I give him the benefit of the doubt—a big pickup has been hired to take us to the farm and a whole bunch of us pile in, carlos and maria, carlos's sons german and edmundo, german's four-year-old son, ingaro, edmundo's wife Irene, his sister, luzmila (the woman from morning guayusa sessions), an indigenous couple from otavalo, both healers, Guzman, the shuar healer, Jamie, chris and me—with our packs and wearing our rubber boots and except for the women and carlos, who sit inside the cab, we arrange ourselves in the back, some of us, including me, sitting on the edge of the bed for the jolting one-hour ride, most of it on unpaved road—you see people riding on the edge of pickup beds all the time in Ecuador insouciantly tempting fate and now I do the same, calculating my chances should the truck roll off the side into a ditch—any such mishap would require an instant reaction in the face of extremely disagreeable odds, in other words, a roll of the dice, in other words yet, basically a matter of holding on tight and hoping your number is still well down on the list—we drive through forest past a few ramshackle homes, the usual garden plots, clotheslines, chickens, going through a stretch of land cleared for cattle ranching and then back into forest, finally stopping at a small stream where we get out and begin the half hour trek to the farm—it is warm and humid and after about ten minutes we stop for a short rest, a blessing from carlos and a drink of kichwa Gatorade, my label, a mixture of aguardiente and herbs that's supposed to give you energy but makes me dizzy as we resume walking on the soft, sometimes muddy trail—my knee is much improved but still a concern and I am careful—it's mostly uphill which is better—the trail winds through thick primary forest and several times carlos stops to point out medicinal plants to the other healers who are here on kind of a tutorial, carlos being widely-known for his expertise—it is difficult to grasp the measure, even the reality, of this environment because it is so dense, literally not seeing the forest for the trees, but it is marvelous being here—as is so often the case in ecuador I must remind myself where I am and that where I am is actually real and that I am really here, which I sometimes question—this always gets me thinking about perception and the nature of reality and being, questions less academic here than at home where everything is so "normal" and taken for granted—that life may be a dream is a liberating notion as in dreams anything is possible—being here with these questions is a sort of tutorial for me also, not about the medicinal properties of jungle plants but in trying to grasp the significance and possibilities of our wispy, fleeting moment of existence—so much wasted energy in struggle and suffering—as I walk carrying my backpack, sweating, a bit dizzy from the aguardiente, surrounded by this strange, humid, breathing entity, the forest, I think about the mostly young people in the occupy movement and how dreamlike their gesture, breaking through a mental and spiritual barrier so formidable it might as well be a nightmare, so iron and brutal in its totality and perceived indomitability, requiring nothing less than a leap into, or from, the unconscious, the world of dreams—that this is happening seems unbelievable, as dreams sometimes are—one wishes for it an equivalent, nay, a greater power than its adversary, which is nothing less than a competing dream of the same human heart, the outcome very much in doubt—I have no idea about the outcome of my modest ecuador adventure or even its meaning—we arrive at the farm, a small compound with two separate clearings, one for general meetings with a couple of open structures plus a small hut enclosing a bucket-flush toilet, the other containing a big thatched roof lodge, the living quarters—there are bananas, yuca, mandarinas, limes and papayas growing at the farm, plus a bunch of chickens, about a dozen fewer than before, we are told, possibly stolen by Colombian workers from the nearby cattle ranch—there are two dogs, one very strange and sick-looking with something like mange—we are surrounded by jungle—after unloading our stuff carlos takes Guzman, the two Otavaleños, jamie, chris and me on an hour hike through the jungle to a waterfall, the path narrow, steep and sometimes challenging, the ground sponge-like and covered with decaying leaves, in places muddy—the rubber boots are a necessity—with my unstable knee I am forced to concentrate every second—an awkward fall here would have nasty consequences—fortunately with all the walking I've done in quito my knee is stronger, though far from perfect—in a curious way the two environments are not dissimilar—walking in the city sharpens your senses, myriad perceptions working simultaneously, constantly aware of the traffic, pedestrians, the rough sidewalks, stoplights, interesting sights, always thinking, navigating, calculating, moving—no stoplights in the jungle other than metaphorical but your senses are on high alert just the same—there is so much to see, at the same time every step carefully monitored—going down slippery inclines I grasp small trees for support but am careful because there might be unpleasant surprises like insects or some larger creature and often they're covered with thorns or sharp protuberances—slipping once I grab a tree covered with little thorns and my hand stings the rest of the day—we stop frequently as carlos points out different plants—there is constant talk between him and the other healers, especially with Guzman, the shuar—the shuar are the fabled headshrinkers of yore but Guzman hardly seems the type, a sprightly, good-looking fellow with a bright, amused glitter in his eye—he has a lot to share with carlos—we pass a camouflaged perch in a tree used for hunting and soon after a deadfall trap designed to kill medium-sized animals, a low passageway bordered by stakes, over which hover two logs, one on top of the other, triggered by a baited trip wire, in this case a thin vine—carlos demonstrates and the logs crash down with whomping finality—this is some serious boy scout shit and all of us are quiet for a few seconds—the logs are heavy and come down very fast—no animal in there stands a chance—the amount of usable plants in the jungle is overwhelming as is the people's encyclopedic knowledge of them and you realize all you've heard about this is true—plants for menstrual cramps, skin problems, stomach aches, sore muscles, dandruff and more—interesting is a plant whose seed pod contents tells you if your wife has been cheating or not, a kind of natural jake gittes without the photographs—most impressive is the *sangre de drago,* "dragon's blood," a tree whose sap is blood red and drips freely from its bark with a cut of a machete, very similar to a rubber tree—the red sap is good for skin problems and, if taken in small doses, helpful in dealing with more serious internal issues—it is also a dentifrice—simply dip your finger in the liquid and rub your teeth—I can attest to its effectiveness—there is also copal, the tree resin that is used in some Mesoamerican ceremonies as incense and by the napo runa for its flammability—in places vines and other plants overhang the path and carlos chops away with his machete—it is humid and my t-shirt is wet and I'm tired from the effort, mostly the extreme concentration, but I mustn't relent, even for a second—the jungle is quiet, birds and animals very much aware of our presence—everywhere the lush green of a hundred shades, dozens of plant species in the space of a single glance—a novice wandering a few feet off the path would be in trouble—carlos demonstrates the subtle method of marking a trail by bending a branch, a practice designed to foil trackers with hostile intent, something still applicable as the war on indigenous populations everywhere in the world by oil, mining, timber and cattle industries and their murderous hirelings is relentless—I think of the documentary Tong Tana and the amazing Bruno Manser—they will not be satisfied until they destroy it all—down we travel towards the waterfall, a quiet background noise that becomes louder until we are there, at the base of a gentle precipitous tumbling of foaming clear water a hundred feet into a pool, the mists a rainbow glimmering cooling our bodies, surrounded by cliffs covered with dense green vegetation dark in the shadows of this quiet hollow—we stand silently for a few minutes and carlos rolls a ceremonial cigarette that we all smoke, native tobacco in a leaf, very smooth and good—a waterfall (kichwa: *pakcha*) is sacred and carlos, Guzman and the Otavaleños strip to their underwear and wade into the pool, next to the falling water—jamie and chris follow but not me because I don't wear underwear and haven't brought my bathing suit—I certainly wish I had—I'm not sure it would be appropriate to be naked—the kichwa and guzman spread their arms, absorbing the spirit of the waterfall and carlos performs cleansing rituals on all of them one by one as they sit on a boulder, his mouth on their heads and hands inhaling the bad energy and blowing his good energy into them, taking mouthfuls of the aguardiente mixture and spraying a mist over their bodies—jamie, serious and intense, mimics the natives and spreads his arms to the waterfall—I rub my face and chest with handfuls of the clear water—the bodies of the Otavaleños are pale and a bit flabby but they are both strong—carlos, my age, is fit and muscular—Guzman, in his thirties, not especially muscular but obviously in good shape—we sit for about fifteen minutes, quietly talking, smoke a bit more of the cigarette, put our damp clothes back on and leave—the walk back is mostly uphill and tiring, but easier on my knee—the couple from otavalo are amazingly fit and lead the way—I am not surprised at this—the jungle is quiet, numbingly green and dim, shafts of light cutting through occasional clearings—my hand stings from the thorns—for the first time I think of insects and realize I haven't bothered to put on repellent, but it's not too bad, some flies but no mosquitoes—ominous rumblings of thunder and dark clouds threaten a storm and we are still some distance from the farm—the thunder booms and reverberates throughout the forest—if it rains as heavily as I imagine it might the ground will turn to thick mud and our climb will be difficult and we will be soaked—nobody seems especially concerned—the thunder trails off and there is no rain—my clothes are wet with humidity and perspiration—finally we are back at the farm—I am tired—inside the lodge everything has been arranged and I have a corner bed with mosquito netting—I change out of my wet clothes and hang them outside—filthy socks, wet jeans and t-shirt—inside, in the kitchen area, the women and edmundo have prepared a late lunch of soup, rice, chicken and a generous helping of chontacuro, the large grubs harvested from decayed chonta palms, roasted in banana leaves—they are extremely fatty with a slightly fishy taste—it takes about three months after the death of the tree for the grubs to be fat enough for harvesting—it's about

4:30—we all take a nap and don't wake until it's almost dark—the women serve *chicha*, a drink made from yuca, whitish, pulpy and slightly sour—to make chicha the women chew the roots and expel the liquid into a large wooden bowl—the saliva creates a fermentation, the longer the process, the higher the alcohol content—the batch we drink is slightly fermented—chris mentions that carlos is going to lead an ayahuasca ceremony that evening and asks if I'm interested—I am, but not certain if I'm ready for such an intense experience, feeling the need to be more acclimated, more in tune—after chicha we have soup and roasted plantains—it is dark—the women clean the bowls and straighten out the kitchen—almost everybody gets ready for sleep but a few gather around carlos, who is preparing for the ceremony—I have decided what the hell, I may not have another opportunity to try ayahuasca—ayahuasca is a kichwa word: *aya*: spirit, *huasca*: vine—spirit vine, one of the most interesting plants in the world, used universally in the amazon in these sorts of ceremonies—I am, however, a bit skeptical—from what I've read and what Mario has told me a true ayahuasca experience entails more deliberate preparation, internalizing the rhythms and spirits of the environment along with dietary and spiritual cleansing, none of which I've even remotely undergone—there is a slightly slam-bam feeling to this gathering, too fast, too sudden, almost casual—nevertheless I decide to do it—candles are extinguished and we sit quietly with carlos in front, the only light coming from the cooking fire in our middle—it is chris, Jamie, the yachak from otavalo and me—Carlos sits cross-legged and pours the brown liquid from a plastic bottle into a small pilche and blows cigarette smoke over it, then waves his feather rattle over the bowl quietly chanting—he hands the pilche to the Otavaleño who sits quietly for a moment and then drinks the ayahuasca, handing the bowl back to carlos—this ritual is repeated until everyone has drunk, each of us pausing several moments in contemplation before swallowing the slightly bitter, earth-tasting concoction—while this happens carlos sings the type of odd, curiously mournful, ceremonial song I've heard in recordings while moving his feather rattle back and forth—the first thing one can expect after drinking ayahuasca is vomiting and, less frequently, diarrhea—I've not had a good bowel movement since coming to the oriente and reflect that I might be in for a rousing stereophonic experience—we sit for what seems like a long time, maybe 30 or 40 minutes, with little happening, at least for me, other than falling deeply into the mood of the fire, the ceremony, carlos's chanting and the swishing of his feather rattle—but there is something going on, a subtle tinge, or buzz, of tightness and anxiety, plus the unmistakable feeling (at last!) of the final stage of digestion kicking in and I borrow a flashlight from edmundo and in a kind of electric haze, barefoot, make my way down the path to the first clearing to the little hut and the bucket-flush toilet—I sit for a long time, thoroughly purged, no diarrhea thankfully, feeling very strange indeed, the jungle close around me—I wonder if some large snake is going to crawl into the hut—I'm not seeing any bejeweled jaguars but I'm not in any ordinary world either—I'm also a little nauseated—I don't know how long I sit but chris comes, maybe a little worried, and I rouse myself, after three trips to the water barrel finally getting the toilet flushed—I walk, dreamlike, back to the lodge, looking out for snakes, leaving chris behind for his own private ceremony—if nothing else the ayahuasca has performed admirably as a laxative—in the lodge we sit quietly for a while but nothing happens for me other than more of the same slightly anxious buzz and subtle disorientation and I decide to go to bed, crawling under the netting and closing my eyes, enjoying a colorful show on the inside of my eyelids, a lot of warner brothers yellows, greens and blues—it begins to rain, lightly at first, then heavily, off and on most of the night, hard on the thatched roof—we are all together, sleeping in the large room—

Trek to a sacred spot

not a great sleep, a lot of yellows, greens and blues saturating restless, vague dreams, roosters crowing all night between bouts of rain—I've got a theory about these roosters—it's because they're wilder and they crow anytime they damn well please, just like a lot of other jungle birds—I used to have some araucanas, the "easter egg" chicken—araucanas are from south America—they have less of the jungle squeezed out of them and the hens usually get broody, unlike their domestic counterparts—anyway, no late night etiquette from these blokes—the frogs are going full blast too, along with the usual jungle birds and their terrific sounds—up early for guayusa and then breakfast, fried plantains, ox milk and yuca—I'm beginning to dislike the bland, over-prescribed yuca—today will be a long three or four hour hike to a large waterfall where carlos will conduct more healing and cleansing ceremonies—chris has asked carlos if he will perform one on me and I look forward to it—today it's Guzman, the Otavaleño, carlos, edmundo, chris, jamie and me—this trek is more demanding than yesterday, the ground more slippery, the path steeper, and of course it's three times farther—because of the rain it's more humid and we're soaked right away and the same battles recommence, utterly attentive to the terrain, ever so careful—I have come to like jamie—he's really an exceptionally earnest kid, very respectful to all and speaks decent Spanish, much better than mine—he's come to stay in the rainforest on a quest or mission of some sort before returning home to attend college—this is pretty unusual for an 18-year-old and I suspect he's had some problems that he's intent on dealing with and this is one rather novel aspect of his therapy—I don't pry—he remains a mystery—something of lord jim about him—this jungle trekking is a young man's game unless you're carlos who's been doing it his whole life and knows the environment absolutely—he and the two healers stop periodically for palavers concerning different plants and occasionally Guzman shows carlos a thing or two—there is no evidence of ego that I can see, only genuine interest and sometimes surprise at what the other has to teach—in general though, carlos is the master—at one point he stops, seeing something a few feet off the path, digs around with his machete and uncovers two very white pigeon-sized eggs—they are from un caracol, churu, *snail*—this is a very big snail and the easy, natural way carlos has uncovered the eggs makes it seem like a stunt, as if they were planted there to impress us—forgive my doubting western mind—we reach an overlook and see the waterfall about a mile away, across the valley, the jungle spread out before us—I'm sweating and my t-shirt is soaked—the kichwa are relatively dry—their hairless bodies are obviously better adapted to this environment—i feel like a European ape, the sweating misfit in the jungle, a touch of the herzogian fool, with none of the grandiosity—we stop for a rest and carlos retrieves a large plastic bottle of *fanta* from his net shoulder bag and passes it around—jamie refuses, giving a short lecture on the evils of plastic—we pay him no mind, drinking and moving on, back into the forest, descending—something glimmers orange and red off the path and we stop—carlos takes his machete and loosens an old rusting coke can—jamie, disgusted, takes it from carlos and stuffs it in his bag—the can is very beautiful—things decompose quickly here—just beneath the rotting surface material is yellowish, clay-like soil, exactly the nutrient-poor jungle subsurface one reads about—about an hour later after a steep descent we arrive at the waterfall, about three times bigger than the one from the day before—we pass around the ritualistic cigarette, take a few slugs of *fanta*, jamie refusing, and carlos and the two healers go down to the pool—we watch as he performs cleansing rituals on them on a large outcropping of granite—before each ritual they drink the sacred water from a small depression in the rock—after a bit jamie, chris, edmundo and i carefully climb down the rocks to the large pool where the noise of the falling water is like a continuous subway roar and the wind from the compressed air blows at gale force—everyone has stripped to their underwear and this time I've brought my bathing suit—the water is cool but not unbearable and chris, Jamie and i swim across and clamber up the rock to receive the cleansing from carlos—jamie goes before me—when my turn comes I lie on my stomach and drink the water from the rock and then sit as carlos performs the ceremony—he puts his mouth to the top of my head, sucks out the bad medicine and then blows his good air into me—he does the same thing to my hands—then he takes the aguardiente mixture in his mouth and sprays my arms and chest—I sit very still and serious—the noise and wind of the waterfall envelope us—I am highly conscious of what carlos is doing but feel nothing—as with most things like this I am agnostic, neither believing nor disbelieving—I leave myself open to possibilities—I am respectful—the ceremony is over quickly—we have not received the same deliberate attention as Guzman and the Otavaleño—it is, I feel, a bit like the ayahuasca session—but I understand the necessarily superficial, passing nature of this experience—again the outsider, incapable of attaining full receptivity and understanding—the yachak performs the ritual as a courtesy, with sincerity I am sure, but knowing the distance that separates us—he believes, despite the incompleteness, that the ritual benefits our wandering souls—despite my agnosticism I would never pass up an opportunity to experience a native ritual of this sort though I would reflexively balk at its Christian equivalent—I *would* participate in the Buddhist—why have i almost violently rejected much of my cultural heritage?—I know very well embracing the rituals and customs of an alien culture is not any kind of answer, though there is much of benefit—as jimmy durante said, these are the conditions that prevail—even someone as deeply absorbed in an alien culture as manuel cordova-rios (*Wizard of the Upper* Amazon) eventually returned to his roots—but I wonder—my disgust with US society is profound and nothing that's happened over the years has mitigated this, indeed it has only increased—milagro, jamie takes a swig of *fanta* and we head back, cleansed and refreshed though soon enough I'm sweating with the effort but it's uphill which is better for my knee—we visit a lagoon, sitting quietly for about twenty minutes—back on the trail carlos stops to replenish his supply of sangre de drago—farther on, he examines the ground and I think he's onto another clutch of eggs but this time he pulls up a bulbous root used for soap—we continue and come across an overhanging vine that chris swings on, tarzan-style and later I disturb a nest of bees, small ones, thankfully, nevertheless moving very quickly to outpace them, receiving numerous though not very serious stings—I'm lucky on this one because there are bees and wasps in the forest that will do a very bad number on you—at the lodge we have dinner, soup, plantains cooked in leaves, scrambled eggs with grated heart of palm, chicha—jamie is going to spent two weeks here alone—after dinner he and carlos walk around the perimeter of the farm discussing food and survival—tomorrow, in the afternoon, we return to rukullakta—

Stone age games

under normal circumstances I wouldn't be very comfortable sleeping in a large room full of people I hardly know but these circumstances aren't normal and it's really better than I'd imagined—there's a together, communal feeling here and these are exceptionally good people—despite the frogs, and the roosters, with their wilder cousins in the forest, I have my best sleep yet—after guayusa and breakfast, chris, Guzman, carlos, jamie and I hike about a half an hour to a small river with a nearby sleeping platform where carlos sometimes goes and we effect some simple repairs—I sweep the roof of leaves with my hand and startle a tarantula about the size of a jacks' ball which scurries under a beam—poisonous but exceptionally shy creatures—finished, we go down to the river to cool off and jamie and chris go for a swim—I hadn't known we were going swimming and to my chagrin I have again neglected to bring my bathing suit—guzman is skipping stones and I join him, this being one of my favorite childhood pastimes—I'm curious about his form, having the cultural conceit that we throw better in the US because of baseball and in this case it's true, his form's a bit awkward—nonetheless it's effective and he's just as good as I am—we're both getting three or four skips—these stones are pretty good, just the right size, though not as many really good flat ones as I'd like—we have a bit of a contest, coming out about even, though he gets off a couple of five-skips, then go for distance, throwing in the direction of an old fiber bridge spanning the river, and here's where I have him, even though my arm isn't nearly what it used to be—I get off some good sidearm tosses with flat stones that sail up the river and land with little splashes under the bridge, 80 meters or so in the distance—the bridge hangs quaintly about ten meters above the water, mostly rotted and no longer usable—guzman and carlos softly voice their approval—they should've seen me back in the day—jamie and chris join us and Guzman, shuar of the old headshrinking tribe, initiates another game, a little like washers, the objective to knock a medium-sized stone off a larger one about 30 feet away—the contest is between chris, Guzman and me and it's a spirited one, pretty evenly matched, but I'm an old washers player and confident, indeed I'm winning and could easily wrap things up but in this case I'm not interested in competition, for various reasons even want my opponent to win, and I take my foot off the pedal—Guzman forges ahead and triumphs, which pleases everybody, though I feel atavistic stirrings of regret—in what's understood as the real world there's no mercy but it's long been established that I don't live in the real world, lack the killer instinct, obtain no delight in putting my foot on the other fellow's neck, which is not to say I wouldn't do it if I had to, which I hope I never do—the thought arises out here of certain dire situations and what the chances of survival would be—in my case not good—I'm older, don't know the terrain and have a bad knee—I'm the guy who keeps his eyes open and stays out of trouble—I admit to observing jamie at first but quickly understood his decency—we're all good guys here but no one really knows, do they, especially concerning oneself—as for the rest of the winners if it's gold they want let the fred dobbses of the world have it all and destroy themselves in a bloody tourbillion, which is the direction we're headed—just stay out of their fucking way—take care of yourselves and your loved ones, the good ones—pick up the pieces and start over—do it the right way, as I suspect the natives I'm with are doing, though I have little hope of ever understanding the mysteries of their psyches and invisible connections to the spirits of this extraordinary environment—how tired already the refrain but never more true that we're so disconnected from the natural world that we've become profound idiots, some sort of bizarre and shameful life form unworthy of this incomparable planet, obese automatons fixated on pleasure and the crushing, soul-sucking security provided by overlords, themselves enslaved to something much larger and more sinister—good god!—but these are decent people I'm with, they represent something better, and there are many like them all over the world, our best and only hope, speaking different languages and customs but addressing the same spirits—how great to be playing stone age games with a shuar of the darkest deepest amazon!

Darkest, deepest dreams

faithful followers and aficionados of maninthemiddle will recognize in the last sentence of the previous post the sly irony that pervades these primitive scribblings—noninitiate or less finely tuned might think I'm hoping in my Westchester soul that the savage I'm playing stone age stone games with might take time out to nail a monkey with his curare-tipped dart and demonstrate the venerable art of headshrinking—obviously the darkest deepest amazon exists in the minds of those with the darkest deepest dreams, but the real amazon has been plotted, scanned, divided, sub-divided, conquered and cremated for the last 75 years, its terrain mapped to the last millimeter and pinned to corporate walls, begrimed with the slobber of CEOs drooling over the untold wealth, animal, vegetable, mineral, within its verdant canopies—as for the shuar, Guzman, I know nothing about him other than he's a peaceful fellow with an air of quiet amusement and intelligence and someone seemingly well worth knowing, as would be the history of his people and the journey that has led them to this point facing the inevitable and its consequences—the inevitable is what's happening all across south America and the amazon, against which the old medicine has no defense other than joyce's silence, exile and cunning, a strategy dependent on a sanctuary under relentless assault from all the usual bloody, boring, depressing suspects—not only is this sanctuary the natural terrain of their traditional homes it's also the realm of the psychic, magical and spiritual, which while obviously threatened by the rapacious, suicidal demands of development and the introduction of new and improved cultural paradigms is also, paradoxically, under assault from well-wishers, the good people trying to "preserve" or "save" their culture but whose interface will necessarily devitalize all that is mysterious and potent, a form of well-meaning parasitism—this is not to denigrate the efforts of organizations like amazon watch, the pachamama alliance, survival international and rainforest action network, to name a few, or for that matter my friend chris, but simply to face squarely the reality of the change—indeed, there is no going back—just as one world language disappears every two weeks so go the old cultures, fading, at worst, to black, absorbed into the brave new genetically modified future, or more hopefully retaining some modicum of integrity and left well enough the fuck alone—unlikely—in the afternoon while waiting at the stream for the truck to take us back we try a little fishing with edmundo and his brother, german, using a round piece of metal about the size of a basketball hoop with a fine mesh net attached, basically a crab net without a handle, maneuvering the object across the bottom near the bank and lifting suddenly, hopefully catching a few silvery minnow type fish in the process—it looks easy and edmundo and german catch quite a few, storing them in a large leaf rolled into a cone—for chris and me it's a different story, as if up against some genetic barrier, like curling your tongue—either you can catch the little fuckers or you can't—we can't—after another ride on the edge (where else to be?) we arrive in rukullakta in late afternoon and in the house chris informs me that Irene and edmundo want me to be a godfather to sacha, their youngest daughter, a request that moves me but a little less so when chris says the children have lots of godfathers but at the very least I take it to mean I'm not a total loser in their eyes—there follows a short ceremony where I hold a rather embarrassed sacha in my arms while edmundo does something with a crucifix, thankfully nothing too elaborate, and I'm asked to give her a special name, which pops out immediately, "flor," and everybody is pleased because unbeknownst to me this is her middle name, a good sign that grants me improved standing, something I'm always happy about—I am presented with a handsome bracelet and necklace of colored beans made by Irene—later, after dinner, we go into archidona, a seedy tropical town graham greene would have liked, for batidos, a kind of fruit shake, at "el sorbette" and have a good time making musica de batidos sucking the dregs through our straws—chris's friend, Roly, the amazon sitcom taxi driver goes by, is hailed with gleeful shouts, and for the price of a dollar we get a ride home—

Lacking passionate intensity

Sunday morning, Baños

Noemy jumps in

Mario tour-1

Mario tour-2

The pitch at Rukullakta

Lavanderia

Rukullakta road

Edmundo jabs

Irene plants

Deadfall

Guzman and Chris

Carlos with some copal

Sangre de drago

Irene

Maria

Chontacuro

Snail eggs

Great-great grandfather (the tree), *ceiba pentandra*

After trekking three hours

Ceremony

Jamie

Chris and Carlos

Guzman, Chris and Carlos

Darkest, deepest dreams

A pistol in pig shit

morning guayusa and then later to tena, about a 20 minute bus ride from archidona, a bigger town that attracts most of the whitewater business in ecuador, to be witnesses in some kind of legal ceremony for irene's sister's ex-husband but the timing is off and instead we go to a battered old bar and sitting around a table next to the sidewalk drinking many rounds of pilsener, ecuador's best, in big bottles as I communicate with irene's father, Enrique, in Spanish, better after a few beers, the same way darts or pool is better after a few, but only a few—too many and darts become lethal weapons, cue balls fly over bumpers and Spanish collapses like a house of marbles and rolls into a *barranca* of gibberish—I am close to that point—Enrique, a tough, stocky guy in his fifties you'd obviously be advised to have on your side, senses it and the conversation lapses into polite entropy—besides, my proficiency in spanish precludes going beyond a third-grade conversation—I'm not drunk but near the point where things could go strange very quickly—enrique is a river guide into Yasuní, the great preserve in the northern oriente, home to the waorani people and some uncontacted groups and said to be the most biologically diverse place on earth—it's a three or four day float on a balsa raft and conditions are not what you'd find in your newfangled eco-tourist gig—sounds good to me—I've been in some unusual drinking sessions in my day and this is one of them, apart from the cell phones and newer cars rolling by we're back in the fifties in this humid amazon night old town bar, a rack of empty bottles on the table, folks with a good buzz—time to go and the company parts ways, edmundo, Irene, chris and I getting the bus to archidona in good spirits and beer hungry and arriving find a small place where I have my first Ecuadorian *hamburguesa*, good Ecuadorian beef and a straight-up cold coca-cola, my first in years, achingly delicious with real sugar, not the corn sugar bullshit of the gmo'd, corn-glutted, corn-holed states—to think, you can't even get real coca-cola in your own fucking country except in some latino neighborhoods—most murkans don't even know the difference—well, if you don't know you're getting fucked I guess you're as happy as a pistol in pig shit and it's all good, init?—I buy some stuff for breakfast in a little market and chris calls the taxi and we head back to the house—tomorrow I go with chris and some runa tea people to hang out at a river near tena—the day after that, back to quito—

Not Huck's domain

I am at the river with a bunch of chris's twenty-something friends from runa tea, including nick olson, feeling old and very un-hip, as it should be, after all, I've had my glorious days too and so it passes from one to the other—still, I envy their energy, strength and enthusiasm—alas—they are a bright, educated bunch with an air of privilege and much to their credit doing something good—if they stand out as exuberant gringos in this brown and poor country, conjuring whatever feelings in the local population, at least they stand out as a group representative of a different impulse, every one of them, I'm sure, attempting to respect indigenous sensitivities and customs, mindful of the terrible history they represent and the contingent nature of their efforts—the river is one of the dozens of small tributaries that feed larger tributaries that feed the amazon and so is considered rather insignificant but compared to what passes for a river in my dear new mexico it might as well be the great river itself—in width it is not particularly imposing, from our location maybe george washington's silver dollar across the Potomac, but its volume and strength are awesome, chill blue waters rolling relentlessly down from those magnificent glaciers and snow-capped volcanoes with an intensity possibly surpassed only by the Himalayan system—this is no animal to be fucked with as I instantly realize the minute I put my puny body in its powerful flow, having to swim twice as hard as I normally would in the little rivers of home—downstream a hundred meters are rapids with large boulders, swept into which you'd not stand much hope—I feel like a high school football player suited up for an nfl game, the best I can hope for a dash onto the field carrying Gatorade for the big boys—I make a few forays, ever so cautious—a few of chris's friends swim across to climb a jumble of large boulders about twenty feet above the river and take turns jumping in and I follow (*I can do this!*), giving it a shot then swimming back across the huge current with visions of tumbling through the boulders downriver, my poor gone ragged lost body chewed and swallowed in jumandy's jungle never to be seen again—no, this is not huck's lazy Missouri swimming hole—the rocks and boulders are river-smooth and stand in obdurate brilliant contrast to the rushing blue water, all around the quiet jungle, tall, deep and green—

Money talks

10/16

in the morning I take my final *pilche* of guayusa and present the yachak, carlos, with my swiss army knife as a token of reciprocity and appreciation—this is not an easy thing to part with as I've had it for years, accompanying me on many adventures and performing yeoman service in deeds large and small, the same knife I once badly cut my thumb with trimming a walking stick on a solo trip at the rio chama—I am a little ambivalent about this gift but I want to give him something of value and apart from my camera the knife is the most important thing I have—I say a few things in broken Spanish and present him with the knife—he is pleased but not overly demonstrative—I have paid for my adventures in the oriente, 25 dollars per day to edmundo and Irene (I am short $50 and will pay them later), some expenses for groceries and now the knife—you always like to think you're part of the inner circle but the reality is that I've been a tourist here in rukullakta—carlos especially is determined to preserve the traditional culture of the napo runa and his son edmundo is working towards establishing himself as an eco-tourist guide—there is some ambiguity then about my status here as I am part client and part friend, forerunner of a hopeful future influx of visitors, a viable business possibly established, possibly not—at any rate I have provided them with some much-needed money that will buy food or some other necessary items—the role of money has its own cultural nuances and I accept the fact that I am expected to pay—after all, I come from the culture of money and it is assumed that it flows naturally from our pores and, relatively speaking, it does—I have no illusions about this and I understand that "Richard from the US," while certainly a good fellow, also means "money from the US," which is just as important as whatever sympathetic qualities i might have—it is an odd dynamic for the guy from the US who can't completely shake the desire to be loved by the natives much as white liberals want to be loved by black folks—this, then, is one part of a complex of barriers that will never be breached and must be accepted if the desire is to operate in a field of diminishing illusions—chris accompanies me to archidona where I catch the bus to quito and then a taxi from the bus station, rio coca, to my apartment on rocafuerte—when I get in the cab there are two shiny dollar coins on the seat that I use to pay half the fare—if there are such things as omens or signs I take this to be positive, though a righteous man would have shared his booty with the driver (which, in a sense, I did), a failure no doubt assuring a stubbed toe further down the road—

Dialing up a little thrill

10/29

it's around 8:50 am and I'm talking with a friend in Albuquerque via skype when the subway makes an unusually loud noise which is odd because quito doesn't have a subway and the thick old walls of this building are shaking and the windows are rattling in their frames like barnaby's bones, moving back and forth, almost billowing, like a scene from *the haunting* while i cower in simian dread of some force beyond anything I've known as the roar and shaking build to a crescendo and after several seconds subsides, the train on its way to the next station—those who have experienced these things and worse than what we get this morning, a temblor, a mere 4.0 on the richter scale, understand the awesome, terror-inducing power of these little stretches, yawns and shrugs the earth undergoes every day all over the place, sometimes with terrible consequences—that this happens while I'm skyping with a friend is fantastic, as if the earthquake gods have dialed up a little thrill for me to share in real time with someone I know back home—and so I'm able to add a little more spice to this bubbling collection of experiences, the ordinary occurrences of the crazy and unexpected that constitutes life in Ecuador and better yet for someone to witness firsthand that I'm not dreaming or making this stuff up—see! here! right now! it's happening!—it's grand to experience a temblor but this is sufficient and I hope never to go through anything more serious—I google earthquake survival tips and find the safest place is away from windows and exterior walls—this sturdy old building is likely safe in all but the most powerful and direct perturbations, but who knows?—I determine that my closet would probably be best, situated beneath a thick wooden lintel, probably a doorway in years past—the terrible part of the experience is not knowing how long it will last and how powerful it will be—I can imagine a few things more terrifying than an earthquake, at sea in the middle of a hurricane would be one, but an earthquake, something that usually happens to other people, is pretty strong stuff and quito is in the hot zone—the last big one here was in 1949 and there's a frightful history with these things in ecuador—

Of referendums, oily lawyers and toothy swimming partners

11/3

Papandreou has offered a referendum for his hapless subjects, rather, the world banking cartel's subjects, to choose between stripping naked and jumping into a vat of burning oil or simply stripping and shivering for the next several years while they figure out how to make some new clothes—the smart money, which would be the bankers' money, says the greeks get the burning oil because there will be no referendum, the overlords never agreeing to such a quaint thing as national sovereignty or democracy—to take the cynicism a step further some say that Papandreou, socialist in name only, has offered the referendum to save what little is left of his reputation and manhood, more quaint considerations steamrolled beneath Maggie thatcher's runaway TINA-machine, knowing full well his masters will never allow it and that his souvlakia is well and thoroughly skewered—beware of greeks bearing referendums and yes, we're still working on maggie's farm, but the occupy movement is alive and the general strike in Oakland semi-successful, as hope, if not burning brightly, is still faintly kindled—while the world quakes and quivers, Susana, her son camilo, and I squeeze into a tourist van around nine-thirty pm and travel seven surreal night hours to cuyabeno, in the northern oriente, sucumbios province, going first through the cold altitudes, stopping once to see faraway snow-capped antisana gleaming portentously in the chill moonlight and then dropping down to the warm and wet lowlands on winding, well-paved jungle roads through infamous lago agrio (formerly nueva loja), a seedy and evil town, the center of operations for Texaco's and now chevron's pillage and despoiling of this once pristine environment with the full laissez-faire cooperation of the Ecuadorian government—plaintiffs from the affected population have successfully, in a judgment without precedent, sued chevron, which has been ordered by an ecuadorian judge to pay 18 billion dollars in fines for the enormous, criminal destruction of the surrounding environment and the health crisis they have caused—starting in the seventies Texaco began dumping its toxic waste in the jungle and continued for decades, taking advantage of the zero environmental standards of a criminally negligent and complicit Ecuadorian government, which historically has never given a damn for indigenous rights and obviously has cared little for protecting its environment vis-à-vis the extraction of "resources"—chevron, which with the approval of the federal trade commission a few days before September 11, 2001 sucked Texaco into its gelatinous, insatiable belly, is of course fighting this judgment fang and claw with every wicked legal obfuscation it can muster percolated in the depressing brains of its bloodless attorneys—the sideshow of sleazy legal contortions continues but this time the bets just might be on the plaintiffs, a bracing and hopeful prospect—driving through the oil country of sucumbios the roads are in good repair with sturdy guard rails and bright yellow lines marking the way, something you would assuredly not see in other parts where there is no oil—it would be nice to think the government is concerned for the safety of local traffic with these gleaming roads but of course this is an absurdity—one glance at the terrible conditions of the homes and towns along the way tells the story—still, even in a country with so much poverty the juxtaposition of the activity of the oil industry, the pipelines, the steady convoy of rumbling tankers, the processing centers with their holding tanks and so forth, determinedly extracting and moving untold wealth from the land next to the run-down shacks and decaying towns, home to thousands, many of whom probably work for this same industry, is shocking—you'd think at the very least you'd see a few signs of the dirty money oozing down to the local level and while there may be some of this that I didn't notice, certainly a possibility, what I saw along the roadside only reinforced the ugly reputation of this rapacious and irresponsible industry—there are those who will criticize my concerns as hypocrisy because here I am using my computer and enjoying the comforts produced by fossil fuel energy and I concede the very small and stupid point but I ask in return what choice do I, or any of us, have?—it is like criticizing someone for complaining that he is choking from exhaust fumes inside the bus because after all he should be thankful he is not on the side of the road walking to his destination—do I have to drop out of modern civilization, get off the bus, and live in purity and isolation for my arguments to have any validity?—we all know there is an alternative to dependency on fossil fuel energy but this entails too much change for the ordinary person used to these faustian comforts, living in willful disregard of their consequences and obviously our masters will never change unless we are at their powdered wattles with our ungrateful peon hands—fat chance there, as they have surrounded themselves with the most sophisticated and deadly security apparatus in the sordid history of class warfare, which is the history of our species—I have no problem imagining my peasant hands around the perfumed wattles of charles koch or scott walker or michael bloomberg or, appointing myself representative of the children blown to bloody pieces with his cowardly and contemptible drone war ("bugsplat"), around the skinny neck of our half-white and fully whitewashed president, the nobel peace prize winner—but in the end this does not work because as a practical matter they are stronger than we are with their praetorian goons and furthermore to do violence to them is to do violence to ourselves and to the goals we have of becoming a better and more tolerable species—it is an uncomfortable and near sleepless ride and around 7am we arrive in cuyabeno, warm, humid and surrounded by jungle, next to the chocolate brown cuyabeno river—we are in the middle of the cuyabeno wildlife reserve which, along with bordering yasuni national park, is considered one of the most biologically diverse places on earth—it seems every place I visit in Ecuador is one of the most biologically diverse places on earth—the cuyabeno river is not a large river in terms of width but there is a good flow and it is impressive, crowded on its banks by thick green jungle—we have breakfast in an open thatched-roofed building next to the river spanned by the old highway bridge that also supports a section of the oil pipeline that slithers its way hundreds of kilometers along the road we've traveled—on the side of the bridge "bienvenidos" is written in fading paint next to the pipeline, an infelicitous but significant pairing reinforcing the subtle feeling of sadness and something not quite right that is always present in the amazon, of inexorable destruction and loss, of the fragility of the natural world against the iron, mindless determination of our ant-like species, which is not to say nature doesn't win in the end, bad news for us but a matter of indifference with her—we go across the warming highway that stretches on into the forest and you get the feeling this really is a faraway place relative to what you know and what you're used to—next to the road there's a large tree hung with the pendulous scrotum-like nests of the crazy oropendola bird, native to the north American blackbird but much bigger and producing wild, full-throated, marvelous sounds that will be the leitmotif of our short stay in the reserve—across the road at the ranger station we pay our fees and receive a short lecture from a handsome indigenous fellow, a siona, about the reserve and the ever-dwindling natural world: the jaguar nearing extinction, the rare manatee, disappearing pink dolphins, continuing oil exploration, and so on—we get into a long boat with a small outboard motor and putter down the river about ten minutes to our destination, the cuyabeno lodge, where we disembark and walk down a boardwalk to put our stuff in a thatched-roofed hut that has a good bathroom and cold-water shower and three beds hung with mosquito netting—after another breakfast in the dining area we get on the boat with about six other tourists and go for a long ride on the small river whose banks overhang with dense foliage to lake cuyabeno, where I and a few others go for a swim in the warm water—again I've not worn a bathing suit so I swim with my pants rolled to the knees—after a bit we head back, spotting some caimans popping their heads above the water—swimming with caimans is not considered particularly dangerous but it is just a tad disconcerting to realize belatedly that you've been sharing the water with ancient predators whose proficiency in killing is surpassed only by one's own species—how far was my gleaming flesh from one of these little monsters in the murky water?—what happens if you step on one?—are there piranhas?—*si, hay pirañas, muchas pirañas—pero no son peligrosas*—our next destination is a small siona village, santa Victoria, which has its own greeter, a woolly monkey that comes up to the boat and makes a big deal of our arrival, especially happy to see our guides, obviously old friends—santa Victoria is clearly a demonstration village of sorts, geared to the eco-tourist trade, and we are given a tour by our guide—especially beautiful is the garden in which is grown mango, papaya, banana, mandarina and the ubiquitous yuca—in a nearby hut we watch two women make pan de yuca, an interesting process not disimilar from the hopi method of making piki, the flat blue corn bread cooked on stone—the women work with skill and economy—we are served pieces of the bread covered with honey—the monkey, adolfo, creates a comic spectacle in the hut and the women shoo him away angrily—back in the boat it begins to rain and the sky darkens dramatically and the ride home takes on a different character—it's a good way from the lodge and we've been out a long time—after an hour it's dark and the guide carefully maneuvers the boat on the narrow river, raising the engine when it gets too shallow—there's another guide in front helping to navigate, shining a flashlight periodically—the rain stops but it's chilly—we pass several boats coming from the opposite direction, mostly locals, families, some merchants carrying goods, one with tourists from another lodge—we go by each other in silence—it's a long time and there's a slight edge to the proceedings and you understand the interesting problems that could arise, one of which the possibility of spending hours in the jungle should the engine fail or the boat hit something nasty and take on water or if we run out of gas—we bump into things and near the end there are problems with the engine but the guide is resourceful and coaxes a bit more out of it and we finally arrive at the lodge where dinner awaits—after eating we talk a while and then go to our hut—the birds, oropendolas and others, are going crazy—extraordinary, fabulous sounds—there are more bird noises here than at rukullakta—camilo and I stand on the boardwalk for a half hour looking at the southern hemisphere stars which are unfamiliar to me—camilo knows his constellations and points them out with his star laser pointer, an amazing instrument purchased on ebay for 12 dollars that shines straight into space—it is an impressive bit of technology and occupies our attention, more compelling even, for the moment, than the stars themselves—

Mystery rain; wonder names them both; an old friend

an all night downpour soothes my sleep but in the drowsy depths of consciousness I wonder if something is not quite right with this rain—it is too steady and goes on for hours—in the morning the ground is dry, not a hint of rain, a mystery I finally uncover exploring a nearby water tank that had been overflowing throughout the night, the water falling onto a piece of sheet metal—water is crazy-money in Ecuador, billionaires lighting their cigars with thousand-dollar bills—what we in new mexico would do with all this water!—there is a profligacy with which it is treated here that is almost astonishing, though the snow pack on the surrounding volcanoes has retreated roughly 30% in the last two decades, attesting to the planet's warming trend—as for the climate change rule of thumb of wet places getting wetter and dry places drier, Ecuador's complex geography would imply that the country is seeing a mix, but this is something I know nothing about, although certainly quito is not lacking for rain and neither, apparently, is the oriente—unlike the melting snow pack that supplies temporary water for the rivers in the southwest, the relatively constant rainfall in Ecuador, allowing for the differences between rainy and dry seasons, provides more or less continuous runoff—there's little chance of rivers running dry here, for now anyway, as you sometimes see in the southwest US—after breakfast we participate in planned activities for the tourists, a short walk in the jungle, swimming in the river next to the lodge, a boat ride and then lunch with about twenty guests in an abandoned compound that looks like an old summer camp rotting away in the jungle—it doesn't take long for things to decompose here, the environment an enormous digestive apparatus, so unlike the arid southwest with its abraded artifacts lasting decades, becoming more and more abstract, weightless and ethereal—the jungle is heavy and wet and whatever the opposite of ethereal is—oppressively present, immediate, where everything is process, speeded up so that one's sense of time is telescoped, focused on the fierce battles small and large between elements co-existing and devouring each other simultaneously—the jungle is history in fast-forward, thousands of dramas acted out each moment, bloodshed, copulation, beauty, deception, competition, cruelty, poetry and death, unrelenting, so that one barely has time to reflect, overcome by the spectacle of life going crazy, crowding in—the desert, its opposite, is space—and death—silent stretches of emptiness that summon a very different spirit from that of the noisy, amnionic jungle, each, as lao tzu says, equally profound: *"If name be needed, wonder names them both: From wonder into wonder, existence opens."*—our siona guides produce a good lunch, tuna, macaroni, ham, salad, bread, soda, brownies and we are well fed—I wander a bit and discover a large colorful caterpillar but there is a commotion and I hurry back to the group to watch a troupe of squirrel monkeys cavorting in the trees overhead—we are as wide-eyed and happy as children watching our agile cousins flip and glide from branch to branch in their playful search for food, in this case fruit—they are obviously aware of our presence but unconcerned—we've had our lunch and now it's their turn, clearly more fun for them, and some of us can imagine not too long ago, a mere few million years, foraging for food in the same delightful fashion—it's not the first time I've been a little envious of monkeys or apes, the true adams and eves, the ones not expelled (or the ones, in their wisdom, deciding to stay behind)—I have befriended a fellow about my age from the coastal province of manabi—gustavo is a powerful guy with sloping shoulders and a somewhat mournful and homely spanish face and a patch of white hair and hands like railway couplers who on the morning walk through the jungle hoisted his five-year-old grandson on his shoulders and calmly carried him for an hour up and down the slippery terrain while the rest of us struggled, slid and sweated, grasping at leaves and trees to keep from losing our footing—gustavo has a wonderful calm about him—I noticed the evening before on the night ride home that he and his wife, mirian, were the most relaxed of all the tourists, snuggling together for warmth and laughing at private jokes—there is a nice easy sensuality to both of them and a feeling of innate class and intelligence—I like their style—Gustavo reminds me of a dear high school friend, now gone, a very physical guy who unabashedly loved the sensuous things of life and from whom I learned so much—we were like brothers and did everything together, duck-hunted, surfed, fished, played sports, drank like crazy and chased after girls like satyrs, with mythological success, I might add—studying was not in our repertoire—came the late sixties and seventies tom and I went different ways—I used a fair amount of drugs but tom got in deep and it ruined him, his adult life a tumultuous ride of dealing, addiction and incarceration, finally dying of a heart attack several years ago—gustavo is tom in Ecuador having taken a different path and I am glad to see it, glad to meet up with him here more than forty years later—

Tommy

the neighbors in the compound bought a puppy about a month ago and there is a new dynamic here in the courtyard, the most vibrant aspect from my perspective being lots of dog shit—his name is tommy and he's a cute little golden retriever or something like that and the whole family is gaga—I look ahead and see tommy as a big dog with a big bark and bigger piles of shit, though when I go out and one of the family is there playing with tommy, usually one of the teenage daughters, I am all smiles and cutesy-gushing myself, *"hola, tommy! como estas tommy? que bonito!"* but what I'm really thinking in my black wc fields heart is goddamn little fucker shitting all over the place and ruining the courtyard and I hope these people keep bringing him inside after dark when he gets older because I can see him barking all night as I lie sleepless losing my mind and thinking of things in Spanish to say to these people—this is really not a good development and Susana, who is the manager of the apartments, is upset also because the family didn't ask about getting a dog, presenting her with a fait accompli—so now in addition to washing clothes and whatever else she does, the good doctor's mother, la señora, the matriarch, mariana, is all day cleaning dog shit, dutifully following tommy's business, piece of newspaper or plastic bag in hand, then scrubbing the ground with water and disinfectant—only occasionally do I see one of the other family members cleaning shit, and never the good doctor, this of course being women's work—most challenging for la señora, I would imagine, is when tommy's process has not been ideally firm and wholesome, which happens quite a lot as I have unhappily observed, the frequent rain making it worse—why they have not tried to train tommy is puzzling—I asked la señora about this but she speaks so rapidly I never fully understand her but the gist of it was that it is too difficult—I don't know what the problem could be—she would save herself an incredible amount of disgusting work—in the mornings shuffling along my hallway to the kitchen I no longer look out at a charming courtyard but rather one of dante's circles of hell where the condemned must clean dog shit for the rest of time—it's not a pretty picture—even less picturesque have been the evenings coming home from work to find a welcoming gift in front of my door and finally the other night the inevitable happening, though fortunately it was only a small part of the heel of my walking shoe and easily cleaned—I immediately had la señora construct *una barrera* of plywood and chairs to frustrate tommy's generous nature—this, for the moment, seems to be effective—meanwhile, depressingly, tommy, and his offerings, grow larger every day—

Inti-Illimani

12/1

in the late 1980s I found myself in Albuquerque editing a small quarterly magazine that concerned itself with politics and the arts, mostly politics, and mostly reacting to the vicious counter-revolutionary crusade in central America carried out by the loathsome Ronald Wilson Reagan, a famous anagram of whose name, as I once mentioned in an issue of this little magazine, spells out *insane anglo warlord*, which he, in company with virtually all US presidents including the pathetic contemporary, surely was—I suppose you could argue the present incarnation in this line of shameless, preening functionaries is not completely anglo, which only demonstrates the corrupting power of the office, acting as temporary titular head of the historical phenomenon known as *"the united states of america and its experiment in capitalist democracy: a tragedy in* ____(fill in the blank) *acts"*—a popular ad campaign in the seventies proclaimed you didn't have to be jewish to love levy's real jewish rye and similarly you don't have to be anglo to love slaughtering people in the service of empire—indeed you must demonstrate quickly your relish in so doing, no hint of wimp allowed—the president must be a manly fellow and mr. Reagan surely was, though he somehow managed to avoid combat in world war II, which in principle is not necessarily a bad thing but another story altogether if you mold a career characterizing yourself as a steely-eyed, granite-jawed, flag-waving patriot ready to kill any and all who threaten our christian-capitalist-democratic-freedom-loving-beacon-of-humanity-normon Rockwell-turkey-eating way of life—reagan was one of the forerunners of the contemporary american-fascist-narcissistic cult of the body (along with his great fantasy pal slyvester stallone), an avid weightlifter who once challenged Mikhail gorbachev to an arm wrestling contest, a comic book president spouting puerile jingoist rhetoric who had the media and majority of the population in cinemascopic thrall while he aided and abetted the killing and torture of thousands of peasants and revolutionaries in central america, now canonized as a great and beloved american president, a fine, genial, warm and folksy fellow, one of the people, one of us, the guy who started his first presidential campaign in philadelphia, Mississippi, the symbolism of which only missed by the irrevocably brain damaged—in those grim days of depravity in central america, wholesale murder sponsored by the US and carried out by its school of america trained assassins, the contras in nicaragua, Roberto D'Aubuisson and his ARENA party in el salvador, killers of Óscar Romero, the Ríos Montt government in Guatemala continuing the ongoing genocidal war against the indigenous population that ultimately claimed 200,000 lives, those days of pregnant women having their wombs sliced open and babies torn out in front of their families, of public rape, of people skinned, of castration, decapitation, disembowelment, dismemberment, burning, torture, once again championed by the genial mr. reagan, those days of cia "dirty tricks" and sabotage and destruction of anything with even a whiff of collectivization or betterment of the common welfare, schools, agricultural and electrical efforts, public transportation, health clinics, water and sanitation projects, we were being told that we were winning the war against godless communism and that it was "morning in America," indeed fine and noble days, but some of us felt just a bit out of nose with the prevailing odor, which smelled more like decaying flesh than bacon and eggs—some of us in fact responded with *contra* efforts of our own,

such as joining peace brigades to Nicaragua, working with witness
for peace or acting as individual volunteers like the martyred ben
linder—my own response was to start a small magazine, *coatimundi*,
and I found myself quickly involved with latin american issues,
learning about the historical role of the US, which had assumed the
mantle of colonial power from the long gone Spanish empire—the
initial relatively innocent step in an escalating spiral of US involve-
ment was the Monroe doctrine of 1823 which was, ironically, viewed
approvingly by Simón Bolívar, but other than the lunatic william
walker nicaragua sojourn in 1856 things didn't really get going until
the smiling bull entered the ring with the Spanish-american war in
1898—I have no desire to catalogue the long bloody train of events
and usurpations visited upon our neighbors to the south and anyone interested can examine the record, but after a 13-year time out
for rural life, art, marriage, babies, divorce and other lively events
in northern new mexico I awoke to the outrages in central america as if to a recurring nightmare first encountered as the war in
Vietnam—amerika was at it again, it had never really stopped, the
normal condition of our republic being war, though now by proxy,
and it was time to become active once more at the inconvenient
urging of what small conscience I possess—so, the magazine—if you
moved in suspect circles then, among strange people who had leftist
latin friends, or who spoke Spanish and went to a university, or who
knew who Augusto Nicolás Calderón Sandino was or what the let-
ters FMLN stood for, then you likely knew something about Nueva
canción, the latin american fusion of traditional and socially com-
mitted music, the exemplar of that genre being the great Chilean
group, inti-illimani, formed by Santiago college students in 1967—I
listened to inti-illimani a lot in those days, loved its energy and
beautiful dramatic Andean melodies, full of the spirit of resistance
and revolution, inspired by such greats as violeta parra, Atahualpa
Yupanqui, Silvio Rodríguez, Mercedes Sosa and victor hara, the
Chilean folksinger killed by augusto pinochet's police on September 16, 1973, five days after the forgotten 9/11 (not in south America)

when US backed right wing Chilean forces overthrew the democratically-elected socialist government of salvador allende—"we can't let Chile go Marxist-Leninist just because its people are irresponsible," growled nixon's batrachian national security advisor, like our current charismatic smiling assassin a nobel peace prize winner, his co-recipient, the truly noble Le Duc Tho, refusing the award—this was the beginning of a 17-year hell for ordinary chileans but not the rich and those associated with US government and business interests—even the notoriously conservative catholic church carefully distanced itself from the terrorist Pinochet regime—thousands of Chileans were murdered or "disappeared" in that nearly two-decade span—victor hara's death has assumed mythic proportions since those days but the reality, carefully reconstructed, is that he was brutally tortured and shot 34 times, his body dumped outside Santiago—the historical record of US intervention in latin American affairs is something I always think about here and I wonder in their deepest selves what the people I meet truly think about the US and, inescapably, how these thoughts affect their perceptions of me—I've gotten some clues from Susana, who is honest and polite, and also from some of my students, once they feel more comfortable expressing themselves, though they, too, are unfailingly polite—the gist of it is that, to put it mildly, the united states is not viewed in a favorable light—more on this in a future posting—but back to inti-illimani—susana has asked me if I want to go to a concert tonight at la Casa de la Cultura, quito's primary cultural center, to see some friends of hers in their band, Illiniza, to be followed by another popular group, Pueblo Nuevo, both of whom perform in the nueva cancion tradition—of course I accept and she picks me up at six, after work—we are hungry and eat at the mcdonald's (*me encanta!*) near la casa and I do like it very much, along with the imperialist coca-cola, and feel no guilt or shame, my belief being a certain amount of these pleasures necessary for the well-rounded and examined life—another option would have been the KFC across the street but we unanimously reject it for mickey d's—you've got to draw the line somewhere—there aren't too many fat people in Ecuador but what few there are seem to be in mcdonald's tonight—after eating we cross the street in the rain and join the stream of people entering la casa's huge mollusk-like concert space, el agora, as if some form of alimentation being sucked into its massive form—it's cold inside and of course I don't have a sweater or jacket and as often happens here there is a long wait and the concert is 45 minutes late in starting and what's more noemy arrives and strong-arms us into the VIP section in front of the stage with its massive speakers more suited to a stadium concert and I think, fuck, not only am I going to freeze my ass off but I'm about to suffer once again one of my pet-peeves of contemporary life, idiotic over- amplification, a full frontal assault on my hearing that will likely flatten my auditory profile even more, a depressing thought, but I notice the guy next to me stuffing bits of napkin in his ears and I tell him what a good idea this is and he reaches into his pocket and cheerfully offers me a whole goddamned napkin which brightens my mood and I thank him profusely—maybe this night won't be so bad after all—I even feel warmer after stuffing napkin in my ears—illiniza comes on and they're good, and the crowd, which is several thousand, responds enthusiastically—they remind me a little of inti-illimani with their energy and between pieces one of the band members speaks to the crowd and though I don't fully understand it is obviously political as he mentions che Guevara and again the crowd erupts—this is interesting—I have just put a photo of che on my wall, with some misgivings, realizing that this is, or should be, a serious gesture—che was a real revolutionary and you don't display these things unless you're prepared to live in a certain way and back your words with certain actions which in some instances might well involve extreme discomfort, if not ultimate sacrifice—there is also much I don't know about che, the reality as opposed to the myth, and now I have an encounter with the obvious that strikes me with a force bordering on the profound—while che's historical significance in the US is mostly abstract, for those of

the white left a romantic story of a dashing, courageous and ideal-
istic young man hunted down and killed with the assistance of the
cia in the jungles of Bolivia, his hands severed for positive finger-
print identification, in this part of the world that has suffered so
much from US imperialism the reality of che Guevara is anything
but abstract—che is a symbol no less here than in the US but he
is a symbol of a lived historical reality beyond what most of the
white left in the US have experienced—the only gringo in the au-
ditorium as far as I can tell, at least in my section, I am in the
middle of thousands of people cheering passionately for che Guevara and while everybody's going nuts I think, well, it's my government, my country, that is basically responsible for killing the man
and responsible for so much suffering in latin america, the awareness of which seemingly a part of the genetic makeup of the people
here—the passionate outburst at the mention of che is exciting and
I cheer and clap too, but it is sobering, and I am cheering as much
to demonstrate disapproval of my country's actions as I am in favor
of the man himself—I wonder if I suddenly found myself by some
bizarre twist in the middle of thousands of cheering Pinochet supporters would I be applauding enthusiastically at the mention of
his name, not in approval obviously but as a matter of self preservation—I have many times wanted not to stand for the national
anthem at sporting events in the US but have lacked the courage,
which speaks to the question of che's photo on the wall, though in
the matter of standing or not standing discretion is likely the better part of valor—after illiniza comes pueblo Nuevo, another nueva
cancion group full of energy and beautiful music and I am by now
caught up in the pure enjoyment and enthusiasm of the audience,
the napkin plugs working fine and the chill of el agora not even
a memory—there are more impassioned words about che and also
salvador allende and again I figuratively pull my head between my
shoulders as now my country is batting a thousand in responsibility
for martyred figures this evening—pueblo Nuevo finishes and exits
to enormous cheering and I think, well, this turned out a lot bet-

ter than expected, really great, in fact, an evening to remember, and the master of ceremonies comes out, I guess to bid us good evening but the energy of the crowd is anything but diminished, rather increasing, and I soon discover the reason because he says our great friends from chile, *inti-illimani*, will be out in a few moments and the crowd roars and I turn to Susana, who's just as surprised as I am—onstage, technicians are frantically scurrying around getting things ready as the excitement builds and then here they come, inti-illimani (to be accurate, I'm not sure which version, there apparently has been a split, but at this moment, who cares?), maybe eight of them altogether, with their glittering instruments and talent and the cheering is tumultuous, and for the next 45 minutes they treat us to their remarkable music, and to be in the midst of the culture that spawned them, to feel the electricity and communication that crosses back and forth between audience and performers, is truly something special—towards the end of the concert, at the height of collective happiness and enthusiasm, the camera pans our section and I see myself on the screen, lone gringo, smiling and clapping with my south American friends—

La Novillada

12/3

we are nearing the end of fiestas de quito, which lasts from the end of November to the 6th of December and which commemorates the "founding" of quito by spain in 1534—quiteños, as do all Ecuadorians, love to celebrate, and even the indigenous population, the ones upon whom the city was founded, which reminds me of Malcolm X's remark about Plymouth rock landing on blacks and all kinds of history book nonsense I grew up with of places in the "new world" being "founded" and "discovered," get into it with gusto—what the hell, it's 477 years since the noble Rumiñahui and his warriors were defeated by Spanish guns, germs and steel—life is hard enough, why not have a party or two?—the official celebration didn't really start until 1958 but it's been going strong ever since and as the majority of the population is mestizo, history is literally in the blood and almost everybody's involved to one degree or another—there are obviously tensions between certain groups and the usual class distinctions exist in Ecuadorian society, but at least by the greater mestizo/blanco population history is felt as something shared—to be sure, the Spanish influence dominates, but underneath are the older indigenous/Indian roots, just as many of the buildings in the old city, el palacio de gobierno, for example, are built upon ancient incan foundations—every day during the ten days or so of fiestas there are celebrations and parades and plenty of drunkenness on the streets and in the *chivas*, the colorfully-lighted party buses that seem like *univision* sets with resolutely cheerful partygoers crammed together bumping and grinding to blaring music—chivas seem horrifying to me and only slightly less interesting than the culminating event of fiestas, the parades honoring the new reina de quito, which I might be curious about if one were in my neighborhood, but the real interest for me is seeing my first bullfight and on this Saturday Susana and I go to the plaza de toros for a corrida, or, to be precise, a corrida de novillos toros, or *novillada*, which features young bulls and young bullfighters—bullfighting is not high on the list of the politically correct these days but I'm curious, about the event, and my reactions to it—the corrida takes place once a year in quito during fiestas and this is the only chance to see one here in the city, although others occur elsewhere in Ecuador at different times—this is the first year the corrida in quito will be conducted under the rules of a recently-passed proposition put forth in a nation-wide referendum considering the outlawing of killing bulls in public: *"Regarding the prohibition on killing animals in spectacles, do you agree that, in the municipality where you live, the spectacles that have as purpose the killing of the animal should be banned?"*—each municipality is given the choice of positioning its collective thumb up or down on the "spectacle"—quito has rotated its thumb to the ground, sparing the innocents in the stands the sight of *la estocada*, the final sword thrust, or killing of the bull, though the fly in the ointment, and it's a big, ugly fly, is that the bull is killed with a *puntilla*, a dagger used to sever the spinal cord, behind closed doors after it has undergone its ordeal in the ring—it's a fine day in quito, a decent amount of sun, the city in high spirits ten days into the fiestas, not unlike the feeling of a Saturday morning before a big college football game, the final *desfile* (parade) for la reina de quito three days off—susana has picked me up in her little chevy spark and after parking in a centrally-located *parqueadero* we take a cab to the plaza de toros and step into a milling, excited crowd across the street from the plaza where Susana immediately runs into a female colleague who makes a face when she hears we're going to the corrida (it seems the majority of polite society in quito makes such faces when the subject of bullfighting comes up), which makes me feel as if I'm slightly perverse and bloodthirsty, but I brush it off, eager to experience this ancient ritual and just as eager to examine objectively my own responses—of all good feelings in life, approaching a stadium before a sporting event is one of my favorites, and I feel a similar excitement, but this is a little different from the usual football or baseball game—for one thing the stadium is smaller, and painted yellow, unlike the monumental drab concrete and steel exteriors of many US ballparks—this and the mood of the crowd gives the occasion a sense of intimacy with an air of something secretly shared, as if a gathering of an ancient order to witness something no longer quite acceptably decent, outside the margins of modernity and enlightened society—as if playing out their roles somewhat defiantly from a century earlier, some of the people, especially the women, are costumed, or posing as, *aficionados*—many of the men are smartly attired but their female counterparts are especially so, dressed *escotado*, which is to say open white blouses plunging dramatically leaving little or much to the imagination, very tight long pants, stiletto high heels and wide-brimmed cordoban hats, so that the impression is one of an elegant, primitive eroticism, at once dominating and submissive, the female, regal, severe, sexual, unapproachable, in wait of conquest by the primal male energy of the bull conducted through the triumphant killer, the matador, the whole ritual an enormous phallic ceremony, the elemental nature of the bull, its brutal masculine reproductive force mastered by the deadly skills of the human now possessing the bull's power, symbolically delivering it to the waiting, suddenly submissive dominatrix—if this seems a bit much I suggest you reserve judgment until you've seen one of these spectacles for yourself, and then you can decide if I'm too excitable and impressionable a fellow—undoubtedly—and this is what I was thinking even *before* entering the stadium—in any case these are commonplace observations expressed more eloquently a thousand times before—the ring itself, *el ruedo*, is an intimate space with beige, sandy dirt and two concentric chalk circles that indicate specific areas for different aspects of the ritual—the *picador*, for example, is not supposed to do his work inside the outer circle—we sit on concrete benches and wait, the stadium only half full, the crowd somewhat subdued—this is the first year of not killing the bull according to tradition, which seems to have reduced the number of spectators, and also, possibly, their enthusiasm—but now comes the procession of horses and toreros: matadors, banderilleros, picadors, presenting to the dignitaries with traditional, elegant style and the crowd responds with an excited roar and the band plays its dramatic spanish music—a moment later there's another roar and an enormous fedex jet lumbers over the stands so close you can practically see the rivets and it's hard to say if this diminishes the proceedings by overwhelming them or adds a weird modernist aspect somehow fitting that proclaims with one wrong turn, one unforeseen hook of its wing, this monstrous bull in the sky could render our anachronistic ceremony into a bloody smoldering scene of horror beyond anything goya might imagine—how quaint the little people below and their play at killing bulls!—you want to see death in the afternoon?—the bullring is in the flight path of the airport and for the rest of the day every ten to fifteen minutes the jets fly over barely skimming the top of the arena, their terrible roaring noise drowning out everything else, stealing the show in their own undeniable way, though the people do their best to ignore them—I reorient myself by checking the program to read the names of the novilleros—they are víctor barrio from spain, josé antonio bustamante from Ecuador and rui fernandes from Portugal, who will fight as a *rejoneador*, in the traditional Portuguese style, on horseback, though in this instance without the *rejón*, which is the lance used to kill the bull—after the formal greeting between toreros and dignitaries there is a ceremony in the middle of the ring in the form of a protest against the new law and against the threat to bullfighting in general, greeted with a hearty response by the crowd—the woman sitting next to Susana, who looks like she might be related to Pinochet, middle-aged, well-dressed with a hint of *escotado*, red cordoban hat, hard-eyed, in fact the wife of a former colleague of susana's, asks me if this is my first bullfight and how do I like it, as much challenge as question, one of the *aficionados* on the defensive, sniffing out the censorious or squeamish—this is my first, I tell her, I don't know yet—many of the people seem to be of a similar type and I get the feeling if this was spain they'd be happier if franco were still in power—none of these bleeding heart referendums then—franco's Ecuadorian counterpart was León Febres Cordero, president in the 80s and a pal of reagan—a few weeks earlier i'd seen *Con mi Corazon en Yambo*, a documentary about the abduction and disappearance of the teenage restrepo brothers in quito during cordero's regime that has yet to be resolved—the eighties was a hard time for latin America and US fingerprints are all over it—bullfighting is cultural politics, an easy divide between left and right, but for me it's a more complicated issue which is partly why I'm here, an open question, curiosity, certainly, not necessarily morbid—I have no particular desire to witness death, though that is the essence of the ritual—clearly the prohibition against killing in the ring sucks much of the drama from the bullfight and I'm not prepared to say on balance if this is a good or bad thing—now the corrida begins with a trumpet call and the bull is released from the *toril* where he has been waiting and the crowd roars in response to this magnificent animal as he comes in a great rushing skittering charge absurdly reminding me of seinfeld's Kramer entering a room, but no kramer this, an unbelievably powerful beast on serious business armed with frightening speed and ill intent, looking for some sonofabitch to obliterate, the banderilleros spilling out like clowns or pests but performing a vital function running into the ring to attract the ferocious charges and tire him out, running behind the *burladeros*, the shelters on front of the *barrera* (wall), for safety until finally the bull pauses to catch his breath, angrier than ever and then the matador, the novillero in his *traje de luces* (bullfighting suit), víctor barrio, a slim good-looking young man from spain, enters dramatically to more cheering and with his *capote* engages the bull in some classic *veronicas* to more cheering, including many *oles!* and it seems to me he's done this well because everyone is pleased and also from my perspective he seems to have the classic style and charisma—susana says the bull is a good one and this also has the effect of pleasing the crowd—the bullfight takes place in three stages, or *tercios*, this the first, culminating in the work of the picador, who comes out on a huge horse covered thickly along its flanks by a kind of heavy fabric armor and also a blindfold over one eye, presumably to lessen the visual terror because the bull is a terrifying animal—there is an odd feeling from the crowd right away towards the picador which is that he seems immediately unpopular, or perhaps this is an unpopular part of the event—it is certainly a less elegant part, with a lot of awkward jousting, snorting and jabbing, the horse clearly not wanting anything to do with this clumsy and fearful business, the picador only slightly more, and you can see it is really dangerous with the bull ramming the underbelly of the horse, fortunately protected by the heavy fabric, without which its guts would be spilling out all over the place—the picador keeps jabbing at the neck muscles of the beast, the crowd displeased—suddenly there's a gale of whistles and Susana voices her dismay—I look closely and see why—instead of sticking in one place and piercing the neck muscles the pic has slipped, slicing half the bull's length, a huge flap of bloody skin hanging like a rug exposing the raw muscles of his neck and back—the banderilleros come running out to distract the unfortunate beast because he is no longer useful for this contest, corralling him back through the gate and into the *toril* amidst shrill whistling sounding like a thousand angry birds—I feel sorry for the bull, they'll never bother stitching him up, and share some of the contempt for the picador who has done such a bumbling, foolish job, violating the *form* and ruining a perfectly good fighting animal—it is easy to see why this is the least popular part of the ritual and why *aficiandos* are so quick to demonstrate their displeasure—a new bull is released, this time coming out slowly, surveying the scene, then rushing at the banderilleros who scatter behind the burladeros—this business of chasing the banderilleros is repeated several times before víctor barrio strolls out as slim, elegant and composed as ever and performs more veronicas with his capote and the crowd, a little peeved from the display moments before with the picador, warms to his graceful passes and soon they're shouting *oles!*—to my untrained eye he seems a good matador, economical in gesture, calm, standing close to the bull as it goes by on its angry rushes—the last part of the tercio begins and out comes the picador once more to a restive, whistling crowd but this time it goes better—still it's a clumsy process and hard to say if the job is a good one or not—the bull delivers some heavy blows to the horse, almost knocking him over, the crowd on edge, gasping—the picador keeps sticking his pic into the bull's *morillo* (the hump of muscles around the bull's neck, on top of its back) as if trying to find the right place—the bull's head lowers perceptibly, the muscles of its neck weakened, blood streaming down its flanks—the whole business is a mauling, huffing, dusty affair, like a couple of bloody fighters working each other over on the ropes with no room for style or polished maneuver but it seems to end more or less satisfactorily with only mild disapproval from the crowd—the first tercio is over and we're ready for the second, the *banderillas*, the barbed, steel-pointed, colored-paper-covered sticks that are placed in pairs by the banderilleros into the bull's morillo for the purpose of further weakening him, as only in this lesser condition will the matador be able to kill the animal—as all this riveting action unfolds, every ten minutes or so a jet flies low over the stands with its terrible roar and people look up involuntarily, momentarily distracted, yet another occasion for me to reflect on how much I hate this modern age, but the spectacle is unavoidable and perhaps worth marveling at in some phenomenal realm—the planes are huge, balloon-like and colorful, appearing close enough to reach out and harmlessly poke, glistening in the sun, moving slowly, as if a cartoon—some of the men are already drunk and happy—two orchestras in the stands play classic Spanish corrida music in accord with the moment or at the urging of the crowd—the weather has been good, plenty of sun, but the usual quito clouds are approaching—soon it will be cool, possibly rain—the stands are a little more than half full—the crowd, perhaps with a mixture of wistfulness and resentment, despite its outbursts, has been relatively subdued—the banderilleros skip out with their sticks raised high and skillfully plunge them into the bull's neck—the crowd roars its approval as the bull tries to shake off the irritants flopping along its bloody flanks—the animal is visibly tiring—this magnificent creature would stomp and gore these little men to pieces one-on-one if the contest were structured differently but it is not normally in the nature of humans to commit suicide—without the ritual process of the banderilleros and the picador and the banderillas, the running of the bull in mad circles of confusion so that even before the final tercio he seems ready to stumble from weariness, the puny matador would never stand a chance, as if a rabbit before a very fast tank—the bull stands breathing heavily, furiously, a baleful eye fixed on his tormentors—it is at this point I think I'd like to see one of these toreros get blasted—a trumpet call begins the third tercio and with great drama and solemnity the matador, víctor barrio, comes out for the *faena*, the final act, having exchanged his capote for the red muleta, under which is the *estoque*, the killing sword, for now a lighter, wooden facsimile for easier use, to be replaced at the penultimate moment by the real item—in this case of course there will be no real item but rather a ceremonial banderilla that will be used for *la estocada*—the banderilleros have been distracting the bull but now víctor barrio walks regally to the center and the two, man and beast, stare down for the final confrontation—at this stage in the ritual the bull is very tired but still very dangerous, in the same way a moderately slow truck with sharp protruding objects would be dangerous—the animal is still capable of quick bursts and full of all justifiable malevolence—I am no expert but understand enough to recognize a matador with some elegance and courage and these qualities are on full display from the spaniard as he allows the bull to charge time and again, though it charges much slower than before, very close to his body, through the muleta as if it were a series of curtains through which each passage signals the entering of a smaller and darker room—there is pathos here also as once or twice the bull, exhausted and turned around awkwardly by the tight movements of the matador, pitches forward on his snout, his tongue sticking out stiffly, his muzzle full of saliva and dirt—the bull recovers, stands and stares, breathing heavily, as if understanding its fate—one feels it has not been a fair fight, the bull cruelly tricked, outmaneuvered, tormented, and now, its energy spent, its rage dissipated, there is little more it has to offer—but here is where the greatest danger for the matador lies because the bull is not finished but still retains enormous power and its purpose, to kill its adversary, is more focused than ever—it's now when the most *cornadas* (horn wounds) take place, the moment of greatest drama, the bull and matador on most intimate and final terms—víctor barrio turns his back on the bull and walks slowly to the burladero and dramatically exchanges his lighter, faux sword, employed to manipulate the muleta, for the ceremonial banderilla, and with as much dignity as possible strides towards the bull with his paper covered barb instead of the *estoque*, and really, after all they've been through, especially the bleeding and exhausted bull, to be killed anyway behind closed doors by a professional butcher with his *puntilla*, I think why not end this in the way it's supposed to end, with the full bloody finality, cleanly done or not, of the ancient barbaric ritual—as sex and death and violence are so intertwined in this spectacle let's take the beastly erotic metaphor to its logical destination and think of the ritual presently performed as an extended sexual encounter where the final act is consummated with a colorful dildo—the bull charges one last time and the banderilla is placed almost delicately between its shoulders, more or less in an acceptable spot, the crowd applauds politely, and the bull is led off into the toril to be later dispatched—the matador makes his circle around the ring in the traditional manner and people cheer and throw flowers, also hats, which he throws back, and there is the feeling of having witnessed an adulterated ceremony, almost a political event, with a lot of smiles and empty gestures—will the matador vault the barrera and commence to kissing babies?—the problem is, the bull dies anyway, and suffers more because it must wait to be killed, the matador, whose life, training and purpose is given to an ancient ritual that, brutal and cruel as it undeniably is, at least in this writer's estimation embodies so much of what is essential in the human condition, is robbed of the fulfillment and dramatic dignity of his calling (howls of ridicule and violent disagreement), and the worst of it, our utter confusion as a (so-called) (evolving) race in coming to terms with the bone-splintering, meat-grinding violence of our nature and by thinking that putting "the killing of animals in spectacles" out of our view and behind closed doors we have somehow fortified the better angels of our nature—there will be five more bullfights this afternoon, all ending more or less the same way, the Portuguese *rejoneador*, rui fernandes, a blond charismatic galloping vision, the poor Ecuadorian, josé antonio bustamante, the least skilled of the three, who must patch his pants with duct tape after a minor *cornada*, the planes lumbering over the stands, a drunken man making a comic spectacle of himself, and I leave agitated, thrilled, troubled—no question I have witnessed something profound and I can see why someone like hemingway would invest so much emotional and literary capital in this absorbing spectacle—but mostly I am angry at the fatuous state of our thinking, the half-measures we take to absolve ourselves from facing the central question of our survival—just who are we, and where do we go from here?

Manabi

12/20

we are on break from classes and at 12:45 pm I fly from Mariscal Sucre International Airport on a medium-sized, thoroughly modern (alas, no 1940s pan am clipper) AeroGal passenger jet to the coastal city of manta, in manabi province—the flight is a tidy, non-eventful 35 minutes for $60—the same trip by bus is 8 hours and costs $10—my fellow passengers are a sampling of the Ecuadorian middle class, comfortably dressed, well fed, compared to ordinary bus travelers veritable millionaires—across the aisle from me are two blond, tanned women in their twenties, their cute little bums pressed comfortably in their seats, dressed provocatively in expensive clothes, laughing and talking loudly, their manner radiating privilege, casual hedonism and catholic virtue—likely they are not supporters of correa and his modest egalitarian economic policies, window dressing at best, but at least offering marginal help to the poor—the more I understand correa the more he resembles obama, minus the drones—the manta airport is small, the weather windy, hot and dry—I had anticipated more humidity, more vegetation, but the feeling is oddly barren, as if I've landed somewhere in the middle east, beirut, without men with guns and uniforms—manta is known as a drug trafficking hub, its port the largest in Ecuador, with a complex network of cleverly disguised vessels ferrying illegal goods of all sorts, not only drugs—manta also has a sizable tourist trade, a portion of which probably involved in the drug market—my friend Mario assures me that a significant slice of certain south American economies, including Ecuador, is ripe with the smell of drugs—as usual, I tend to believe him—the narcotics trade is a tick from the drug-consuming north swollen on the blood of latin America, itself involved symbiotically—if there's money to be had a country (or person) will do virtually anything, including sacrifice its citizens in slaughter—never do ordinary people profit, indeed the reverse—no coincidence that as income inequality increases in the US the rest of the population not only struggles economically but also politically—a few days ago the senate passed the new defense bill authorizing the expenditure of 662 billion dollars, which is but the tip of the iceberg in terms of real military spending—included in the bill are provisions empowering the military to arrest on home soil US citizens suspected of "terrorist" activities or associations and to detain those citizens indefinitely at Guantánamo Bay without recourse to due process and habeus corpus—the peace laureate, after a few minor quibbles concerning the military encroaching on *his* power to do the same (he already has absolute authority to determine which US citizens to assassinate) has indicated he will sign the bill—without so much as a squeak of protest from a somnolent US citizenry, the military will now have the unbridled authority to break into your home in the middle of the night and drag your sorry ass off to Guantánamo and keep you there for as long as it pleases with no obligation to leave even a sticky note for your friends and relatives as to your whereabouts—but those who never raise a finger or word in protest against the policies of the state will probably be safe, something germans in another time figured out quickly enough and something good citizens everywhere have always instinctively understood—I pass through the diminutive manta airport terminal and outside in the parking lot I am greeted by my new friend, Gustavo, whom I'd met on the trip to cuyabeno six weeks ago, the same Gustavo who reminds me so much of my old high school friend of bacchanalian nature and passion, a catholic who assuaged his troubled conscience over riotous Saturday night adventures with heartfelt prayer and genuflection at the following day's mass—my own conscience naturally and thankfully unburdened of this particular impediment I marveled at his agony but sometimes went to church with him anyway, sinner, heathen, even a bit of a jew, enjoying the solemn mystery of the latin mass and keeping a surreptitious eye on certain female parishioners—I shake gustavo's massive paw, exhaust one-half of my Spanish vocabulary in greeting and get into his old chevy v-8 pickup, immediately at home in this quintessentially new mexican truck, horn falling out of the steering column, balky ignition switch, Styrofoam cups and papers littering the floor, dust everywhere, cracked dashboard, cracked windshield, seats worn through to the springs, big rumbling engine, tailgate secured with bailing wire, rusty tools, straw, dirt in the bed—gustavo, white hair, craggy, doleful, iberian visage, with the slightly weary but comfortable air of a man who has eliminated all but the essentials from his life, wearing an open, short-sleeved shirt, faded jeans and old leather boat shoes without socks, steers the big old rumbling truck east along the highway towards his home in rocafuerte, about 30 kilometers away—in keeping with the new mexico feeling the land between manta and rocafuerte is brown, dry and barren, with flatland to the north and bleak hills to the south dotted with the odd looking ceibo tree, which appears very much a cousin to the African baobab—a little awkward because of the language barrier, we don't speak much and I'm content to look out at the dusty landscape, different from anything I've seen so far in Ecuador—approaching rocafuerte the terrain changes with more water draining from the highlands, supplying increasingly green and fertile fields growing sugar cane, corn, peppers, bananas, palm trees and, surprisingly, rice, lots of it, green wispy stalks sticking up through flooded fields looking like parts of southern Louisiana—rocafuerte is obviously poor, with dilapidated houses of cinder block, rotting wood, bamboo, sagging balconies, tin roofs, old vehicles puttering along the highway belching exhaust fumes, people young and old riding rusty, creaky bicycles with balding tires, the road in disrepair, chickens everywhere, gardens, pigs, distressing amounts of garbage alongside the road (ecuadorians are notorious, unrepentant litterers), but despite the poverty there is a richness immediately apparent, certainly the abundant agriculture but also the activity everywhere, families gathered outside, friends hanging out, talking, the sense of community obvious, people waving to Gustavo as he drives past—we arrive at his property, hidden behind a large sliding metal gate activated by remote control from his truck, and descend the steep driveway to the parking area—immediately upon entering there is a small ferris wheel, like one of the roadside bikes of dubious structural integrity, something of the sort you might see in a park in montevideo or buenos aires, or so I imagine, certainly the sort of delightful thing you would encounter in a fellini film or Márquez novel, used many times, says gustavo, but not recently—gustavo is a retired mechanical engineer, having worked in the oil and maritime industries, and has a metal shop on his property next to the highway in which he tinkers and which caters to the occasional passing customer—we walk down a cement path lined with flowers, through an arbor to the front porch where hangs a comfortable-looking hammock and enter the house, a solidly middle class affair, not at all typical of the area—I stash my things in his sons' bedroom, their pictures covering the walls, two muscular, bronzed, handsome young men in bathing suits, swimming, surfing, scuba diving or smilingly saluting the camera with bottles of pilsener in the company of young blond women, and meet gustavo and his daughter Irene in the dining room, which has a china cabinet with glass doors and a long dark polished wooden table with overhanging chandelier, where the housekeeper, consuelo, serves us almuerzo, soup and a plate of chicken, rice and salad—irene is about 25 with an abundance of her parents' sensuality—one often hears that the best-looking women in Ecuador are from manabi, and, if true, mirian, gustavo's wife, is no exception, today working in portoviejo, the provincial capital, returning later this evening—consuelo, in her thirties, quiet and deferential, is also a handsome woman, dark, like most Ecuadorians, with a good figure, her self-effacing manner revealing the social dynamic between her and the family—with my bad Spanish and gustavo's bad English, communication is poor, but somehow we are able to understand each other—after lunch Gustavo takes me on a tour of his property, lush with different kinds of fruit trees, mangos, papayas, naranjillas, limones, tamarindo and more that I don't register—there are chickens, ducks, geese, two cats and two dogs—he shows me his *taller*, his workshop, cluttered with old tools, blackened and scarred heavy work tables flaked with metal filings, huge bench vises, welding equipment, heaps of scrap metal, all in grimy disarray, obviously the environment of a retired person who putters absently when the mood strikes and not the organized workplace of economic necessity—still, he does attract the occasional customer, and for this has hired a young man, Fernando, a good-looking guy, dark, wiry, with a pleasant, gentle manner, like so many Ecuadorians, wearing dirty blue gym shorts, ragged t-shirt, backwards cap and flip-flops—inside the shop it is hot—latin music emanates from an old dusty radio on one of the oily tables while vehicles roar by outside—they confer briefly about a job and then Gustavo and I get into the truck to pick up his youngest son, jose anibal, who, along with his younger sister, maria estefania, is a product of what Gustavo describes as a troubled time in his life when for several years he left mirian for another woman—they live virtually around the corner and as we wait outside in the truck for his son Gustavo explains that the mother has not spoken to him in years—this is related in a tone of sad resignation, as if internally reflecting on the absurd situation he has created for himself—to his credit anyway, I think, at least he's maintained a relationship with his children and appears to share some of the responsibilities with his former lover—that Gustavo and mirian live a stone's throw from his two out of wedlock adolescent children and former mistress who never speaks to him seems extraordinary, even comical, but I realize this fits a developing awareness I have about this country that begins to crystallize here in rocafuerte—I've felt this in quito, this quirky, sometimes exasperating quality to daily life, full of frustrations and unexpected events, a difficult adjustment for someone from a more ordered culture like that of the US but a necessary one unless you really have something against your teeth and want to grind them down to the gums—until now I've only played with the idea but finally the connection is unavoidable—I've not read much latin American literature but I did read *one hundred years of solitude* twice and delighted in its magical realism, something I'd always considered the purest fancy and the product of a whimsical and rich imagination, but the true wonder is that Márquez, great writer and brilliant imagination that he is, in the end, like all artists, humbly serves as but a conduit for the communication of a far greater reality, something so powerful and profound and absurd that any human with a spark of sensitivity and wit cannot help but be moved, and sometimes, as in the case of a Márquez, inspired to the creation of art—I see now that what Márquez wrote, his magical realism, is absolutely a reflection of this seemingly illogical, sensuous and thoroughly marvelous culture, that all his kaleidoscopic flights of whimsy and phantasmagoria are grounded in the mystery of this unique confluence of the human and natural world that is latin America—jose anibal, a talkative stripling of 14, jumps in, sitting in the middle, and we drive to portoviejo past more watery fields of rice and sugar cane with smoke on the horizon from burning stubble as I divide my attention between the sights and jose anibal's incessant questions delivered in rapid Spanish despite gustavo's admonishments to slow down for the linguistically-challenged gringo—I do my best to understand and respond, noticing that Gustavo, while clearly loving his son, is slightly irritated by his nonstop chatter—I can only imagine the emotions both must feel in what is an unusual situation but no more unusual than countless relationships in my own country, and there is a touching affection between them, though Gustavo has the air of a man awakened to a parallel universe wondering how did I get here and who is this chattering person sitting next to me calling me papi?—after about 20 minutes we arrive in portoviejo, a poor, bustling, small city looking like so many other provincial semi-tropical cities all over the world, a myriad of color, haphazard, curious architecture, much of it from the sixties, buildings in moldering disrepair, volumes of colorful cheap merchandise, electronics, plastics, clothes, shoes, thousands of people on the sidewalks doing what people on sidewalks do, shopping, walking home from work, smoking, shouting, spitting, talking with friends, holding hands, eyeing each other, eating food purchased from one of the hundreds of sidewalk venders that clog these thoroughfares, skeins of power lines sagging over narrow streets, buses, trucks, cabs jammed together honking and spewing exhaust fumes, and Gustavo, clearly displeased and anxious about having to drive his big truck in this ruckus, finds a small parking lot down an alley and we get out and walk to a dingy, dark little cave of a pet shop, the purpose of our trip to buy some fish and a five-gallon tank for jose anibal—our mission accomplished, jose anibal clutching his tank containing colored gravel, small electric pump and a plastic bag of fish, mollies, a few angelfish, a couple of goldfish, we drive back to rocafuerte, where Gustavo at his old lover's house deposits jose anibal after a tender farewell with words of fatherly advice and a kiss on the cheek, seeming saddened and relieved as he watches his son pass through the gate—driving back from portoviejo we'd stopped for a cup of sugar cane juice and I'd had some with ice, realizing the mistake afterwards and anticipating a bout of diarrhea later—the cane juice was delicious and made with a hand-powered grinding machine into which the stalks are fed—I've been pretty good about minding what I eat and drink but it's impossible to be perfect about these things, nor, I believe, would you want to be—it's late afternoon and after stopping at the house for my bathing suit we go to crucita, a fishing village about 15 minutes away, a few small colorful fishing boats being dragged up on the beach for the evening, a mass of giant frigate birds circling, and I go for a swim while Gustavo watches, the water very warm with gentle waves and filled with small round jellyfish of the non or only mildly stinging variety—after my swim we go into a typical seaside bar across the street for five or six pilseners and Gustavo talks with the proprietor, a garrulous fellow with ambitious plans for a big new bar in anticipation of increased tourist trade—he shows us the wooden architectural model a friend has made—we're there almost an hour and it's dark by the time we get home, greeted by a slightly peeved mirian, who serves us a modest dinner of soup and leftovers from lunch—whatever irritation mirian has dissipates quickly and soon she and Gustavo are teasing and laughing, clearly very comfortable and happy in each other's presence—Irene, on the other hand, seems upset about something and is quiet—tomorrow we get up early for a walk on the beach and a swim, something Gustavo and mirian do regularly—at 9:30 we bid each other goodnight and I read for awhile underneath the mosquito netting, mailer's *existential errands (purchased at my friend carlos' used book stand—more on him later)*, vastly enjoyable, the author at his brilliant and outrageous best, really strutting his stuff—

The money catch

1 2 / 2 1

it's not unusual for me to sleep poorly my first night in a new place and this night is no exception—I'm ok until the electricity stops around three am, shutting off the air conditioner, a rattling old GE, and activating my waking brain, one electrical system powering down, another firing up—i remain on hyper-alert the rest of the night listening to gustavo's mad roosters and the growling yellow-eyed trucks with their mysterious cargoes pulling from the coast, destined for points east and elsewhere—as usual in such scenes I drift off just before dawn (not before cock's crow but in spite of), but not for long as a few minutes later comes gustavo's knock on the door, surprisingly light for his heavy hand, though resonating like an executioner's call—it's time to get up and go with him and his wife for their customary matutinal perambulation on the shores of the equatorial pacific—I stumble around their sons' room cursing silently, pulling on my wet bathing suit all different kinds of ways before getting it right—Gustavo and mirian are waiting in the truck and I wedge myself into the front seat feeling tired and a little strange, especially with mirian, whom I hardly know and who is much more reserved than Gustavo and who I suspect may be less than thrilled to have a strange gringo staying in her house for a few days, perhaps one of those situations where the gregarious bear-like husband impulsively opens home and hearth against the natural inclinations of the wife, but she is friendly enough and greets me smil-ingly, asking how I slept, a conventional and polite question under the circumstances concerning one of our curious human common-alities, an experience easily communicated across barriers of cul-ture and language, in this context a little embarrassing for I am slightly neurotic about sleep, a battle I have been waging my whole adult life, though generally, in Ecuador, I have slept surprisingly well—it doesn't matter very much if mirian really cares about my sleep, likely she doesn't, but it is the sort of question that acknowl-edges our shared humanity and even if formally posed eases my dis-comfort and allows me to contribute, albeit modestly, to my end of the conversation—I ask about the electricity shutting down and Gustavo explains that this occasionally happens and we talk about a few more simple things and then I turn my attention to the scenes along the road as we drive towards crucita—one of the things I love about Ecuador, and I see this all the time in my neighborhood, is the openness of life, the visibility of people and their daily rou-tines, unselfconsciously going about their business, and here in ro-cafuerte, because of the rural setting and climate, with people living outside their homes almost as much as inside, it is even more evi-dent—there's a warm, sleepy, early morning sensuality to the peo-ple as they get ready for the day, the women especially marvelous in their casual loose clothing, sweeping, burning trash, feeding chick-ens, tending to their children, cooking—the men are loading trucks, or fixing them, repairing their homes, making things, some waiting to be picked up for the day's labor, but there are others doing noth-ing, sitting with their morning coffee alone or with friends, watch-ing the traffic—some are already nestled in their hammocks—they will maintain this posture more or less the whole day, perhaps re-treating inside for a siesta as the weather warms, because for many in rocafuerte, as in all of Ecuador, there is no work—even at this early hour the road is filled with bicycle traffic and it is common to see people carrying things as they ride on their rickety old bikes, sometimes very large loads, construction materials, bamboo poles, bananas, chickens, and together with the green and wet fields dotted with white egrets, the simple homes and modest businesses, it is a wonderful sight that stirs my imagination and when I see an old man pushing a pig in a cart the fantasy is complete: I am in the middle of a novel by Gabriel García Márquez—gustavo parks the truck at the same place as the evening before and we get out for a brisk walk up the beach, into the middle of a mass of fisherman and their small blue and white vessels hauled up onto the sand with the morning catch as great numbers of big frigate birds with their distinctive forked tails circle and dive aggressively, sometimes swooping in and grabbing fish right out of the plastic bins carried by the men—there is a swirling bustle of colorful activity with men shouting and moving about, the morning work finished, teams gathered together to maneuver the boats on heavy wooden rollers for safekeeping up near the road, pushing, straining, everyone yelling spirited directions at the same time with much laughter and excitement, a seemingly chaotic scene recapitulated for the ten thousandth time and you wonder why it all seems so random and disorganized, but of course it is not—the ocean is calm, as it usually is, and while most boats are putting up for the day some are going out, waiting for the right moment to advance, pushed through the waves by family members, friends or other fishermen—the majority of the catch is mackerel and sardine but bigger fish end up in the nets too, thresher and hammerhead sharks, tuna, bonito, billfish, and these are loaded into the backs of trucks and taken away—occasionally sharks are left on the sand—there is a large open shed where the money catch, the mackerel and sardine, is piled and sorted for the first stage of preparation and shipping, with dozens of workers, mostly women, working energetically and rapidly midst much shouting and laughter—back at the house for breakfast we have good Ecuadorian coffee, which is made by adding essence of coffee, a kind of syrup, to hot water or milk, pan dulce with *sal prieta*, not someone who works for the gambino family but rather a delicious mixture of ground peanuts, corn and other spices that is the staple seasoning of manabi, each household concocting its own variety, queso and cooked sweet bananas—after breakfast Gustavo goes to his *taller* and I sit in the backyard on a comfortable chair with mailer's book and soon fall asleep, a huge and very handsome reddish brown rooster resting under the table next to me—I fancy he likes me but obviously it's the shade that has his affection—I sleep most of the morning and then it's time for almuerzo, prepared by Consuelo, fish soup, rice and fish with onions, avocado and *aji*, the hot sauce found everywhere in Ecuador which, like sal prieta, varies from place to place—it is delicious and generally not very spicy—gustavo and I discuss ecuadorian culture, which, given our limited vocabulary in each other's language, is a bit like butchers discussing brain surgery, but I understand very clearly his statement about south Americans not reading very much—he takes me up to his biblioteca, a tight, dusty, dry space with a few ancient moldering books and several dozen old reader's digests in Spanish from the 70s, but the most interesting thing is a collection of small, dead, dessicated *murciélagos*, likely of the fruit variety, cluttered about the window sill—gustavo says something about needing to clean them up and we go back downstairs, his point about limited enthusiasm for reading, at least as far as he is concerned, sufficiently proved—later that afternoon i go with Gustavo back to his ex-lover's house and we wait for jose anibal, who jumps into the truck, still chattering, wearing a reindeer hat for the Christmas performance at his school—jose anibal and I sing a round of Rudolph the red-nosed reindeer and soon we're in the actual town of rocafuerte, a smaller, dustier, more bedraggled version of portoviejo, where Gustavo drops him off and where later he will pick him up—if these interactions are any indication, their relationship is fragmented at best, with most of their dialogue centering around jose anibal's anxious relationship with his mother and gustavo's advice to calm down and not take things so seriously, difficult words for a fourteen-year-old to assimilate and indeed, jose anibal appears not to pay much attention—before returning home Gustavo drives to fernando's place to pick up a dish his mother has prepared, driving a couple hundred meters down a rugged dirt road bordered on one side by banana trees and small rice fields, and we are in the middle of southeast asia, a secluded green and watery world unseen from the main road, astonishing in its picturesque charm and beauty, and again I wonder, trying not to succumb to some sort of romantic rural Márquezean fallacy, how much superior is the wealthy person's life in north America to this materially poor but in so many profound ways, exceedingly rich existence—fernando appears from his house, which resembles something you might see in a production of *porgy and bess*, and hands the dish to Gustavo, smiling and waving at me—for dinner we have soup, rice, tomatoes and onions along with the dish fernando's mother has prepared, banana and pork, which is most delicious—then after a short conversation with mirian, Gustavo and Irene, who still seems to be pouting about something, I bid them good evening and retreat to my room, positioning myself under the mosquito netting for a half hour with mr. mailer's excellent book—tomorrow, another walk on the beach—

Last day in Rocafuerte

after a better night's sleep i go again with Gustavo and mirian to the beach, which is the same as yesterday, the fishermen and the frigate birds in their ancient *pas de deux*, a marvelous sight that I hope continues for another ten thousand years, though I wonder what this beach will look like in the not-so-distant future—the fishing is good here, the fish stock and waters still relatively healthy, but if things continue the way they are going, with Ecuador and all of south America, with evermore mouths to feed and determined to "develop" after the western model, then there can be nothing but waste, pollution and emptiness—that this process is well under way is as evident as the equatorial sun, with a depressing inevitability that feels like a greek tragedy—the president of ecuador talks a fine environmental game but jumps into carnal embrace with Chinese and Canadian mega-companies to mine and drill in the most precious natural environments remaining on earth, with their equally precious indigenous cultures struggling to survive in a changing world—will the time come soon when the quaint little vessels of crucita are replaced with factory ships to harvest the mackerel and sardine in massive numbers, threatening their survival and decimating all other species in the bargain as in so many other parts of oceans all over the world where the fishing has gone mad to feed a human population gone equally mad?—this will be my last day here—tomorrow morning I'll take a bus from rocafuerte back to quito and after new year take another bus to archidona to visit chris and my kichwa friends in rukullakta for a couple of days, possibly including a half-day rafting trip—gustavo and I go for a swim and after a few minutes mirian begins gesturing from the beach—a bit farther out is a group of large black creatures, likely dolphins, surfacing and diving in the distinctive manner of marine mammals, and when Gustavo starts making his way back to the beach I follow suit—we've seen several thresher sharks and a couple of small hammerheads on the beach this morning and though they pose minimal threat the idea of sharks in the water together with these animals close by stimulates that part of the brain that objects strongly to the idea of offering one's body as nourishment for predators—it's almost certainly not sharks cavorting behind us but they are large, and, who knows, could they be orcas?—the imagination is in equal measure marvelous and terrifying and as Gustavo and I make our way towards shore the needle is in the yellow zone of circumspection, perhaps cowardice, red of course being unbridled terror—while our species may have originally emerged from the sea it's been a while, and the lower the water level on my body the higher my level of comfort until at last we're standing next to mirian, our toes gripping the sand, watching the dolphins or small whales, whatever they are, swimming not far from where we've just been, perhaps twenty of them, quite large and dark—if dolphins they're bigger than any I've seen before—mirian says they're whales—whatever they are they're about the size of orcas, though with none of the telltale white markings—later, another trip to rocafuerte, this time with maria estefania, jose anibal's sister, a year or so younger, at first shy but soon talkative as her brother and unbearably cute to the point where I want to put my arms around her for a big (humbert?) squeeze—birdlike, pretty, a little flirtatious, maria estefania has me captivated—gustavo buys a few things in one of these typical Ecuadorian stores that has piles of brightly-colored plastic goods and then we get some ice cream, frozen hard as stone—like jose anibal, maria estefania is deposited at her mother's house—I can feel Gustavo mentally exhale as she passes through the gate—that night we get a visit from Gustavo and mirian's youngest son, jose, in his late twenties, one of the dark, handsome, muscular boys in the photos, even more striking in person, with a movie star's charisma—his parents are doting—he is formal towards me to the point of suspicion—in the morning, when I leave, he is friendlier—

La reina de La Reina del Camino

back to quito—gustavo deposits me at the small, cage-like depot in dusty little rocafuerte, seemingly as relieved to take leave of my presence as he is with poor jose anibal and maria estefania—I purchase a ticket for quito—10 dollars—gustvo is a decent sort, but there's the feeling I have somehow bored, or disappointed him, much of this owing to our lack of real communication, our deficiencies in the other's language—we were curious about each other, and so there is some frustration, as it would have been fascinating to get into things on a deeper level, our origins, histories, cultural differences and similarities—I recognize in Gustavo as well an independence of spirit that I also possess, which borders on selfishness and can lead to the understandable irritations and frustrations of those close to us—but he and mirian have been gracious hosts, have opened their home to me, tolerant of this strange gringo in their midst, and for this I am grateful and consider myself fortunate—how many others have this opportunity?—if people had the time to pursue their interests and passions, were not chained to the grinding exigencies of economic necessity, there would be more opportunities such as I have had, though I'm not rich and have to work while here—yes, gustavo and I are kindred spirits of sorts, wolves of a different kind, but wolves nonetheless—gustavo worked for years as an engineer on ships, ingeniero de un barco, sailing all over the world—now he's settled in rocafuerte, retired, married, puttering in his taller, comfortably middle class with his little estate, fruit trees, marquezian ferris wheel, remote-controlled metal gate and two out of wedlock children around the corner—I wait for about half an hour, watching the activity in the streets, people aware of my presence, but discreet—rocafuerte is a very poor town, with the idleness of poverty, people on rickety bicycles, hanging out, a few hawking fruit, vegetables or cheap candies—it is warm, but not unbearably so—dusty—this is a dry part of Ecuador, apparently—finally the bus arrives and I board with my red mochila and look for a seat in the rear, thankfully in the nearly empty bus, alone, but I'm certain by the time we're halfway to quito (the trip will take over six hours) the bus will be full and I'll have a seat mate—I have my copy of existential errands out but I know I'll never read because what I see outside will be more compelling than anything mr. mailer has to offer, and indeed, it is, the verdant landscape, the small, colorful towns and busy streets, tiendas with their cheap plastic goods, the smoky eateries, hornados, the sidewalk fruit and vegetable vendors—ecuador is dollar-poor but food-rich, which is its saving fortune—when the world crashes and people have only their smart phones to eat, places like Ecuador will be seen as paradises—compare Venezuela, historically which, foolishly, has put all its eggs in the petroleum basket and neglected its agriculture, relying on food imports, though growing conditions are ideal—for now, with oil prices high, mr. chavez can implement his "revolution," but should the price plunge, as it surely will (the risible invisible hand), the Bolivarian project will be in trouble—to be fair, chavez inherited this over-reliance on oil (historically Venezuela a de facto oil colony of the colossus of the north), and I have read that he is trying to diversify the Venezuelan economy, including develop its agriculture—correa, too, has based his "revolucion ciudadana" on oil exports, specifically to china, but again, with a drop in global prices...the countryside rolls along, endlessly fascinating, mysterious—after about two hours the bus, almost full now, stops at an eatery and we all pile out to stretch, go to the bathroom and get something to eat—as I'm about to get back on the bus I'm approached by a small, dark, attractive woman who introduces herself, anita, saying she noticed I was reading a book by norman mailer—of course I'm surprised that anyone on the bus would know who the hell the old pugilist is, and she explains that he was a favorite of her deceased husband, a one Lloyd price, and did I know who he was, had we ever met, all gringos in Ecuador of course familiar with each other—the first thought that comes into my head (well, not exactly the first) is the r&b singer (lawdy miss clawdy!), but no, that couldn't be, and she explains in her halting English that he was an ingeniero, and that he'd died a year ago—they lived in a house they'd built together in the village of San Plácido, in manabi province, from where she was returning to her apartment in the north of quito where she lived with her teenage son, Francisco—now, I'm a normal male, if a bit long in the tooth, and the predictable wheels are turning—we return to our respective seats, she in front, I in back, next to a young indigenous fellow with his ear buds—the landscape passes by with a slightly more romantic coloration, the ubiquitous tv blasting some ridiculous movie of tropical violence and mayhem, the usual sinister villains, the muscular, sweating hero, the voluptuous heroine, their smoldering, tragic love—at the quitumbe station in the north of quito I hasten to locate anita, who is waiting outside (mirabile dictu!) and get her phone number—we agree to have lunch soon—

Año Viejo

12/31

there's a hint of lunacy in the air—it's new year's eve but attention here is focused on exorcising the nastiness of the last 365 days (*Año viejo*) rather than celebrating the nastiness of the next—I am supposed to meet Mario at 2 pm on avenida amazonas, where the action traditionally resides—the more I know Mario the stranger he becomes—he has an odd collection of older, male expatriate friends, French, dutch, german, US, all single, retired, with an air of mystery, as if a group of ex-spies or smugglers, but in fact their pasts are fairly mundane, mostly business—they are uniformly tall, gray, English speakers, marginal spanish (though they've got me beat, multilingually), with a hint of queerness, not necessarily sexual—I have met them over the course of several get-togethers with Mario where the scene is invariably the same, a group of old guys drinking coffee and whiskey sitting around listening to Mario hold forth in his usual manic staccato english, finally telling him to shut the fuck up, good for a few minutes until he launches in again—tony, from the US, my favorite of the group and a bit atypical, is a retired merchant marine captain with property in ecuador, a big, amiable guy with curly gray hair and a deliberate manner who thinks uncle sam is finished—tony keeps urging me to go to a whorehouse with him in the central part of the city, but likely it won't happen—30 bucks—he says the women are young and good looking—I

184

wander up and down taking pictures on amazonas, which is closed to traffic and jammed with revelers—monster masks, families with little goblin children, stages on the sidewalks with blasting music and huge puppets (muñecos), different from those of the handmade variety that will be burned on the sidewalks later, in the manner of effigies, to rid the world, or at least the immediate vicinity, of the previous year's devils—many have faces resembling well-known politicians, including correa and US presidents—others are burned to exorcise misfortunes or character defects such as cancer or intemperance—there are also many *viudas* (widows) about—on this occasion they are men dressed provocatively as women, survivors of the dead year, letting it rip one last time before the new year descends—most of the "women" are true cross-dressers—I see cross-dressers mixed in with the working girls on my walk home each night on the corner of guayaquil and esmeraldas—later in the afternoon I will have an encounter with a group of these viudas—I meet Mario in front of hotel mercure on amazonas, and we go directly to a sidewalk café where I meet yet another of his older expatriate friends, this time a guy from Switzerland, rudy, tall and gray, with raw cheeks as if just sandpapered—something about mario's friends makes me instinctively recoil and I must make an effort to engage with them—I wonder if I fit the profile of mario's collection—it seems very much like a collection—sometimes I think Mario is actually crazy—he is definitely manic and tolerates no more than a few seconds of someone else speaking before rocketing off on a cackling, spittling tour de force that leaves his leaden companions staring—but the inner circle is wise to this routine and soon they're shutting him up, which he takes in stride, almost touchingly, as if a small boy—in a few minutes he's blasting off again—mario's a man whose head is exploding—but the thing about Mario is he's an interesting cat with a lot to say so a bit of forbearance is in order and I, for one, have learned a few things listening to his wild words—we're not long at the café, leaving rudy behind, thankfully, but, distressingly (I had wanted to roam up and down amazonas with Mario as guide), off to a nearby apartment where there are a couple more of these same variety of friends drinking irish coffee and telling Mario to shut up, but not before he tells an interesting story about driving a rich left-wing student friend to a jungle redoubt near the Peruvian border in the eighties, fleeing the forces of febres cordero—after a couple of hours, buzzed with the coffee and whiskey, feeling weird and claustrophobic in this little apartment room with these people, I get on the bus to centro historico with Mario and his dutch friend, chris, have a plate of *seco de chivo* in an indoor mercado, then bid them goodbye and i'm on my own, heading home—it's around six and things will get crazier in quito as the night develops but I've seen enough and I'm a little tired and I've never been too crazy about new year's celebrations anyway—walking down Venezuela I pass a couple of people trying to burn a muñeco that looks like Reagan but is probably correa—the thing is balky and it's a struggle—finally they get it going in a half-hearted way, straddling the gutter and the sidewalk—a female cop comes along and tells the people to drag the smoldering muñeco onto the sidewalk, which they reluctantly do—the muñeco is bizarrely lifelike and there is a fascination in watching it burn—the burning paint of the muñeco gives off thick dark smoke—it is poorly constructed and falls apart bit by bit—I arrive at bolivar, close to santo domingo plaza, and there is a commotion, lots of loud rock music and a jam of people in the streets—about a dozen viudas are dancing like lewd valkyries, stopping cars and humping hoods, door handles, fenders, each other, not allowing the cars to continue until the driver gives money—a quarter suffices—many of the cars have families with young children, who stare bemusedly at the viudas' frenzied grinding and humping, the crowd laughing and cheering wildly—the viudas are perverse, erotic, and except for hairy muscular legs and arms look convincingly female—there's a wild sexuality in the air—I'm snapping away with my little camera and suddenly a bunch of them spot me and come running over screaming and lift me into the air, supine, carrying me into the street—just before being lifted into the air I manage to put the camera on video—the crowd is yelling and laughing like crazy—I am physically overpowered and realize the foolishness in resisting—there is no danger and everyone's laughing and so I go along, a little embarrassed but laughing myself, at myself—it all happens so quickly—two of them spread my legs and another hops down the street, turns, and runs back towards me, jumping into my spread legs and giving a thrust as everyone cheers—they let me down good-naturedly and gently—ruffled, smiling, not terribly self-conscious, I step back into the crowd—hardly anyone looks at me, caught up in the spectacle on the street, the viudas already into something else—I am absorbing some sort of lesson here as the viudas approach another, younger gringo with his girlfriend, but he snatches his arm away from them and hastens off, embarrassed—maybe this is the difference between old and young—I have been swept into a spectacle much larger than my insignificant ego and sense of propriety and ultimately, I understand, it is of no personal consequence—what matters is the ceremony, whatever it means—all of us bit players in something immeasurably grand—get over it—

Back to Rukullakta

it takes around five hours, portal-to-portal, to get from my place
on rocafuerte to edmundo and irene's house in rukullakta—first a
cab to rio coca, the terminal in north quito, then a bus to Cumbayá, which stops in front of a supermaxi (department store, re-
grettably named), and from there the last leg, about four hours, to
archidona and a short cab ride to rukullakta and the little blue cinder-block house across from the community building and soccer
pitch—Cumbayá is a middle/upper-middle class bedroom community near quito in the tumbaco valley—around the supermaxi you
might think you were in white plains—the ride from Cumbayá to
archidona is a journey away from this glassy suburb to reassur-
ingly less developed working class districts, then climbing into the
dramatic cloud forests to the east with their expanse of emerald
heights, granite cliff faces, brilliant cultivated squares of potatoes
and corn, grazing cattle looking like tiny lead figures clinging to
the steep slopes covered with abundant grass, cleared of forest, a
cornucopia of grass, silver tumbling rivers below—in the cloud forest it seems always to be raining or the air saturated to the point
of bursting—descending, approaching the oriente, the air turns
warmer, the vegetation changes, the land flattening and spreading
to the horizon, a vista inspiring the mind's eye towards the great
basin that contains 20% of the world's fresh water and much of its

remaining mystery—the indigenous population has changed also, from the sierra to the lowlands, the colorful garb of the mountain culture replaced by a raffish assortment of t-shirts, shorts and flip-flops better suited to the warmth and humidity of the oriente—constant from one place to the other is poverty, especially reflected in the hodgepodge of cinder-block and wooden dwellings that line the highway in the oriente, in various states of seeming imminent collapse, sometimes colorfully adorned in moldering paint, always chickens, small gardens, clotheslines, young women with babies, the occasional earnest, rickety business, diminutive saw mill or manufacture of building blocks—also evident upon entering the napo region are the *oleoductos*, the oil pipelines snaking parallel to the highways, the rusting arteries carrying the country's economic blood—there is an extreme paucity of work for the local population and this is everywhere apparent, not only the visible signs of poverty but the general lack of industry and associated energy so that you see a lot of people simply doing nothing, reinforcing the stereotypical image of the tropics—but perhaps for the need to keep warm the exigencies of survival are no less critical here than anywhere else and everyone must do at least the minimum to stay alive—concerning this, to the casual observer, much is hidden, the hundred-and-one ways of surviving as a member of a deracinated culture trapped on the margins in a rapidly changing, consumerist, technological and rudderless world—these activities exist, but from the highway you would never know—this is my second time here and I am excited—I arrive in colorful, disheveled archidona around four o'clock, the air warm and humid, thick clouds above—I get a cab near the bus stop, a yellow cab driven by a young mestizo who speaks nearly indecipherable Spanish but I understand his immediate preoccupation which is wanting to buy my sunglasses—he's a thick, disagreeable sort, stupid in his treatment of me as a stereotypical gringo, an offensive if harmless combination of aggressiveness and condescension—eventually we find edmundo and irene's house and he charges me two dollars, double what I should pay but the hell with it—little sacha, my ceremonial goddaughter, spies me first and runs into the house to inform her parents—there are warm greetings with a bit less of the usual shyness—most of my conversation is with edmundo—chris is elsewhere—I have brought gifts: for sacha a journal and pen, for her older sister Jennifer colored pencils, for edmundo playing cards and for Irene a picture frame—I am staying in the same room as before—chris arrives, not feeling very well and looking thin but with enough energy to play soccer on the dirt field with 11 other villagers, including edmundo—carlos, the yachak, comes by and greets me warmly, as does his wife, maria—this makes me feel very good—for dinner we have black beans and noodles—chris and I had talked previously about a rafting trip with edmundo and Irene and tomorrow we'll go to tena to make arrangements—edmundo and Irene have a friend, luis, who is a guide—chris and I will split the cost for them—about an hour after going to bed it begins to rain heavily and continues most of the night, crashing down on the metal roof—thankfully there are no crazed roosters and the family next door refrains from turning on their radio full blast at three am—in fact they don't turn it on at all—I get a good night's sleep—

Mr. Beckett, Mr. Jumandy

1/3

waking around seven I go to the choza, the thatched hut attached to carlos and maria's house, for a guayusa session that lasts more than an hour—I follow the conversations more closely this time, still not understanding very much, but it is good to be in the dark, smoky, warm enclosure next to the small fire, good to watch maria prepare the guayusa in the old way, repeatedly dipping the pilche into the charred metal pot and pouring the dark green earthy liquid back into itself until ready—I receive the offered bowl with a soft "paga-rachu" (thank you) and listen to the women talk quietly in a murmur that could be a river flowing outside the choza, their soft chuckling conveying a knowing humor, laughing at the foibles of the people in their lives, humor that in its intimacy captures the stumbling fallibility of all people—to be near this is comforting and I linger, drinking a second and third cup of tea, not at all anxious to leave—some of the women take the tea in their hands and rub it onto their faces and forearms, it is good for the skin, and with my last cup I do the same—carlos comes in and we say hello—he sits for awhile, stirs the fire, and leaves—german, one of carlos's sons, and his three-year-old boy, ingaro, enter the choza—german, a pensive sort, sits and stares at the fire, sipping his tea—ingaro stares at me, a stranger—the women dote over him—carlos comes back with a clutch of small drums, sits next to the fire and begins tightening the heads with waxed thread—he gives a couple to maria to work on—carlos talks quietly as he works on the drums with his strong dark hands, laughing along with the women—carlos remains a mystery—I know he has done many things in his life and that now his passion is to preserve what's left of his people's traditional culture—I wonder what he really thinks, if he fully understands the crushing reality of the future—probably he does—there is a peacefulness about him and maria that suggests they have come to terms with this future and have determined to live the rest of their lives in observance of their traditions, in addition to doing what they can to insure that their work, or at least their spirit, continues—he obviously recognizes that this preservation of culture is a possible economic lifeline for his community, at least an alternative, and a healthy one at that—edmundo, his son, shares this vision—chris, still not feeling well, has slept late—he comes in somewhat sleepily, says good morning, "alli-puncha," and softly shakes everyone's hands, sitting next to me, receiving a pilche of guayusa from maria and joining the conversation, laughing along with everyone else—I understand little but it doesn't matter—I am relaxed and feel for the moment a part of this company—later, Irene, edmundo, chris and I take the bus to tena, a lively and small Amazonian city dotted with marvelous 60s flash gordon architecture, a hub for adventuring and rafting, many gringos—after a few dead-ends we hook up with the wife of their guide friend and discuss plans for the following day over *batidos* (*licuados*, fruit smoothies) and ice cream in a particularly colorful yellow and green science fiction building—there's a US football game on one of the TVs that are everywhere in the world and chris tries to explain some of the rules to edmundo, whose eyes glaze over as if listening to a lecture on tupperware marketing strategies—we will meet Irene and edmundo's friend, luis, tomorrow at 11 am at his office in tena and from there proceed to our rafting trip—much of the day is still before us and we decide to go to the caves—*cavernas de jumandy*, just outside archidona, is where the legendary leader of the napo people went to evade the Spanish after the revolt of 1578, almost exactly 100 years before the pueblo uprising in New Mexico—as in New Mexico the rebellion ultimately failed and jumandy was captured and executed—but they survived for awhile in these caves, much as Geronimo survived in the dry mountains and rugged terrain of the southwest US and mexico—the caves are in the side of a steep hill and have been carved out over the millennia by powerful streams, the same streams that feed the misahualli river, a tributary of the napo, in turn one of the major tributaries of the amazon—at the entrance to the park is a large swimming pool and fiberglass water slide, fed by these streams—because of the torrential rains the pool is filled with mud and has been drained—two workers wearing shorts and rubber boots clear the mud with a hose and push brooms—it is warm and humid and the men work slowly and without much effort, taking breaks and joking around—the hose has numerous small leaks that shoot thin jets of misting water, refracting colors—where I'm from this is a waste but here it's like worrying about conserving air—we pay our money and go into the cave with a guide—there are two caves and we choose the shorter one—with us are two giggling teenage kichwa girls who flirt with chris—the stream is rapid and the footing precarious—we have been given headlamps—the air is warm—the noise from the stream reverberates against the cave walls—I am wearing my river sandals but proceed cautiously, as there are holes and it is slippery—my knee is better but one wrong turn and I'm fucked all over again—once more I think about the difference between tourist attractions here and the US—these caves are unchanged since jumandy's time—there are no vending machines, electric lights, hardhats, hand rails, directional signs, footpaths—we have signed no wavers, insurance policies, last wills and testaments and have no thread of theseus to guide us back through this labyrinth should our guide slip and crack himself unconscious or worse—and it is a labyrinth—we've taken several turns and without a guide it would be difficult to get back—I don't imagine the batteries to our headlamps are scrupulously monitored—in total darkness this would be a frightening proposition—even with our guide, who is confident and attentive, obviously very well acquainted with the caves and knowledgeable about the history, there is an edge of anxiety—I can't see very well and am continuously adjusting the weak beam of my headlamp—the ceiling is low and there are stalactites—we're all bumping our heads—everyone speaks in low voices and there is nervous laughter—the stream is powerful and threatens to knock us off our feet in more challenging crossings—irene in particular is anxious and we take turns helping her—a couple of times we pass small returning groups, one of them a middle-aged European couple, a buxom woman wearing a flimsy bikini practically falling off with the exertion of hiking, the man clad only in a jock strap and blue bandana—their bodies are streaked with mud—in the darkness and mystery of the cave they seem like members of some eleusinian sex cult and they set the kichwa girls off in a round of giggles—perhaps notions of cultism are not far-fetched as shortly we pass a huge phallic stalagmite know as jumandy's penis which stands at the entrance to a narrow passageway and must be grasped for support as you pass by—this elicits more giggling from the girls—i try to imagine what it was like for jumandy and his warriors here, in terror of their merciless pursuers, navigating with their torches in the utter darkness, communing with spirits in hope of salvation—we come to a small waterfall at the base of which is a deep hole, the circumference wide enough for one person—chris and I take turns submerging ourselves in the hole, the falling water beating down—it takes a bit of screwing up one's courage before getting in but it's safe and revivifying—our guide then takes us to a side chamber and tells us to extinguish our lights—for about ten minutes we sit in absolute darkness, mostly silent, time and perception bending and stretching, accompanied by a nudging, gnawing fear bordering on terror, assuaged periodically by the guide's voice with stories of jumandy and the nervous giggles of the kichwa girls—long an admirer of samuel beckett, I finally comprehend as no stage experience could ever communicate—it is the end of the world and nothing remains but a disembodied human voice in complete darkness—the voice speaks a strange language and I understand little, but it's enough to reassure me—but there is a terrible poignance because it is the last human voice in the universe and all that is left for me, the last listener—it is the voice of the guide (who is the guide?), winding down—soon, silence—rather than depressed I am amazed and energized almost to the point of giddiness, and happy too when we pull up stakes and move out of this dark place, this reminder of human loneliness and isolation—finally we arrive at the exit, a narrow opening through which we crawl, emitting the most extraordinary beautiful light I have ever seen, a silvery-green effusion of life and escape—later, walking home on the highway, irene spies a dead boa on the other side and lets out a shriek—the boa is a powerful totemic animal—edmundo, chris and i cross the road—the snake is about five feet long and has been run over—there is a strong odor—edmundo hides the animal in the bushes and sticks a branch in the ground to mark the spot—he will return later to get the bones—

On the river

1/4

another night of torrential rain with vivid dreams of waterfalls and flooding—an army of trolls stamping their feet on the metal roof—it is still raining heavily in the morning and there is discussion about canceling the rafting trip—luis is not answering his phone—we decide to take our chances and go to tena anyway, hoping the rain will subside and indeed on the way it does—selva verde, luis zapata's guide business, is on avenida José Antonio Santander, whoever that esteemed gentleman might be, off one of the main streets of tena in a typical storefront enclosure protected by one of the metal roll up doors that every business in ecuador possesses—luis is not there but his assistant, alvaro, a friendly, well-built guy of about 18 says he's expecting us—we stash our stuff and come back a few minutes later and luis, an immediately imposing figure in his mid-thirties with a strong mestizo face and a mouthful of smiling white teeth, his powerful body wrapped in spandex, is there—the first thing luis does when we shake hands is pointedly squeeze the biceps of my right arm with his left hand by way of gauging my strength and likely what position I will occupy in the raft—I have no illusions of being an imposing physical specimen but I'm not exactly a weakling and this little reconnoitering squeeze miffs me more than I care to admit—but luis is the boss and he's got a business to run that depends on these sorts of physical calculations and I don't begrudge him, though I'm put off by his intimate appraisal, this touching—I've done my share of river paddling, certainly a lot more than my three companions, though about this luis knows nothing—but I'm not here to prove anything and I know I can take care of myself despite being by far the oldest of the group—an hour later we're at the end of the road next to the Jatunyacu river unloading the raft and the gear—the jatunyacu is a couple of hundred meters wide, clearly an energetic bit of water, surrounded by jungle—upstream, to the west, green mountains dominate the horizon—the sky is overcast, a bit of a mist—a big old rusty suspension bridge crosses the river here, passage to the communities on the other side—I take a walk on the bridge about halfway across, carefully stepping on the motley collection of planks, the river 50 meters below—some locals with large bundles walk past, ignoring me—luis gives a thorough run-through of procedures and techniques and then we're in the raft, into the choppy river, a big series of class three rapids ahead—not impressed with my biceps or youthfulness, luis has put me in the middle position across from Irene (I'm with the woman!)—chris and edmundo are in front—luis is in the back with his paddle, giving instructions—alvaro, the assistant, is paddling alongside in a fiberglass kayak—he plays in the waves like a duck—it is marvelous to be on this wild river, the dark green mountains behind us shrouded in mist, the quiet jungle crowding both banks—we hit the first rapid, larger than anything I've experienced on my little new mexico rio chama, the raft wildly bucking up and down in the four and five foot waves generated by the powerful, fast-moving river, huge boulders everywhere, all of us shouting and yelling, paddling like mad, immediately soaking wet—getting through we rest for a few moments and then another rapid is upon us and we're swept ahead, churning, bouncing, twisting and paddling, pitching into the troughs of waves that threaten to engulf us, flip the raft over, luis yelling like ahab, and then we're clear for a moment, raising our paddles together in a triumphant salute, exhilarated, though my kichwa friends look a little shaken and unusually pale, especially Irene, who doesn't seem to be enjoying this at all—noticing her discomfort we try to rally her spirits with teasing and laughter, to little effect—but there's no time to ponder her condition because there are more rapids ahead, just as powerful—though rivers are an integral part of life in the oriente they are considered extraordinarily potent and dangerous, an accurate assessment, and it is likely most of the people who live here are not expert swimmers, which is understandable—this is not the sort of water in which to practice your strokes—even if you were an expert you'd stand no chance in conditions like this—luis mentions a german kayaker who died on this river a couple of weeks ago—they never found his body—a couple more wild rides, a short respite, and then we're into another one, the biggest so far, and suddenly a really big wave rises up and the raft yaws violently and chris flies off as if an invisible hand has reached up and snatched him—we stare for a second, dumbfounded, and then the same thing happens to Irene, the same invisible hand, poor terrified irene, of all people, and she's quickly swept away, alvaro in his plastic kayak immediately giving chase to the small gasping figure bobbing in her life jacket—edmundo is shocked at seeing his wife in the rough water and helplessly watches, not knowing what to do—there is really nothing to do except hope that chris and Irene remember to follow luis's instructions to float on your back and remain calm while the kayak and raft try to pick you up—we dip into another big wave and edmundo topples over backwards and hits the water with a splash, rapidly floating away—in less than thirty seconds we have lost chris, Irene and edmundo, in that order, with luis and me furiously paddling, not so much to rescue our mates but to maneuver the raft through this stretch as not to be spun sideways and lose the raft completely or be pitched over ourselves—while paddling we scan the river to see if everyone's safe—alvaro has caught up with Irene and she's pulled herself onto the kayak, obviously exhausted, as much from fear as physical exertion—edmundo is bobbing clear of the rapid and by now we are all in calmer water—I don't see chris but then he appears, next to the raft, looking rather pale himself, but safe—I grab his life jacket and pull him aboard—next comes alvaro with his enervated cargo flopped across the stern of his kayak and chris and I pull irene into the raft, where she more or less collapses, and finally we get edmundo, stunned but okay, and chris and I pull him over—thankfully we've hit an extended calm and have time to recuperate, most of our attention focused on Irene who finds nothing of our humorous attempts to cheer her up the slightest bit bracing or amusing—chris excitedly recounts the adventure in Spanish, laughing maniacally, while edmundo tries to laugh but is too freaked out and concerned about irene to muster more than a grim smile, while luis, who has remained calm throughout, scans the river—obviously he's had people go over before but I don't think three at once—I never felt anyone to be in imminent danger, perhaps it all happened too quickly, but there can be no doubt my attention was fully focused—at length we arrive at a spit of gravel and stone jutting into the river and beach the raft, luis and alvaro hauling out food from the cooler, bread, cold cuts, mayonnaise, mustard, ahí, pickles, olives, potato salad, soft drinks, fruit, cookies, brownies, arranging everything on the overturned raft neat enough to please queen or king—for some time now the sky has been clearing and it's hot, the strong equatorial sun bearing down—we're quickly set upon by biting flies but it's of minor consequence—hungry and tired from our efforts we each find our own warm smooth white cushion-sized stone on which to sit and eat our sandwiches, the wide blue river rushing past, jungle all around—irene regains some of her spirit and receives our teasing good-naturedly—nothing would be better now than to take a nap but it's too hot and obviously we need to get going—back on the jatunyacu we soon enter the napo, larger than the jatunyacu, farther downstream larger yet, eventually joining the amazon in peru, near iquitos—throughout our trip we've seen indigenous people in dugout canoes and also people with curious gas powered machines along the shore, panning for gold—we've been on the water several hours and we're tired—arriving at the tourist town of misahualli we haul the raft through the square and deposit it next to the road—a handful of small monkeys cavorts in the plaza, stealing from tourists, partaking of one of the national pastimes—on the way back to rukullakta, luis, behind us on his motorcycle, is stopped at a checkpoint and his bike is confiscated because he's left his license in tena—the police do not allow him to return with us—

The general exhorts, I follow

1 / 8

I meet anita at 12 o'clock in plaza santo domingo at the statue of Antonio José de Sucre, one of the heroes of the Battle of Pichincha, which took place on may 24, 1822—the general gestures in exhortatory fashion towards the Pichincha volcano, where the great battle was fought and won, a key moment in the Ecuadorian war of independence—*adelante!* says the general, and I take his command to heart, smiling at the attractive ecuatoriana as she somewhat shyly approaches me walking across the plaza, disembarked from *el trole* at the santo domingo parada—she has travelled from her home in the north of quito, a long trip, about an hour—the comely anita, wearing a white blouse, jeans and large blue sunglasses (in which I see my own, sunglassed, smiling, funhouse reflection), plants a warm kiss on my cheek, smelling faintly of fruity perfume—if my Spanish was sketchy to begin with, it now has the momentum of traffic on 10 de agosto *en la hora de pico*—no importa!—*adelante!* says the general, and off we go, anita taking my hand, up avenida venezuela for lunch at a restaurant near la basilica, the largest cathedral in quito, and maybe all of latin America—we are shy with each other—anita does most of the talking as I try to decipher her words while holding hands (already!) and negotiating the traffic, pedestrian and vehicular, on the narrow sidewalks and streets of the old city, trying not to trip, bump into pedestrians, or get crushed by a car, an undertaking summoning all my capabilities, the stereotypical self-conscious stumbling older gringo with his latina, secretly delighting in this fortuitous turn of events and the possibilities to follow—why not?—we have lunch, which I pay for, of course—it is understood that the male pays for everything all the time in latin America, especially males from the north, and I do so gladly—*los almuerzos tipicos* are cheap, around $3—from there we go up the avenue to la basilica, an imposing neo-gothic structure hulking above its surroundings, with two huge towers fronting the avenue, each with a large clock whose times have stopped and note different hours—I am not one for churches, but the cathedrals of quito have captured me—la basilica is my least favorite, however, huge, somber and forbidding, lacking the grace and character of the four others I'm familiar with, la iglesia de santo domingo, of my neighborhood, la iglesia de san Francisco, la iglesia de la compañía de jesús, (known as *la compañía*) and la catedral at plaza grande (*independencia*), and I'll add a fifth, *el belen*, next to alameda park, one of the oldest, and certainly one of the most humble, churches in quito, reminding me of old Spanish colonial churches in new mexico—the *mudéjar* (Moorish) influence on the architecture of *la catedral* is particularly striking, and the latin American baroque-*mudéjar* style of *la compania*, along with its overwhelmingly complex, gold-leafed interior, is an unfailing marvel—but no man-made structure can compare with the female form, and anita diminishes the ponderous basilica as so much feeble, human pretension—up we climb, to the catwalk above the vaulted ceiling of the interior, as if traversing the back of some monstrous, rough beast, up the narrow ladder, anita above (father forgive me), to the roof, which offers a grand panorama of the city and the distance beyond—it's all very glorious and I am delighted to be way up here on the roof of la basilica in the company of this attractive woman, with a soupçon of vertigo adding to the adventure, mystery, and hint of peril that has flavored my time in this beautiful country—and now the possibility of romance—a myriad of feelings here, and I love it—I am blessed—an impulse to make the sign of the cross makes me smile at myself, the old companion I know so well, his follies, foibles, and small adventures, his absurdities, this superstitious impulse being only the most recent in a long train of random thoughts and urges, occasionally acted upon, as this very excursion to the middle of the globe—what am I doing here?—who knows?—who cares?—what does it matter?—that I am here is all that is necessary—I am indeed in a wondrous place and fully absorbed, as I have been from the start, which is how it should be, always—we stay for about 30 minutes looking out over the city—it is a relatively cloudless day for quito—the cement exterior of the cathedral is rotted, no doubt from the pollutants of the city's air—iron reinforcement rods protrude like bones under the crumbling skin of the towers—chunks of cement will fall, probably already have, to the sidewalk far below—the whole cathedral will fall, eventually, as everything does—these ruminations snap me back to the sweet corporeality of my companion, who has become somewhat reflective herself—we walk back to santo domingo plaza in an afternoon thunderstorm shielded under my valiant K-mart umbrella with its two broken ribs—at *la parada del trole* we exchange chaste *besitos* and plan to meet again soon—

La Liga

we're halfway through the 1ˢᵗ eight-week cycle of the new year—as usual I'm teaching two classes, two hours each, from 2 to 6 pm—the first class is a delight, the second, less so—in general these students are bright, if uninformed and less imaginative than one would wish—techies—my teaching style is that of a counter puncher, which is to say I need some signs of life and enthusiasm from my students—of course I throw the first punch and it's got to be sharp enough to elicit a response from at least a segment of the class—it is this response I thrive on—the more lively the feedback the more animated my own, and so on—I am good at keeping things going as long as I have some help from my students—the 2-4 class is full of bright, interested students whose English is pretty good—the 4-6 class is in stark contrast—the first bunch laughs at my jokes and makes me feel like Jaime escalante, the second stares at me blankly and makes me feel like a guest speaker from the klingon language institute—the eternal plight of teachers, a plucky if somewhat hapless lot—if the board was a mirror students in the second class would see some interesting faces in response to their own maddeningly wooden expressions as with my back turned I write obligatory and tiresome points of grammar and syntax—in addition, this time around, both classes are unusually large—teachers love to complain and I'm no different, but in reality my schedule is ideal and the workload is much less than the average working stiff's—I work about 24 hrs a week, 20 paid, and make more money per hour than the average Ecuadorian—it's just enough to get by—the conditions are much better at this school than others where I have worked in Albuquerque—most students call me "teacher" and are unfailingly polite and respectful—I stand by the door at the end of class and bid each student goodbye—I recognize the majority are here to fulfill a requirement and are less than wholly interested in learning English—their speaking skills are fair, their writing skills better—they are smart enough to absorb the minimum and regurgitate this for the exams—some students in the second class find a certain humor in their poor skills and joke with each other about it—I do not find this amusing—these students will likely fail—the majority of the students are in their early twenties and are the vanguard of ecuador's technological future—likely there are some geniuses in my classes—though not of its stature, epn is considered the MIT of Ecuador—it was founded in 1869 by the catholic conservative president, Gabriel Garcia Moreno, later assassinated by liberals, for the moment suspending their credo of tolerance—tolerant Garcia Moreno was not, but he founded a good university—for a while I've been bugging Susana to go to a soccer match and today she picks me up at nine-thirty to see her favorite pro team, "la liga," play at their stadium, Estadio de Liga Deportiva Universitaria, commonly referred to as "la casa blanca"—la casa blanca is in northwest quito, a good drive from my apartment in el centro historico—they are playing olmedo, from riobamba, to the south, not considered a very good club—both teams play in ecuador's highest professional division, Serie A—we park in an underground lot in a shopping center nearby and join the stream of fans on this sunny morning, passing people hawking liga jerseys and caps, ticket scalpers and food vendors—the food is traditional, mostly fritada, fried pork with two types of corn, "choclo" and "mote," a small potato or two, a piece of cooked "maduro" (banana)—fritada is delicious, especially with a bottle of *orangine*, an Ecuadorian soft drink, my favorite variant being *orangine de mora*, the blackberry flavor—if there's no *orangine* the devil's coke will do—susana buys a couple of tickets from a scalper—the markup is not severe, maybe ten percent—casa blanca is a large stadium seating 55,000 and from the outside looks 50 years old, the white paint chipped and faded, streaked with black mold, but in fact was built in 1997—the climate here ages everything quickly—inside the usual excitement seeing the emerald, impeccable field, in the middle of which stand two enormous inflated idolatrous objects three or four meters high, one for the worship of credit, the other beer, steadied uneasily by flimsy guy ropes, the beer idol toppling over once, likely inebriated, the credit holding strong, a reassuring omen of fiscal soundness—the president, an economist and devout catholic, would be pleased in the recesses of his pagan soul to see this—the humans at the base of these totems struggle to keep them upright and when the moment arrives they quickly and unceremoniously disconnect the air and the two bozo-like objects deflate rapidly and are dragged off, reduced to their essence as heaps of malleable plastic, products of the true god, oil, ecuador's blood, that which buttresses the young president's confident and well-rested countenance—the crowd, which is thin, warms to the occasion as all the while on either end of the stadium the true fanaticos have been manufacturing a constant din of drums, horns and wild cheering, setting off garish pink and orange smoke flares, manipulating great banners in support of their beloved futbol clubs, jumping up and down with excitement—there is a competition between the two ends to see which can generate the most noise and enthusiasm—this is not a big rival for la liga and consequently there are fewer fans than usual—the players come out onto the field with hearty disapproval for olmedo and great noise for liga, looking very smart in their white uniforms, and the game begins, the home team immediately displaying its superiority, scoring goal number one within minutes, almost casually, as if toying with their outmatched opponent—it's the first professional soccer match I've seen and it's exciting, the constant noise of the crowd, the wonderful skill and speed of the players—quickly liga scores another goal and the crowd, which has grown and fills about half the stadium, roars as if Ecuador has won the world cup—at halftime it is 2-0 and the little humans race out with the inflatable idols, struggling to blow them up with electric-powered pumps, the huge ungainly objects flopping around like players fishing for red cards, finally erect for two short anticlimactic minutes, then deflated and dragged off—la liga comes out first to thunderous cheers, energetic and radiating deadly confidence, still sharp in their white uniforms that contrast so smartly with the brilliant green grass—olmedo comes out minutes later, as if reluctant, to hearty disapproval and shrill whistles, looking dispirited and interested only in getting things over as quickly as possible—within seconds liga scores the third goal and again the fans rejoice as if it's a championship instead of a glorified exhibition match against an inferior opponent—liga begins substituting, as does olmedo, and about half the players on the field are those who started—it makes no difference as liga's second players are equally superior—before the end liga strikes twice more and rooting interest centers around keeping olmeda from scoring—throughout I have been watching one of olmedo's players whose style and pluck I admire, a wiry, speedy black youth who keeps getting knocked down but bouncing up every time with spirit and energy, coming close to scoring a couple of times—finally he's knocked down one time too many and stays down, exhausted, and the trainers come out with the electric cart and carry him off—he's replaced by another player, a pudgy guy with wild curly hair who plays with reckless energy but not much skill—I look over at the sideline and the youth is up and looking fine—this of course happens all the time in futbol and has happened three or four times today—you think they're dead and the cart comes out and wheels them off and when they hit the sideline they're up and bouncing, racing back onto the field—final score: la liga 5, olmedo 0—

The West Bank; old Quito; an impatient guide

2/18

Palestinians in the west bank have recently installed a modest solar and wind electrical generating system supplying power to 1500 people and Israeli authorities are threatening to tear it down—the west bank, Palestinian territory, is "administered" by Israel—Palestinians are required to obtain permits before they can build anything on their own land—as befitting a low-minded and cruel occupation virtually all requests for permits are denied, forcing Palestinians to build "illegally"—israeli praetorians then march in with court orders to destroy any such constructions because they've been built without the required permits—it is a wonderful exercise in diabolical circularity—a key component of the Israeli method is to wait until the structures have been built, allowing the nurturing of a modicum of hope, and then to bring in the wrecking machines, Hyundai, Caterpillar, Volvo, et al, to deliver a double blow—one can only marvel at the depths of such psychology—and of course it is an effectively demoralizing tactic, having been used over and over again throughout history, as any people with a memory of their own oppression will recognize—but any people with such recognition also understand that the spirit of resistance is inextinguishable no matter how vicious and demented the oppressor's tactics and even if squelched for the moment rise up in the future with a vengeance—I have been to the occupied territories and seen these things—the stench of a base and cunning meanness lies thickly everywhere—israel is a police state—the peace center in east Jerusalem where I stayed has recently been destroyed for the fifth time—the two-story house next to the home I helped rebuild with other international volunteers was destroyed a month after we left—the illegal settlements ("settlements" sounds quaint, they are huge, state-of-the-art gated communities, small cities, with malls, public parks, swimming pools, etc, using a grossly disproportionate amount of water, roughly 86%, in a parched land) continue to be built all over the west bank, internationally recognized Palestinian land—the pace of house demolitions accelerates—something terrible in the course of history has been done to the collective psyche of many jews that inhibits an objective view of what exactly is going on—this is a literal fact in Israel, where most citizens have never been to the occupied territories—the continual invocation of the holocaust comes from a people mortally traumatized—but the holocaust is one stop, albeit an unspeakably horrifying one, on a historical journey that has molded a particular stance separate and against the world—this seems to be a part of the jewish character, the jewish memory—the separation wall closes israelis in as much as it keeps others out, more of the timeworn pattern of willful alienation, impossible to disentangle from the historical reality of suffering, oppression and horror at the hands of others—all this is terrible, tragic, vexing—and now we seem to be approaching some sort denouement with the state of Israel—admittedly I don't approach these issues from a disinterested vantage point—my father was jewish—I grew up with images of the holocaust and attitudes inherited from him, a tough secular jew ready to knock the teeth down your throat if you so much as raised a kike-suggesting eyebrow—I taught a unit on the holocaust every year complete with film footage of the camps being liberated—I have shed more than a few tears over the holocaust—but now my sorrow is for the palestinians—there is a marvelous photographic exhibition of quito from the 1800s to the present at centro cultural metropolitano, in plaza grande (plaza de la independencia)—I have returned about five times, never tiring of the images—there are many pictures of the old city, including a few of my street, rocafuerte, from as far back as 1850—things have hardly changed—there are several pictures of the terrible earthquake of 1868, one showing the rubble in santo domingo plaza from surrounding collapsed buildings, another showing before and after images of the great cathedral at san Francisco plaza with its two towers, one destroyed by the earthquake, the plaza filled with refugees—there are sepia-toned pictures of the surrounding hills of quito at the turn of the century, rich agricultural land fully utilized, now filled with apartment buildings creeping to the summits like a massive accretion of mineral deposits—there's a wonderful picture of *aguateros*, the indigenous water vendors, collecting water at the fountain in san francisco plaza—there are several pictures of *calle guayaquil*, the street I walk virtually every day, instantly recognizable, even from one hundred years ago—on guayaquil where now stands the lovely and recently restored teatro nacional sucre was a *carnicería* that serviced much of the city, the open space fronting it a *plaza de toros*—it was only a matter of dragging the dead bulls a few feet to be butchered—the plaza is now filled with thieves, whores and pickpockets and serves as a space for street theater and concerts—if this sounds Elizabethan it's because it is—I have fun with panoramic photos trying to locate my section of the old city—I love the photos from the fifties, sixties and seventies showing the transition from banana to oil republic, the obvious US influence, the advertising for pepsi-cola, Goodyear, Revlon, camel cigarettes, zenith and more, the wonderful styles of dress, the old cars—these were the years of united fruit, the alliance for progress and the "enlightened" strategy for fighting communism, of right-wing dictators and left-wing protests and, crushingly, the discovery of oil in the mid-sixties by Texaco and the beginning of the transformation of the basic economy from agriculture to petroleum—the pictures from the eighties onward interest me less, depicting what I consider the drift to a depressing state of affairs, a perception surely reflecting my age, a strong nostalgia and the foolish romanticizing of earlier depressing states of affairs—I have really wanted to go with an intelligent quitaño for informed commentary and did have the opportunity to go with Susana once but only for a short time—I have asked Mario to come with me and today we meet in the plaza—I hardly recognize Mario, wearing what looks like plaid pajama bottoms, with a white t-shirt, and in high form even for him, his crazed bean fairly spinning in manic energy—I wonder if he's a cokehead—though we have made plans for a "tour" of the exhibition it is clear his priorities have changed—what he wants above all is to have lunch with a couple of his strange friends and we go through the first part of the exhibition hastily, Mario manifesting obvious boredom, dismissive of the pictures as old material he's seen a hundred times, not considering in his rampant egoism for even a moment that it is I who am the newcomer and the one most interested in learning about the history of quito, having asked him respectfully as someone I consider to be well-informed to provide commentary and insight—we go through about one-quarter of the exhibition and Mario is simply too bored and impatient to continue, taking his leave to eat lunch with his ghastly expatriate friends, inviting me to come, but I am secretly fuming and politely decline—we part company and I continue my perusal of the photos—at this point I'm not sure I want to see Mario again, and I'm not certain he doesn't feel the same—

Cunning low and high

3/7

one is advised to be careful in quito—any number of larcenous characters prowl, looking for victims, women and tourists at the top of the list—I've had three encounters, the trolley, the bus, and most recently sitting on a bench in ejido park, early for work, killing time, checking out the sights—comes a middle-aged woman poorly dressed to sit on the opposite side of the bench, nonchalant, right on time for her own work I suppose, checking sights like the obvious stranger near her with a shoulder bag not of the expensive variety, rather ragged actually, but filled with something—what?—loose change? passport? pocketknife? tickets to tonight's ballet at teatro sucre?—too enticing to ignore—I feel her presence, the itching, compulsive desire to probe, explore, waiting patiently for the precise moment, the gringo lulled by the warm afternoon sun, distracted by the strangeness of this place, perimeter defenses relaxed—I know what she is about—I wait, sensing her desire, her low cunning, her practiced patience—five minutes—I have not looked at her since our first buenos dias—more minutes pass—it is time—I turn suddenly and there, like a reptile, like a crocodile slowly and innocently floating towards its prey, her hand, resting on the bench, inches from my bag—she snatches the hand away like some retracting anemone but it's too late—I smile and bid her goodbye—angrily she turns her head as if the one aggrieved—walking home in the early evening a few days later on veintimilla, near amazonas, I come across an unexpected sight—out of a large black SUV parked next to the sidewalk step five men dressed in dark suits, laughing and talking loudly in english—they are from the US and they are looking for a place to eat—one speaks with a Spanish accent, presumably their guide, and is recommending a restaurant on amazonas—they are in their thirties and forties, well-fed, comfortable in their expensive suits, in high spirits, exuding a brash confidence as if commanding ownership of the sidewalk and surroundings, anticipating a good meal and perhaps some entertainment later—my reaction is an immediate, involuntary loathing and fear—symbols of the arrogance and power I despise—I'm close, right in the middle of them—my attitude gives me away—one of the older ones is aware of me and we exchange hostile looks—nothing like an expensive suit and a certain demeanor to put things straight—years ago I asked a student, a tough gang member, what kind of person frightened him and he claimed no one—normally a response of this sort is nothing more than bravado but this guy was genuine and I more or less believed him—then I asked how he felt when he saw men wearing suits and carrying briefcases walking towards him—he hesitated and offered an answer that was less than convincing—it likely wasn't something he'd thought about very much—it was as if, somehow, these types didn't exist—but they surely do—another world than his own, another realm where people in fine clothes make the rules and enforce them with steel and blood—

San Plácido

3/15

when we parted company after our time together for lunch and the climb to the top of *la basilica*, anita invited me to visit her in San Plácido, the village in the cloud forest about 45 minutes by bus from Portoviejo, the capital of manabi provence—it is between class cycles and I have called—she is somewhat surprised to hear from me but I have no major plans and I would like to see San Plácido, and her—I have hard enough time understanding Spanish in person, especially when rapidly spoken, anita's style, but understanding on the phone is worse—I gather that she will meet me in Portoviejo at the bus station the afternoon of the 15th, and that we will take the bus together to San Plácido—when I arrive at the station in portoviejo, however, anita is nowhere to be found, and so i buy a ticket for San Plácido and go by myself, on a rickety old bus packed with campesinos laden with goods purchased in the city—this is not an entirely rational move, as I have no idea where her home is, nor, of course, can I be sure if anyone in San Plácido knows, or even if she will be there—but there is much about this entire Ecuadorian walkabout that is not "rational," whatever the word can possibly mean, and so, in this regard, for better or worse, I am consistent—at least I am not hitchhiking, though once I get on the bus I wonder if that might not be a safer alternative—it is a slow, meandering trip on the groaning, exhaust-spewing conveyance that is at least 30 years old, held together by layers of colorful paint, an eccentric matron with the right combination of artfully applied makeup, managing to make herself presentable, even a bit charming, if not wholly functional—as we climb higher into the cloud forest I think of *the little engine that could*, and *scuffy the tugboat*, with some bolero as background music—in front is the usual picture of jesus, beatific and protective—it soothes me, but I am apprehensive, too, for not only am I fearful that the bus will fall apart, I am not sure when or where is the stop at San Plácido—it is late afternoon and cloudy when I, along with one other passenger, a teenage boy, depart the old bus at the roadside stop just outside of the central part of the village—I walk up the road to a handful of modest structures that apparently is main street, San Plácido, and in a small general store ask about the home of the widow of the deceased gringo—there is much befuddlement, which is surprising because San Plácido is tiny, clearly the sort of place where everyone knows everything about everybody, and surely the gringo with *su esposa ecuatoriana* would be a topic of interest—I don't know if the two guys in the store are being purposefully vague but then an older gent, plainly *borracho*, comes in the store and says of course he knows the house, which is close by, and offers to walk me there—it turns out the house is directly across the street from the bus stop—it is now dark and raining—there is no one at the house, a white, single-story, brick affair with a blue roof and front yard enclosed by a wire fence against which a dark, short-haired, medium sized, fierce-looking dog throws itself, barking furiously—the old guy departs, wishing me luck—suerte!—maybe this time it's run out—the rain intensifies—I take out my trusty K-mart umbrella, bending forlornly with its broken ribs—I am alone in a small hamlet tucked away in the cloud forest—as the dog is in the front yard I figure anita can't be too far removed and hopefully will soon show up—there is a house across the street with its lights on and I walk over—beneath a front porch and dim light bulb a thin, unshaven, middle aged man in a dirty yellow T-shirt sits drinking a beer—he informs me that indeed, anita lives in the house across the street, but he hasn't seen her since the morning, but as the dog is outside, she should be returning soon—the man's wife appears and regards me suspiciously, saying little—she is heavy, with short, graying hair and wears a bulky green sweater—I marvel at the man's T-shirt—it is cold—they ask me if I have anita's number—stupidly, I have neglected to add her to my contacts but I try a number in the call log that might be hers but for some reason it won't go through—there is a smaller house next to theirs, with no lights on that I can see, but a woman, curiosity aroused by the strange conversation, appears and says she has anita's number and will call her—amazingly, anita answers and tells the woman that she is on the bus to San Plácido from Portoviejo, and should arrive in half an hour—milagro—somehow, apparently, I have missed anita in Portoviejo—I hear "gringo" as the woman talks to anita—so, there's a new gringo in town—the word's already out—by tomorrow morning all of San Plácido will know—an hour goes by talking to the couple under the porch as the rain continues to fall—there is no traffic on the highway and, with no street lights, the darkness, surrounding mountains and rain increase the sense of mystery and isolation—the bus is very late—the heavy woman opens up and does most of the talking as the man, now drinking aguardiente, still in his T-shirt, lapses into a morose silence—he has not offered me a beer but I would decline in any case—it is too fucking cold—the woman tells me that they have a farm and animals and that life is very hard—their children have gone to live in the city where life is better, a story I've heard many times—finally, out of the caliginous gloom, the colorful old wheezer pulls up, air brakes belching, door creaking open, and anita, wearing a flowery dress and high heels (tacones!), steps carefully off and comes clippity-cloppity up to the porch—I thank the couple for their hospitality and together, sheltered under my broken-winged umbrella, anita and I walk across the street to her house where we are greeted by her dog, rex, less unfriendly, but putting me on notice with some hard pokes on my legs with his fearsome muzzle—I spend four days and nights with anita in her little house under a constant, at times torrential, rain, the summits of the surrounding mountains obscured by heavy clouds—when the rain subsides during the day we go for walks in the dripping forest resonant with strange bird calls and other sounds that anita says are monkeys—the last day anita accompanies me on the bus back to Portoviejo, and I return to quito, wondering, as I look out the window, if the last four days have not been a dream—

Walking home-A

3/22

evening class gets out around 5:45 each day and since October when I decided to forgo the madhouse trolley I've been walking home from the university—in all the trip takes about an hour and, together with my walk from the trolley coming to work earlier in the afternoon, my total walking time is about an hour-and-a-half each day—sometimes, Saturdays, I'll take another long walk, a regular being a stroll to the mariscal district, a seedy, colorful tourist hub and nightspot where I visit the excellent Confederate Book Store and chat with the owner, bill grochowski, a man of interesting if not entirely politically correct perspectives, sometimes actually buying a book, then heading back to rocafuerte—that's a good two hour perambulation—arriving in quito last august my knee was in bad shape but with constant walking plus some exercises in my apartment it's much better—not only are my knees improved but all other parts of my legs, too, and I actually have these days what passes for a little spring in my step, sometimes heading across santo domingo plaza breaking into a little run just for the hell of it, bouncing up the steps to the upper level of the plaza—at work I always use the stairs, never the elevator—at this altitude you feel it by the time you've reached the third floor, actually the fourth since around here the first floor is called *planta baja*, or PB—heading across campus after work it's usually about

218

six o'clock and since we're in the middle of the rainy season the
clouds are low and the pavement is wet and the sky is getting
dark—normally the rain quits around four or five but sometimes
it's still going—in such circumstances i gather myself into a thin
profile under my sagging little umbrella (time to get a new one,
but I'm sentimental) and begin the trek, which, under most conditions, is usually enjoyable—there's nothing striking about this part
of the politecnica campus, a mélange of unimaginative buildings de-
voted to the grinding pursuits of different branches of engineering,
though that of the mechanical variety has its attractions, especially
bridges—correa is a big bridge builder, which on balance seems positive, though I am not sure—if the result is to bring commerce,
development and the dominant culture (*especially* the dominant
culture) to the countryside I'd rather them torn down—obviously
there's nothing much to be done about it and to accept these in-
evitabilities with something like wisdom and soul-saving equanimity is far and away the supreme challenge, though I don't think I'm
up to it—traversing the dripping campus in the early evening takes
about ten minutes, passing the dreary technical buildings, the only
points of light and life being the students, as everywhere, full of life
and energy, young Ecuadorians dark and attractive, much laughter, couples holding hands, groups together talking loudly—I always marvel at the difference in perspective and energy that age
delivers, between mine and theirs, their lightness of heart and ur-
gency for the moment, the world, troubled as it is, still offering
something like promise, the spirit and resiliency of young souls,
the natural condition of their moment—I don't begrudge them, nor
do I envy them, their innocence, naiveté, their superiority, looking through the lens of youth at a universe that if impenetrable at
least seems somewhat accommodating, for them a perspective necessarily exclusive of others, without which existence would be in-
supportable—let the fathomless yaw occupy the lonely thoughts of
the old as they face the inevitable, some comforted with images of
angels, waterfalls, emerald vales and zaftig virgins—not this trav-

eler—the closest I come to paradise is for at least one of my drifting atoms joining forces with others in a hunk of dark chocolate or a brooch settled in the soft canyon of a pair of beautiful female breasts, virgin or otherwise—I sometimes see former students and we acknowledge each other warmly, though it is rare that I remember their names, an occupational affliction—there are two arresting sights going through the campus, the first a modern, concrete building of the brutalist mode constructed sometime late in the previous century, a dark gray largely windowless star wars redoubt of modestly swooping affect that has fallen into disuse, probably because it houses pursuits generally considered insubstantial in this hardheaded environment, which is to say the arts, specifically of the performing variety—it also houses, distinctly ad hoc in nature, a rather forlorn collection of biological specimens, which glimpsed through the front door actively discourages ingress—it is an odd building completely out of character with the dull surrounding boxes, as if in fact it did swoop down from space in search of temporary parking and disgusted with its neglect soon to fly away in hopes of finding more agreeable digs—the other notable sight is pichincha, massive and darkly green, looming over quito, this time of year its upper reaches invariably covered with clouds, the white sprawl of the expanding city creeping up its flanks—pichincha is to the west, a handy signifier, similar to the sandias in Albuquerque, which points one to the opposite cardinal direction—heading out of the campus, through the entrance gates with the guards and their guns, turning to the west and pichincha, I'm on the street named ladron de Guevara with its rumbling herds of elephant-like buses belching diesel fumes, their brakes straining and shrieking, engines roaring, in the midst of students walking to and from evening classes on the typically rugged, cracked old quito sidewalk that poses its own challenge to safety and survival, one of a dozen things monitored more or less simultaneously on even a casual walk in this or any other busy urban environment, my level of awareness a notch higher as a stranger though feeling slightly less so after eight months—on the left is the old cec building, still in use, a mid- twentieth century house of pedagogy vaguely stirring the dread of past academic nightmares and a bit farther west, "llantas y servicios," a large open air building for repairing tires that never seems especially busy except for the occasional "zzziipp!!" of a pneumatic wrench and a clanging tire iron, then the *preuniversitario* ernest Rutherford, one of several private institutions named after famous physicists, the other two I'm aware of being albert Einstein and Stephen hawking, whose purpose other than making money is to augment students' preparation for the rigors of quito's high tech universities, one of which of course is epn—I suppose the trendy choice would be hawking but the Rutherford name carries a certain distinction while einstein seems dated and better suited to the Bronx, but no more of that, for now we come across a busy traffic hub where *ladron de guevara* becomes *patria* and in the middle of this circling, swirling, snarling, fuming traffic the marvelous seal fountain with its delicate, spouting pinnipeds, something straight out of the 1933 Chicago world's fair, lovely, quaint and anonymous in the bustle and overshadowed a bit farther down *patria* by the grand *casa de la cultura*, quito's principal location for Ecuadorian culture, which includes a museum housing ecuador's best collection of pre-columbian artifacts as well as theaters and performance venues such as the agora, where in December I saw inti-illimani—architecturally, *casa* is a juxtaposition of forms that manages to survive and leave the viewer with a favorable impression that does not diminish over time—looking west, standing east of the hub and fountain, one sees *casa* with pichincha towering in the background, the buses and cars in constant noise and animation—the rugged sidewalks are crowded with students, the mad buses rumbling and pouring diesel fumes as I walk down patria towards 6 de diciembre, passing the large digital clock that gives time and temperature, usually around 18:18 and 13 celsius when I walk by, past the large and very popular mcdonald's, always careful crossing the entrance to its parking lot—drivers are aggressive in quito and there is barely thought of pedestrian right-of-way, which takes a little getting used to though most drivers will stop if you are planted directly in their path, reassuring evidence that automobiles have not completely robbed quiteños of their humanity—I've learned to put many of my responses and attitudes on the shelf out of respect and the necessities of survival but occasionally a little of the old posturing surfaces and if first at an intersection I'll sometimes continue with all the self-affirming determination of a true new Yorker, my birthplace, while the driver waits—some quiteños are polite and friendly and will give you first passage with a smile and a wave, others you sense mean business and it's in your best interest to defer—quito's streets are choked with buses of all varieties and the system is much less formal than in the US—there are bus stops proper and improper, meaning that in some places, along ladron de Guevara, for example, there is only a general area for getting off and on, determined by any number of factors, not the least of which being gender and attractiveness—I've seen buses stop for a sexy quiteña even if a bit beyond their usual area where under similar circumstances if it's a man they might continue—here and in many other parts of quito buses are hailed like cabs, as long as it's in such designated sections—entering and exiting can be a challenge also, this too depending on gender—males must frequently negotiate a slowly moving bus whereas females are granted the courtesy of a complete stop—young men ride shotgun with fabulous insouciance on the bus's steps calling out stops and hustling fares in raucous competition with other buses, a reminder that it's all about the serious business of making money—on the sidewalk in front of mcdonald's is a small portable fritada stand owned by an indigenous woman that always does a brisk business—*fritada* is fried pork served with *choclo* (corn), *mote* (another type of corn) cooked *maduro* (banana) and small potatoes and kicks the shit out of mickey d's any day—these stands are legion all over quito and I have a favorite on veintimilla I hit up once, sometimes twice a week before work, probably the cholesterol equivalent to eating at mcdonald's but it's cheaper, tastes better and I walk a lot—more on this particular place and other favorite eateries later—on the northeast corner of the busy intersection at 6 de diciembre and patria you face another temple of obesity and impacted arteries, KFC, which together with mcdonald's and the diesel fumes from the buses creates an unhealthy atmosphere that I'm always anxious to escape, crossing patria and 6 de diciembre, alert even with a green light, walking a short way alongside ejido park down patria and its mad traffic, on the opposite side big money buildings like the Hilton colon and banco internacional, taking a left just past the arch onto a path diagonally through the park that leads to the northbound trolley stop on 10 de agosto—I won't take the trolley, that's just where the path empties, 10 de agosto, which is the second leg of my journey home—ejido park, roughly 1/8 the size of new york's central park, has a bad reputation but I've never experienced a bit of trouble except for the woman on the bench whose number I had from the start—by the time I'm walking through ejido it's getting dark and the first few times I was nervous and on notice but the path is well-lit and reminds me a little of dorothy's yellow brick road because of the dotted yellow line on the red bricks demarcating pedestrian and bicycle traffic, though no one pays any attention to that—at this hour it is mostly people walking home just like me, ordinary folks, couples, men in suits talking animatedly, few paying me any mind, some looking with the curiosity I've grown accustomed to, at this hour almost never an acknowledgement—activity in the park is winding down but if it's not raining there still might be a volleyball game, some soccer, a smattering of old men playing cards on benches—you are aware sometimes of shady characters lurking about but at this hour of relative activity it's a long shot for anything to happen—even if a long shot however, something *could* happen, in the same way something could happen in Albuquerque or new york—everybody's a little uptight in quito—I wonder how I would react facing a knife or gun—it happened once in boston, a knife to my throat from behind—I willingly gave up my wallet—quiteños get nervous if you walk a little too closely behind them—it takes about five minutes to get through the park, to the next leg of my walk, down 10 de agosto, a different scene altogether—

Walking home-B

a couple of the sections in the tube-like glass structure at the ejido northbound *parada* on 10 de agosto are shattered in a spider web pattern, which I find a bit surprising since you don't usually see this kind of willful damage around quito—the city is old and there's a lot of poverty but destruction of the purely anti-social variety is rare, especially in my circumscribed travels—maybe other parts of the city have more—the trolley is relatively new, this, the older section, about 15 years old—one feels, despite the terribly crammed riding conditions, that quiteños take a certain pride in their metro system—I feel sorry though for the people who are dependent on the trolley because it can be hellish, especially during peak hours and when the weather is bad, which it usually is during rainy season—in the evenings as I walk home i look at the trolleys going past, the people stuffed together like animals, their faces sometimes literally pressed against the doors, the windows fogged with their breathing, soggy clothes and wet hair, and I feel a sense of condor-like liberation, though I may be trudging through puddles with soaked feet, my pants drenched with the spray from passing vehicles, my knees groaning—these slight discomforts are nothing compared with the physical and emotional travails of being on the trolley in such dantesque conditions—once past the ejido *parada* I cross 10 de agosto, facing pichincha, mindful of moving briskly be-

cause the green light is short, just before reaching the corner looking for the small brass key embedded in the asphalt that I regard as a
kind of talisman, feeling a twinge of disappointment if I don't spot
it—I wonder about this key, how many others have noticed it, what
they think—it is of the sort that would open a small lock, probably dropped on a hot day, perhaps years ago, and pressed into the
asphalt by passing vehicles—crossing bogata, mindful of traffic as
always, heading south towards centro historico, you hit the rugged
sidewalk on the west side of 10 de agosto, buckled and broken as
if having suffered through many of its own small earthquakes, immediately facing the steady aggressive flow of evening pedestrian
traffic so that the usual vigilance is required, careful not to trip on
some rogue section of sidewalk while simultaneously negotiating
the flow of humanity, the majority giving respectful berth but always a few heading at you in a more challenging manner—I am not
averse to facing these types of confrontations but here it's out of the
question and I go out of my way to avoid them—I must suppress
natural responses in this regard as it is an absolutely losing proposition and I seek always to communicate an impression of respect
and peacefulness—at the same time a certain hint of swagger and
physical confidence is required lest the more predatory regard you
as a target—as always a certain balance is essential—I have visual-
ized and practiced mentally my physical response, obviously a last
resort, should ever one be required—I think of my walk home as
divided into three parts, prosaically, A, B, C, the walk down 10 de
agosto being part B, the longest and most demanding with its frac-
tured, broken sidewalk and crowds, the most typically urban with
its bustle and street traffic and small businesses, clothing stores
with blond haired mannequins and their pointy nipples, technology and music stores, restaurants, *panaderias*, bicycles, refrigera-
tors, *farmacias*, Chinese *almacenes* (department stores) and the like,
much energy, noise, music, the recorded, amplified voices advertising goods and sales: *"remate! remate! remate! siga! siga! siga! remate! remate!..."*—soon I'm at the alameda *parada* and up the stairs where

indigenous women sell fruit and streams of workday refugees head resolutely home—this marks the last leg of the 10 de agosto run, on the periphery of the old city, but first a careful crossing of the wide *avenida de santa prisca* which empties into 10 de agosto like a river carrying its lethal detritus of buses and cars, the first time a daunting excursion but now quite relaxed with eyes wide open of course, still observing fellow quiteños for cues on making the crossing, not infallible guides always as once it almost got me squashed by a very large bus—one evening after crossing, a few yards down the sidewalk, there was an explosion on *santa prisca* that turned everyone's head and in the middle of the boulevard a bus with a blown tire sat like a fat man with a ruptured aorta—the stretch after *santa prisca* is a long one, passing the *archivo nacional* and an open-front book store that I like, for many weeks admiring a handsome political map of Ecuador that I finally bought for $22—across the street in alameda park stands an impressive monument to simon Bolivar, a kind of classical/futurist meld from the thirties, very dramatic, and then, further south, the ugliest sight in quito, the abandoned *filanbanco* building, dark and graceless, looming like a board-game piece that nobody wants, testament to the corruption of one of the viler breeds of our species—it has sat there like a death star for over ten years, the statue of Bolivar straining in its direction, as if wanting to smash it to pieces—what to do with such an ugly piece of shit?—my fantasy is to have it gutted and filled with flora and fauna from the amazon, a fine tourist attraction—triple canopy with a spiral staircase—five bucks a pop—10 de agosto has now turned into guayaquil and in another two long blocks i'll be well into *centro historico*, my neighborhood, the place I have grown to love, but first banco central, the trolley stop, and the wide brick sidewalk where so much happens, including the vendors selling illegally, ready to pack up at a moment's notice, where one night dozens of yellow baby chickens I first thought wind-up toys ran peeping all over the place while their frantic owner chased them down—

Walking home-C

if I've been walking fast down 10 de agosto I make a point to slow down on guayaquil, in the old city, because this is a marvelous and unique place, and I want it all to sink in—I'm not especially observant and feel the need to train myself here because it's different from being in nature where you are attuned to the quiet and solitude—cities are noisy and packed with distraction and the very act of navigating in these fish tanks disrupts the connection between that quiet part of our selves that communicates with the transcendent and mysterious—any city worth its salt has places of meditation, churches, temples, museums, concert halls, parks and the like where people can go to re-establish and strengthen the connection between this inner space and whatever exists beyond—the old city by virtue of its antiquity is conducive to a certain form of meditation—it's common to hear of the "timelessness" of the old streets of x, or the "timeless beauty" of cathedral y, but living in a place like the old city it really is possible to think of time as a static entity, a stationary fluid through which generations swim—as if a subtle reminder of this one of the first things you run into on the narrowing street of guayaquil is an Indian store selling incense, fabrics, soap, bollywood movies, rolling papers, pipes, posters and small statues of hindu deities, the owner, a plump, sensuous, middle-aged, Spanish-speaking Indian woman given to wearing colorful saris and a perpetual frown—I bought some sandalwood incense once and never went in again, though I always look when I walk past—it is a typical open front store with a roll up metal door—it's around here I invariably remind myself to slow down and take things in, the sidewalks and streets narrower, the walking more challenging—the trolleys roar past playing their little warning jingles, familiar snippets of "la cucaracha," "Rudolph the red nosed reindeer" and something that sounds like "that's amore" (*when the moon hits your eye...*), and if it's raining, splashing water, people good-humoredly jumping out of the way, jockeying for position in the well-known places where puddles are deeper in the street—the trolleys make me nervous, their terrifying bulk speeding along inches from the sidewalk—i don't want to get too close, imagining any number of bad scenes, not the least of which being clipped in the back of the head by one of the massive side view mirrors that come close to a sidewalk busy with all manner of pedestrian traffic including vendors, usually indigenous women, selling barbecued *cuero* (pork rinds), *plátanos* and *tamales*—I pass a section of really old buildings, one housing a dilapidated but functioning hotel in which I've had a perverse notion to rent a room for a night, and in the other buildings two interesting small businesses, one for cleaning and restoring hats, the other a progressive book store, "libreria progreso," the man in the dimly-lit and mysterious hat store constantly working on an array of bowler hats favored by the kichwa, the good fellow next door whom I've come to know a bit, Arturo, seemingly always involved in animated conversations with exotic leftist-looking intellectual types, his little nook of a store filled with photos of che, fidel and Regis debray—the first time I went into his store I bought my picture of che after introducing myself in bad Spanish, feeling a little intimidated, but Arturo put me at ease, speaking slowly and simply—keenly aware of the terrible history of gringo intervention and dirty tricks I made it a point to communicate my disgust with US policy in latin america, past and present—now when I visit we get right into things, the only inhibiting factor my clumsy, plodding Spanish—Arturo has an animated style of speaking, sometimes acting out his points with extravagant gestures, often, I suspect, to facilitate communication with his linguistically-challenged interlocutor—in a glass cabinet on a lower shelf is a collection of erotica, of no particular political persuasion—I would visit more often with Arturo but by the time I pass his store it's going on seven and I'm hungry and tired and he's usually getting ready to close—a little beyond arturo's store is the old farmacia fybeca with its polished brass fixtures, gold-lettered windows and black and white diamond-patterned floor, its white-coated pharmacists patiently taking orders behind a long counter—this is on the corner of esmeraldas and guayaquil, a hangout for hookers and transvestites, all very interesting, and then the block of *el teatro sucre*, on this side the trolley stop next to a wide open kind of mini tenderloin filled with more hookers and shady characters, one of the places I walk with a little extra attitude, the clinking turnstiles of the *parada* marking the passage of harried quiteños pushing their way out the exit onto the wet, crowded sidewalk, music blaring from the open front stores overlooked by a couple of impressively ugly buildings from the sixties, a common sight throughout the old city—I negotiate the throng, nodding to some of the tough-looking characters I've come to recognize—across guayaquil is the lovely and recently restored *teatro nacional sucre*, venue to excellent musical shows, the plaza many years ago a bull ring, the theater in those days a carnicería—now the plaza is a busy place full of interesting types, some less than honorably intentioned—there are concerts too, and, almost always in the evenings when I walk past, street performers surrounded by curious, good-natured crowds, los borrachos and trolls out in force—if it's late and I'm especially hungry I'll stop at the next block at La Tradición for a glass of steaming *morocho* and *un empanada de pollo*, a full meal for $1.40, sitting at the front, if there's a table, to watch the activity in the streets—the two are a natural pairing and very delicious—a steady diet of *morocho y empanada* would clog your arteries in a year which is why I restrict myself to once a week and even that's probably pushing it—about two weeks ago on a Friday I had my heart set on *morocho y empanada* at La Tradición but the whole neighborhood was blacked out, a rare occurrence, and I was disappointed to think of missing my favorite meal as well as the chocolate ice cream cone to follow at a pizza place farther down the block—to my surprise and utter delight however, La Tradición was open for business despite the loss of electricity, its interior lit by dozens of candles, creating a charming and mysterious atmosphere, the woman at the counter taking money and making change, as usual, from a drawer—the blackout had transformed a lively and unique environment into something completely different, intimate and equally compelling, and I marveled at the difference between this and my experience in Albuquerque when the electricity fails at commercial establishments—apparently the unfortunate people of Albuquerque lack the resources, mental and material, to conduct business when the power goes out, a condition that seems to have bedeviled much of the world—happily there are exceptions to this pathetic state of affairs, such as La Tradición—when the matrix self-destructs or is finally destroyed by the last remaining humans, I will be making a beeline for La Tradición—this same night, happy with candle-lit *morocho y empanada*, my bliss was compounded discovering the pizza place down the block still open for business and eager to sell their melting ice cream, not for the *descuento* I was hoping for though you would hardly call one dollar for a fat delicious chocolate ice cream cone *exorbitante*—the next part of the walk on guayaquil is up the hill which takes you past another wonderful restaurant, *heladeria san agustin*, normally closed at night, with the old st. augustin church on the other side of the street—farther along is the the *parada* at plaza grande with its urgent, milling crowds and fiercely clinking turnstiles, the sidewalk becoming even narrower from here on out so that the maneuvering for position is constant—one of the biggest challenges is passing slower walkers because it usually means getting onto the street and dealing with the threat of being crushed by a trolley—if the gutters are filled with rain you have the robin hood/little john situation of competing for the best sidewalk position with oncoming pedestrians to avoid being soaked by passing vehicles, usually a losing proposition for all concerned—it is these moments when I love quiteños the most—a good rain storm brings out a kind of festive humor and philosophical acceptance of things beyond human control and a wonderful politeness too, displayed by the exaggerated dipping and turning of umbrellas to avoid contact—I've been drenched many times by passing trolleys along with the people next to me and invariably our reactions are smiles and sometimes laughter—there is a sweetness to this culture, although many will tell you how much worse things have gotten—despite my few encounters with thieves I have never felt threatened or afraid walking home—now I'm on the home stretch headed towards santo domingo plaza, passing clothing stores, fabric stores, relojerias, the adult movie theater and the security guard with his mild-mannered german shepherd, past the chirping stoplights, the massive old white convent as i look down its long sidewalk corridor and old polished paving stones and arched portals reminding me of poor van gogh at saint remey, crossing Bolivar and finally onto the plaza, on guard here a little bit but never a problem, the statue of old general sucre gesturing towards pichincha, the great church ahead and the thick arch, survivor of earthquakes, through which I pass, usually a small gathering of afro-ecuadorians at the entrance or close by, a place laid claim to, large, imposing women, drama, loud voices, the arch smelling of urine, the strong lights embedded in the sidewalk casting up, blinding, garish faces, Lautrec, Ensor, jack the ripper, never a problem though Susana has warned me, never a problem here or rocafuerte itself, old rocafuerte, la loma, la mama cuchara, the last stretch passing the little police station, none of my usual hostilities, the small stores selling colorful plastic items of utility, buckets, bowls, dish racks, cups, the music store and its bootleg CDs blasting cumbia, merengue, salsa, the doors, my friend who nods hello, by four o'clock each afternoon *borracho* and out in the street directing traffic with his whistle, the panaderia, *sansi pana*, busy and well-lit, where I buy *cachos* (croissants) for the morning at 15 cents apiece, another, smaller, music store, merengue, salsa, my eyes whirling, taking it all in, not forgetting the dog shit on the sidewalk, mad taxis and motorcycles racing up and down the street much too fast, more tiendas and their colorfully garbed native vendors so sweet when you get to know them, selling fruits and vegetables for next to nothing, the school kids going home in their blue uniforms, a flowing, chattering, laughing, high-spirited river through which you must pass, the many small restaurants serving seco de pollo, menestras, sopas, cuero, platanos, some a little fancier than others, some no more than a grill on the sidewalk, past the decrepit *grande hotel* full of glass windows straight out of the sixties where scruffy giant Europeans and gringos come piling in with their huge backpacks ready for Ecuadorian adventures, the hot dog stand and its fine *vendedora* selling thin dogs in thick buns and salt-saturated papas fritas that will kill you, but she's a long-legged beauty and the reason I bought some in the first place though never again, my favorite little *restaurante* with its sidewalk grill where I buy seco de pollo or menestras once or twice a week for $1.50 from my friend zoyla, the abuelita, from here a short walk to my place, unlocking the heavy front door and if it's dark taking care not to step in any of tommy's shit in the courtyard as he greets me enthusiastically, wanting to play, up the stairs, stepping over the barrera, unlocking my front door and turning on the lights, feeling good, allowing myself to fully acknowledge at last how tired I am, and I am home—

Bienvenidos to oil country

Adolfo, woolly monkey (on the right)

Swimming partner

With Susana and Camilo

Tommy, on point

La barrera

Mirian and Gustavo

Thresher shark

El Oro

Frigate birds

The money catch

Wholly upside-down mackerel

Afternoon game, Rukullakta

Chris, in goal

Edmundo

Rio Saludo

Beavers

Oleoducto

Arriving at Martín's grandfather's

Rio Aguarico, with pipeline crossing

Chris and Martín at Dureno 1

Burn-off

First well in Lago Agrio

Waste pit

Emergildo

Carlos

Maria de Lourdes y Carlos

Amigos

Hard Rock in Archidona

4/13

it's chris's birthday tomorrow so I get a substitute and take the bus at cumbaya for archidona, arriving about five hours later, taking a cab to rukullakta—everyone's here and doing pretty well, though Irene has been out of sorts for a while and edmundo is concerned—as usual I have gifts for all, Irene, edmundo, Jennifer and sacha, which they accept graciously—the gift for edmundo and irene is a large loaf of freshly-baked bread—there's a subtle feeling of something not quite right around here—money's scarcer than usual and irene's depression or whatever it is has cast a slight shadow over everyone's mood—edmundo is preoccupied with paper work and Irene is simply preoccupied—edmundo leaves to take care of some village business—there's a soccer game and chris joins while i watch—after the game (irene has disappeared) chris and i have a meal of sweet tea, pasta and ketchup, typical when things are especially tight—we look for some of the bread i've bought but it's been eaten already—later chris and I meet up with two of his young friends, students from the US working in rukullakta, and janet, his kichwa girlfriend, and we walk in the dark to the "hard rock café" in archidona, a little joint blasting merengue, salsa and reggaeton (a kind of latin hip hop reggae), a big tv screen with music videos, packed with gyrating kichwa and locals drinking pilsener and having a good time, good vibes, chris and janet dancing right

away in "perreo" style which surprises me a little—perreo is associated with reggaeton, with a lot of what you might politely call syn-
chronized lower body contact—irene and edmundo are here—I'm
in a booth with them and a slightly drunk kichwa woman and i
ask her to dance—she's dark, in her forties, with a faraway look
and smiles at me a few times as we dance but otherwise ignores
me completely—when the music stops we go back to the booth
and a kichwa man comes over with bottles of pilsener for all of
us—he's a short, agreeable, kind of biker-hippie looking guy, very
handsome—later I find out he's the woman's husband and that she's
suffered some kind of tragedy—it's late, around midnight, and I've
danced a lot, with this same woman and a few others, and with
Irene, who's sexy and has a wandering eye—I get the feeling Irene
is very dissatisfied in general, very bored—she's a decent person but
doesn't have edmundo's depth—anyway it's late and I'm thinking
about how early everyone gets up in rukullakta, that it's going to be
a sleep-deprived weekend, but edmundo, Irene, chris and janet are
ready to go and we get a ride home with their friend roly, who is
ubiquitous, the amazon taxi driver—

Birthday boy

4/14

thankfully no pre-dawn radios or roosters and after a decent sleep I go to carlos and maria's choza where preparations for chris's birthday party this evening are underway—the women have made a bucket of *guarapo* and a larger bucket of *chicha*, both fermented for a few days, which means there will be some happy people tonight—chicha of course is chewed yuca with added water, the enzymes in the chewers' (women's) saliva breaking down the material and turning it into a drinkable beverage that ferments with time—the longer the fermentation, the stronger the drink—a few days is enough for a mild kick—guarapo is prepared the same way, using yuca, but with the addition of ripe plantain—guarapo is brownish in color and delivers a bigger jolt than the paler chicha—the choza, bluish smoke from the cooking fire gathered at the ceiling, hums with good female kichwa energy and laughter no doubt centered around the bawdy and scandalous and I assume a few comments about me but that's the price you pay for the privilege of being here—there's a big batch of locro (thick soup) going filled with chicken and vegetables, and fish wrapped in banana leaves steaming over coals, tended to by some of the younger women—chris is expecting about 50 to 75 people and has spent excellent fullbright money to buy supplies for the party—I stand a little self-consciously with the women gathered round the table preparing food, including the jovial, round, semi-toothless maria, carlos's wife, her face painted in the traditional way with vegetable dye, her marvelous chuckling laughter that seems to come from the earth up through her body and out her smiling mouth, spreading warmth and humor throughout the choza, a comforting emanation that signals all is sane and well in the universe—despite the unaccustomed surroundings I feel a sense of security and normalcy, the mundane tasks recapitulated for centuries, the comfortable sense of belonging and intimacy—community—the other women are related to the family and share the mirth and quiet talk, I of course understanding nothing but content to be here with them cutting fruits and vegetables, bananas, papaya, watermelon, strawberry, mango, yuca, broccoli, garlic, onion, feeling very much the dorkish alien gringo but sensing too that in some way my presence is accepted and perhaps even appreciated—unlike the kichwa of the sierra with their colorful garb (a custom imposed by the Spanish hundreds of years ago), the women are dressed in typical oriente fashion, aggressively and unselfconsciously informal, shorts (though maria always wears skirts), t-shirts (never braless), sandals, many slightly overweight but none obese, beautiful black hair hanging in wisps, their hands covered in pulp and peelings holding sharp knives slicing through the fruits and vegetables quickly, laughing and chuckling in a mixture of Spanish and kichwa, none of it comprehensible to me—octavio, the father of chris's girlfriend, janet, wanders in and out of the choza, at ten o'clock already a little drunk—the darkskinned octavio, about 50, of medium height and solidly built with strong construction worker's hands, is a typical wisecracking alcoholic with a bit of a smirk, aggressive enough to make an outsider like me slightly uncomfortable—the evening before, drunk as usual, he made a couple of joking remarks at my expense standing with chris and one of edmundo and irene's neighbors and I grinned good-naturedly as one must under the circumstances, but I confess to not enjoying it—chris says it took him a while to get used to octavio but he's grown to respect him as a hard-working, responsible person despite his drinking and aggressive manner—octavio claims to be impressed with my beard, saying it marks me as a wise man, but his tone is mocking—this morning he stands close behind me and speaks to the women in the choza, making them laugh—then he comes beside me and addresses me directly in inebriated Spanish that I can't understand and the women laugh again, though softly and discreetly, their eyes downcast—in another time of my life standing in a bar with a guy like this there could be a problem, but obviously not today—I am at so many disadvantages here the only thing I can do is grin like a *burro* and swallow my dollop of manure—after a while octavio gets bored and wanders away—I fervently hope he doesn't return—obviously a big part of my discomfort with octavio is my bad Spanish and non-existent kichwa—if I could humorously turn some of his remarks back on him I wouldn't feel quite so helplessly self conscious—janet, chris and I go into the forest to gather large leaves for tonight's dinner plates—we cut the leaves from the trees with knives and janet, with her long black hair, in a mini dress and sandals, ties them in bundles using strips of plants—janet is 19, slim, dark and beautiful, very quiet around me, in most respects a typical young woman, but seeing her in the forest deftly tying the bundles of leaves she is anything but ordinary—I watch discreetly as she performs a task practiced by generations of her people—there may not be much more of this after her—janet is of a generation with more of a foot in the modern world than in the old—she and chris talk quietly in Spanish, obviously very close to each other—we get about 50 leaves and return to the choza—that night around seven the festivities get started in the meeting house next to the soccer field, about thirty people sitting on benches around the perimeter, mostly people from the community, dressed semi-formally, the men in long pants, clean shirts, some of the women in dresses, others in pants and blouses, talking quietly, many of the men smoking cigarettes, kichwa pop and cumbia playing from edmundo's huge speakers but not too loudly—some people stand outside, as if not quite comfortable or ready to enter—children run around laughing and playing—the first serving of *guarapo* is passed around in *pilches* by women in traditional dresses, some with faces painted with vegetable dye, bracelets and necklaces made from different sorts of beans and seed pods—I receive the offered guarapo with a "pagarachu" and take a good deep drink, draining the pilche, as is the custom, everyone watching and smiling as I swallow the beige, sweet, thick liquid swimming with small pieces of yuca and plantain—we sit like this for a while, waiting, chris, his usual gregarious self, smiling, the man of the hour, as always in his curious dual role as participant/observer, subject/object, walking in and out, his 23rd year newly-minted—I admire him much and envy him too, a lifetime of intellectual and existential adventure ahead, a very thoughtful guy with great sensitivity and talent for interacting with others, as evidenced by his relationships with the people here, their obvious affection for him—it is remarkable to me to see someone so young with such purpose, anthropology a calling well suited to his temperament and observational, reflective gifts—more guarapo comes around followed by chicha and I'm feeling an energy I hadn't before, a pleasant buzzing of the cheeks along with a kind of elevated sensation, as if my neck were an inch or so longer—people are smiling and so am I, nodding at kichwa I have seen before and some I have not—the woman I'd danced with at the hard rock cafe comes in, somber as ever, along with her husband, then carlos and maria, who greet me warmly, followed by my bête noire, octavio, seeming unusually sober and preoccupied—there's a nice feeling in the room, no doubt helped by the generous amounts of chicha and guarapo being passed around, but the kichwa love gatherings and parties and are interested in seeing chris's birthday celebrated in the traditional way, knowing he's in for a lot of good natured thrashing—the odd, apparently universal custom of being spanked once for every year of your existence, as if the regular lifelong spankings one absorbs, psychic and otherwise, isn't enough, is observed in kichwa culture as well, with particular if harmless sadism involving not only hearty smacks on the ass, one for each year, but also a whipping on the back with *ortiga*, a plant in the nettle family—there's an interesting relationship to physical pain in kichwa culture—ordinary and often not so ordinary mishaps, bumps and bruises are laughed at by both victims and observers, as if an essential, ongoing lesson in toughness, though if the accident is serious there is no laughter but instead commensurate concern and response—this morning as I was standing at the table in carlos and maria's choza helping with the food, two children were playing roughly and, I felt, dangerously, in a hammock and sure enough one fell out landing hard on his back—hurt and stunned, the boy, about six, clearly wanted to cry and for a moment everyone, including the girl he was playing with, looked to see if he was okay, and as there was no apparent concussion, blood or broken bones everyone started to laugh and so did he—I have seen this several times—but there is a line, when crossed, where empathy and care come to the fore, and I have seen this too—in regard to physical pain an interesting kichwa custom is the disciplining of children with pepper smeared in the eyes (a milder, much less vicious version of the pepper spray employed by the sadistic, bloated goons in the hire of the corporate state, as we have seen in the occupy movement), the purpose ameliorative more than punitive, the pain, while intense and momentarily blinding, lasting but for a few minutes, the whole process conducted in the form of a ritual—chris tried this once as an object of study and attests to its stinging effectiveness and also notes the subsequent care of those administering the punishment—of course there are degrees of seriousness and sensitivity, some families showing more of it than others—the symbolism of the punishment is interesting, as if eliminating an old behavior (vision), the guilty momentarily entering a kind of purgatory (blindness/pain) and coming out of it with new, chastened sight, a fresh start—contrast this straightforward "primitive" punishment with the psychological pain and torment dished out by the church, for example, in western culture, and decide for yourself which has longer-lasting harmful effects—there's an over-and-done-with aspect of the pepper punishment that is diametrically opposed to the crippling guilt and anxiety laid down by the church and other such powers which seem more designed to keep the mind in a state of permanent bondage than health—it's obvious also that the poorer classes have a different attitude towards physical pain than those above them economically, more of a focus on strength and toughness, as life is necessarily a tougher business for those with less, a lesson learned and reinforced from the beginning—after the third or fourth round of guarapo and chicha some women in traditional garb come out with the locro that's been cooking much of the day, the thick soup filled with chicken, yuca and vegetables and everyone gets down to business—after a bit the women circulate again, this time with dinner, served on the leaves janet, chris and I had gathered earlier, each aesthetic offering resplendent with a large piece of fish and a generous helping of rice—there's a wonderful grace, dignity and humor in the women's manner, very colorful in their dresses, making every effort to see all well provided for, the guests responding with politeness and enthusiasm—chris's friends from runa tea, nick olson and his English partner, have arrived and they sit near him and enjoy the meal—there is an air of anticipation surrounding the evening's festivities and chris is in a happy mood, the center of attention, sitting with the lovely janet, at last with a moment's respite after the work she's been doing all day—the meal is finished and the women come again to collect the leaves, plastic utensils and food scraps, deposited in plastic garbage cans—I reflect on the ubiquitous all-conquering plastic, used as much here as anywhere else in the world, so normal now in the daily lives of indigenous people—somewhere in the pacific swirls the enormous gyre, everywhere beaches choked with polymer hell concocted in satan's laboratory, lasting hundreds of years—a depressing thought quickly banished—events move to the birthday boy's celebration and punishment and dignitaries gather in the middle of the room to make speeches and conduct the ritual—carlos begins with some words in spanish and a blessing in kichwa but before that he has presented a few people with ceremonial necklaces made of colorful beans and I am pleased and honored to be one of the recipients—others present their testimonials to chris, followed by the young man himself with a short speech, then sat down by carlos and presented with necklaces and small handmade ceremonial items—there is a gleeful anticipatory tension in the room, with some calling out and making jokes at chris's expense—one of the larger young men is summoned and chris is instructed to jump on his back, which he does self-consciously and a bit awkwardly, but smiling also, as he must, but what follows will be done with affection and fun without the slightest hint of malice—with portentous flair edmundo removes his belt, a black leather strap with a chrome buckle, and doubles it over—the crowd laughs and hoots as the man carrying chris, a strong guy with thick black hair bends over with chris on his back, as chris, his clothed and vulnerable rump exposed to the crowd, laughs and jabbers in spanish, a broad smile on his bright, crimson face—there will be 23 blows delivered by 23 people, and edmundo delivers the first with a huge windup and gentle slap that causes laughter and much good-natured urging for harder blows—22 others follow, males and females, each in his or her own fashion, drama and force irrespective of sex, though the males tend to hit harder and with more flair—I deliver my smack with as much fanfare as I can muster—with their turns the teenage girls giggle self consciously and get it over with quickly and rather lamely—I imagine chris's ass a little sore but this is only the first part of the birthday beating, the lashing with the ortiga branch next, the onlookers, their appetites whetted, eager for the more traditional punishment with the stinging nettles—the green nasty-looking branch is revealed, brandished by a smiling carlos—chris's smile is broader, his face, if possible, even redder—the people in the room are shouting and laughing—the guy holding chris is getting tired and with a little jump hoists him farther up on his back—carlos rolls up chris's shirt exposing skin and everyone hoots and hollers—carlos bends over and makes a show of examining chris's back, smiles, makes a comment, raises his arm and comes down with a soft blow that disappoints everybody—this crowd is out for blood, or at least some good welts—edmundo takes the branch from his father and gives a sound whack that causes the birthday boy to yell out, more to please the crowd, I think, because I doubt it hurt that much, but then, after 21 more, it might be different—as with the belt everyone takes turns and when I deliver mine I see that chris's back is red with a network of raised lines but he's laughing—the ortiga branch is in worse condition, sad and limp, oozing fluid—at last the ritual is done—the guy lets chris down and stretches—people come over and examine chris's back—janet gives him a hug—he's laughing and talking like mad, takes a long gulp of guarapo from an offered pilche—someone cranks on the music—people start dancing, kichwa, runa tea people, townies, chris and janet—roly the taxi driver is here, animated, smoking cigarettes—a lot of people are smoking—I'm sitting next to a young kichwa man of about 20 with a shy but inquisitive manner and we have a halting, friendly conversation—the music is blasting—he offers me a cigarette and I accept—the last of the guarapo comes around but there's still plenty of fermented chicha—the music is kichwa pop, cumbia, salsa, with some reggaeton for spice—there is a dj—I love the sweet rhythmic innocence of the kichwa music—the floor is full of dancers and I'm damned if I'm just going to sit so I get up and go over to the woman from last night and take her (gently) by the hand out to the floor—she's more distracted and unhappy-looking than ever, only once or twice acknowledging my friendliness and then fleetingly, with the barest of forced smiles—after the song she retreats quickly to her seat and waiting bottle of beer—her husband is talking to some friends and nods to me when I return with his wife—he seems to be enjoying himself—the kichwa style of dance is consistent with the music, a sort of gentle up and down with little pelvic action, the opposite of hard core reggaeton *perreo*, a kind of throwback happy style I find exceptionally charming, the joy of dancing with only the barest intimations of later stops along the continuum, though as the night progresses things will change—for now this is still a birthday party, a family affair, not some bacchanalian mash—I had decided earlier that if I got the chance I would dance with maria, carlos's wife, and now I go over—she gets up in her colorful dress with a broad semi-toothless smile creasing her beautiful brown face marked with geometric lines of vegetable dye and we dance in the signature gentle rhythmic up and down style favored by the majority, adhering to a certain decorum, though there is nothing prudish or inhibited about these people—the older tend to dance this way and I am perfectly comfortable, feeling no pressure to display my sexy moves or dispel gringo stereotypes—the younger couples dance more sensually and aggressively, naturally enough, and when the reggaeton comes on, or something that sounds like reggaeton, chris and janet get right into their thing, a level beyond everyone else, and I wonder what people think of this though no one seems to pay the slightest attention—after we finish maria sits down rather abruptly and I am left to briefly ponder the gulf between us, between cultures, personalities and again the impediment resulting from my lack of fluency—irene hasn't been around but now she appears, emanating an aggressive, sexual energy, obviously a bit high, though with her I'm beginning to understand it could be nothing more (or less) than a swing in her mood—she's wearing tight jeans and an orange jersey and gets right into the dancing, switching partners and flirting openly with the men, edmundo aware of her, apparently unconcerned, this obviously an old routine—not for the first time I wonder if there's a bit of the horns about edmundo, if irene's sexual posturing has gone beyond mere flirtation—he's much more agreeable, stable and gentle than she is, and much wiser too, seeming to tolerate her behavior with the perspective of an older brother, though certainly she's caused him considerable pain—irene's always been a little reserved around me but after last night at the hard rock café in archidona her attitude has loosened and now she comes up and asks me to dance and swept up in her energy I dance more aggressively myself, an occasional glance at edmundo, who's drinking beer and talking with the dj, seemingly unaware of Irene—the music stops and there's a slight awkward moment but Irene's attention is captured by something else and she's gone before I can even say anything in my second-grade Spanish and I'm left by myself feeling a bit foolish but the music starts in and surprisingly, Jennifer, edmundo and irene's oldest daughter, asks me to dance, though her manner is self conscious and I get the feeling she's been put up to it by someone in the family—not that it matters—I'm glad she's asked me to dance and I feel more or less part of the proceedings and though jennifer disappears quickly when the music ends another kichwa female, a woman in her thirties and pretty damned sexy requests a dance and I'm pleased and full of illicit thoughts but even the remotest chance is thwarted by my piddling communicatory skills and she too filters away after the music—in such circumstances in more commonplace surroundings my English has usually proved wanting as well and it's not difficult to remind myself of where I am and perhaps more importantly who I am, which is to say an older gringo gent more safely and wisely restricted to the realm of fantasy in this particular situation and most others for that matter—it's true, I can vouch for it, the mind is forever 16 even as the body marches on to oblivion, our primary drive reproductive after all, everything else commentary, occasionally dramatic, mostly mundane—it's getting late and the intensity of the music and dancing increases, the elders merging into the darkness and disappearing—carlos and maria are gone—it's around 11—a kichwa woman I've never seen before is dancing with inebriate abandon—she's in her late thirties or early forties, good-looking, others getting into it too, drinking more, a bottle of aguardiente passing around, voices raised, laughter—chris has told me some kichwa will party until sunrise, which means seven hours or more of this—I'm thinking about sleep, slipping away over to edmundo and irene's house, shutting myself in—the earlier crowd has been displaced by a different bunch, noisier, drinking, shouting, or maybe it's the same people acting differently—but it's as if there have been two separate gatherings—in fact there *are* different people here, likely those who've been waiting for things to get interesting—chris and janet appear and disappear, dancing crazy perreo then suddenly gone—roly the taxi driver is dancing with the new wild woman—I keep looking at her, trying to be discreet—my somber dance partner is drinking beer and laughing but then she and her husband leave, as if for some pressing matter—only the hard core remains—this is not my scene, even if I don't feel at all uncomfortable—but I've been sitting and watching for about 15 minutes and there's nothing here for me, no one to dance with, everyone else mashing down drinking and partying—the children and elders have vanished—edmundo is gone, where I have no idea, but irene's here, a little drunk, dancing near me with a younger guy in his early twenties—my Spanish is good enough to understand a suggestive remark he makes to Irene as she laughs—I am actually a little shocked at this but it reinforces my notion that irene has something of a reputation—the runa people get up and leave, nick saying goodbye, remarking that this party will likely go on for many more hours—I wait a few more minutes sitting and watching, then exit the building, walking carefully in the dark, the noise and laughter echoing behind me, the little blue house nearby, on the other side of the dirt road—thankfully the door is unlocked—no one's there—there's a dim light on and I go into my cinder block room and lie in the dark on the moldy bed listening to the music and faint bursts of shouting and laughter, but it's not too bad and I figure I'll be able to get some sleep, which I do, but about an hour later I'm awakened by the music turned full volume crashing out of edmundo's huge speakers reverberating throughout the village as if some rock concert in a soccer stadium—I resign myself to a sleepless night but can at least appreciate the unusual circumstances though after a while the music, the laughter, the drunken shouts sound like any other wild party and I wish it would go away—there are periodic lulls that last for 10 or 15 minutes and I drift off thinking at last it's over but then everything kicks in again louder and crazier than ever—I try to visualize just what these wild kichwa are doing, wondering if chris and janet are in there dancing too, wondering about Irene, wondering what happens during those brief quiet moments—I have accepted the reality of an all-night kichwa party but cling to the faint hope that maybe it will end sooner than usual, but I suspect it won't—then everything goes quiet—I hear people walking around, calling to each other, laughing, voices receding, the sounds of a party winding down, tired people going home at an eminently sensible hour, about 4 AM, which, under the circumstances, gives rise to a pleasant sense of well-being—at least I'll be getting three or four hours sleep as compared to the possibility of one, maybe two—I drift off for about 10 minutes and am awakened by the front door bursting open and drunken, laughing, shouting people piling into the living room, in the grip of some kind of unsettling, manic energy, whooping and wild—they've dragged the giant speakers with them and in a few minutes the music is going full blast, the shouting and shrieking rising above it—only a thin door separates me from this alien, unrestrained bacchanal—I have no idea what the hell they're doing—dancing, of course, but what manner of drunken kichwa revelry can this be?—there's a lot of ribald whooping and shouting, as if couples are taking turns dirty dancing surrounded by inmates from a local asylum having a collective out-of-body experience—there seem to be about 10 or 15 people—I try to visualize just what the hell is going on, but I'm effectively blind and captive to my imagination, as if locked in a steamer trunk onstage at a rock concert—the option of going out and joining them, or at least watching, which occurs to me, is dismissed—I dread the possibility of some drunken reveler crashing against my door, which is only wedged shut—there are bumps that cause my heart to jump—I picture the door flying open and drunken kichwa piling into my room—as with the partying in the building across the street there are moments of relative quiet, though the proximity of so much psychic and physical energy leaves me anything but calm—with each lull I hope the party's over but each time it starts in again with renewed energy, the whooping, the shouts, the clapping hands—I'm still curious about what the hell's going on out there, accompanied by an insincere urge to check things out, but really, it would take something like my room catching fire or a boa constrictor crawling into my bed to get me to the leave the room—I can't imagine what the reaction would be if I suddenly appeared—I listen for chris's distinctive high-pitched excited voice but can't hear it—strange voices, yelling, laughing, ululating, spring break in ft Lauderdale, no, not as bad, infinitely better, indeed, extraordinarily better—I think I hear irene's voice, right in the middle of it—where is edmundo?—what about that damned octavio...and these are my last thoughts because then, inexplicably, against all the laws of morpheus, as if some benevolent oriente dream spirit has reached in and touched my forehead, I fall into a kind of turbulent sleep, dreaming I'm in the engine room of a WWI kichwa submarine, a creaky orange rusting nautilus, the engine a strange raucous music, shouting drunken sailors, red and turquoise waves all around, dancing pink squids, water, water, everywhere—some time later I awaken to quiet and the thin light of morning filtering into my room—the party is over—

Encounter on Montufar

I spend the day with anita and Luis Fernando, her teenage son, a slim, likeable fellow, at el parque metropolitano in the north of quito near atahualpa stadium, a huge park almost twice as big as central park in nyc—we take a picnic, relax, walk around, watch a spirited soccer match—it is a good day, nice weather, families, kids, dogs—this is really an impressive place with grand vistas, thick forests, open meadows, outdoor sculptures, ponds, llamas, birds, tourists—it's nice to be with anita and Luis Fernando, but I have a little bit of the blues—something haunts me, the weather, the park's vastness, a feeling of not quite belonging, though that's not uncommon for me—there is something else, and that is in three months I'll be leaving Ecuador, back to the dreary, eviscerated culture, the old routines—nine months have flown by like the proverbial something—I've had a good, rich time here and have grown to love the culture, the warmth of the people, the humanity—what strikes me most of all and what I appreciate profoundly is the humility of everything, the attitudes of the people, the institutions, so opposed to the hubris of the states, the arrogance of being number one in everything, the strongest, the richest, the most sophisticated, the tensions inherent in most all interactions born of the ethos of dominance and superiority—what an intensely lonely and unhappy place is the united states!—the greatest shame and sin in the US is to be poor (or old) and everyone commits his life to escaping this disgraceful character defect or at least covering it up by consuming as many glittering items as possible, usually electronic, burrowing deeply into solipsistic virtual worlds, sliding further into debt and loneliness, cut off from real community—ecuador is poor with a capital P and one of the results of this is an utter lack of pretension, an utter lack of pressure and expectation to be rich—why bother?—thus, by necessity, attention is focused on more basic things, family, friends, preparing good meals, appreciating the few items one possesses—to be sure, the western corporate model is creeping into the equation, the materialistic values encroaching, brought about by ecuador's improving economy, the driving force being the curse of oil—many parts of quito could be downtown Toledo or Oklahoma City, or anywhere in this world of cities, the new glass and steel buildings, the flashing electronic signs driving the consumerist message into the people's brains, the ubiquitous cell phones sucking away at everyone's time and consciousness, smart devices creating vast hordes of zombies, slaves, the staggering, polluted gridlock that is the streets of our brave new atomized world—this is what I hate and what I will be returning to, the epicenter of techno-consumerist misery, though to be sure my beloved new mexico is much different than the rest of the woeful conglomerate, our status as colony of the military industrial complex notwithstanding—we leave the park and walk to the ecovia station, where I bid goodbye to anita and luis fernando—yes, the dreaded ecovia, the bus, heading towards la marin, that den of thieves, pickpockets and cutthroats, but it's Sunday and still light, about 4 o'clock, and the bus, while crowded, is full of Sunday adventurers, couples, families, enjoying their last hours of freedom before work the next day, the mood pleasant if a bit subdued, perhaps wistful, though that could be me—but I'm not completely wistful because this is the scene of the great pocket slashing episode and my fearful stumbling walk home through the mean streets around la marin and though I've been on the bus a couple of times after that, I'm still a little uptight—at least this time I know where to get off and I won't get lost walking home and it's still daylight, all very reassuring, but nevertheless I'm on full alert, a prudent attitude in these circumstances—the streets are crowded and there's the usual representation of seedy, even dangerous-looking characters, but I've got the walk down, the attitude, and I really do feel confident in my abilities to navigate these streets, deal with most contingencies—after all, it's been many months since I've had a problem and I've been walking miles every day with no incident—a bit of the swagger has returned, no doubt about it—I turn down montufar, a narrow, hilly street perpendicular to rocafuerte—today montufar is virtually empty and I walk several blocks, approaching rocafuerte, the old buildings in the late afternoon crowding over the rugged sidewalks like a gallery of silent observers—most of the tiendas are closed—a few dogs, pigeons—emptiness—I pass a middle-aged couple on the other side of the street walking in the same direction—we're the only ones about except for a figure coming down the block toward the couple—the person, I now see it's a short, crazy-looking black man with wild hair and wearing a red windbreaker with the sleeves rolled up to his elbows, is fast approaching—I figure I'm ok because he's on the other side and if anything he'll hassle the couple, but suddenly he veers off and crosses the street and comes directly up to me jabbering in Spanish—he wants money, money, dinero—his eyes are wild and he's got no front teeth and he's a powerful, thick guy, with big forearms and hands, a miniature leon spinks, a miniature *crazy* leon spinks with crazy hair more like don king but thicker and he's right up into my business, jabbering away, really aggressive, but I'm cool because I'm a *veterano*, having walked several months on the streets of quito without incident, able to handle all situations with aplomb, and I speak to him calmly, almost soothingly, communicating my unfortunate lack of resources, sorry, my brother, that kind of thing, but he starts patting my left pocket to determine its contents and here is where I begin to realize this really is a loony fucker and probably dangerous too and I start walking faster to get away from him, saying hey, hey, and suddenly he thrusts his left hand into my left pocket, I'm astonished at how quick and powerful and unerring a motion it is, but before he can get anything, and actually all I have in that pocket is a small swiss army knife, I grab his thick wrist and yank it out of my pocket, yelling *puta!* which surprises me a little, discovering this is the word that comes to the fore, my first genuine cursing at someone in Ecuador, and in a flash my assailant turns tail and hauls ass down the block and even if he'd gotten my wallet I could never have caught him, nor would I have probably wanted to—I am shaken—the couple on the other side of the street is abreast of me and looking on in concern—I make the universal circling motion with my forefinger around my temple—the guy was nuts, yes, but it also could have been worse—I see the error of my laid-back ways—as soon as I saw him making a bee-line for me with his crazy eyes I should have gotten the hell out of there, pronto, making noise, a big fuss, airhorns, whistles, bells—va-moos—but no, I'm the cool gringo, everything under control—now, instantly, the world is a darker place, i am the outsider again—but there is a difference compared to my first months here—as i approach my apartment i see familiar faces and say hello—they return my greetings—this is my neighborhood—i know the sidewalks and the buildings—on montufar i had been too comfortable in a situation i should have recognized as threatening—but this doesn't dilute the connections i have forged over these months—lesson learned, more to come—

Lago

5/19

I am on a bus headed towards lago agrio, an oil boom town just south of the Colombian border, riding through a soggy, green landscape after passing through the andean cordillera, now snaking alongside the rio saludo where Chinese beavers, guests of the Ecuadorian government, are busily constructing yet another massive work, a hydroelectric project that will be completed in a few years—the company is called sinohydro, one more tentacle of the neo-maoist dynasty of glorious Chinese state capitalism that is competing with the more established western industrialized countries, together collectively taking down what's left of the world's ecosystems, replaced by more dams, cities, cars, pollution, wars, mass insanity and other wonders of the age—as much as I love Ecuador there is no question that it is a country eager to replicate as quickly as possible the western techno/consumerist model, the only difference being they're going to do it their way, dammit, with no interference from or domination by the bloody ugly giant from the north—no, they've invited the Chinese and get a slightly better deal for their environment to be obliterated, the maoist-yuppie beavers all too willing to oblige—the oleoducto, the oil pipeline that bisects the country carrying crude from the oriente in the east to esmeraldas on the coast, slithers into view alongside the road like a fat rusty serpent, undulating, dipping out of view, reappearing, inexorably rushing along—I am meeting chris at the Hotel Lago Imperial in the afternoon, where we will spend the night and meet up the next morning with Martín criollo, who will guide us the next few days to some of the places around his home fouled by the oil giants Texaco/chevron, as chronicled in the documentary *crude*—Martín is a cofán from dureno, a community east of lago agrio—this situation, the pollution ("pollution" is too mild a term, rape and plunder would be more apt) has become an international cause célèbre, pitting impoverished indigenous communities in the amazon against a billion dollar oil giant backed by the cleverest, most ethically-challenged lawyers money can buy, with western governments hardly disinterested observers—the irony here, if not blatant hypocrisy, is that while chevron is now out of Ecuador and the Ecuadorian government is supporting legal proceedings against the company, oil extraction from the oriente continues unabated, carried out by petroecuador, the national petroleum industry, aided and abetted by Chinese companies and other worthies, most notably old mr. cheney's halliburton—when it comes to oil all the bastards are up to their elbows, including the smooth-talking, charismatic mr. correa—it should be noted as well that it was the Ecuadorian government that willingly allowed Texaco to come in and begin the pillaging of the amazon and its people in the first place, so the sort of righteous huffing and puffing by the government now plays just a tad cynically, like the parent who sells his daughter into sexual slavery and is later outraged at the treatment she's received—to be fair to mr. correa, it was not *his* administration that let the US oil company in, but of course it's the Chinese now given the red carpet—I have heard a lot about lago agrio and am interested to see it—originally called nueva loja, it was established in the sixties as part of the government's land reform program that gave incentives to mestizo poor scattered about the country to settle in different parts of the oriente and turn "non-productive" land into something generating more cash, part of a larger, global developmental trend encouraged and financed by institutions such as the world bank and international monetary fund, with the usual pound of flesh in return—it meant money for governmental and business elites, a bit of land and marginally better life for the settlers ("los colonos"), environmental destruction, conflict and cultural dissolution for the traditional inhabitants—all this was before the discovery of oil in nueva loja by Texaco in the late sixties, which turned a bad situation into something much worse—with the oil bonanza the gringos informally renamed the town lago agrio ("sour lake") after the texaco headquarters in texas—it stuck—lago agrio has a notorious reputation as a boom town with all the attendant vices of such places and, as it is next to the colombian border, has the added elements of being a hub for drug trafficking and safe haven, of sorts, for guerrilla groups, including the farc, *fuerzas armadas revolucionarias de colombia*, a Marxist-leninist group that's been fighting the Colombian government since 1964—the two groups, drug traffickers and guerrillas, are inevitably intertwined—it also has a large refugee population forced to flee the country as a result of the decades-long conflict—part of the reason I am interested in seeing lago (people frequently refer to it as simply, "lago") is because for the last couple of months I've been watching the HBO series *deadwood*, a semi-fictional account of the old boom town in south Dakota, its rampant and anarchic growth powered by gold rather than oil—*deadwood* is the first tv series I've watched since *the fugitive*, in the sixties, with david janssen as the dour, long-suffering richard Kimball, and I'm really into it—the language is impossibly neo-Shakespearean but even what I don't understand I enjoy, and the characters are compellingly high-comic and gritty, all representing cultural archetypes that become etched ever more deeply into one's consciousness with each episode—*deadwood* seems crazy and over the top at first but soon it becomes apparent that something profound is going on, not only about US history and culture but also the development of human communities—as for lago agrio, it is a fascinating place and much safer than it was ten years ago when murders were commonplace, usually drug-related, a kind of opportunistic infection invading a compromised host—now lago, like the ever-aspiring mafia, is assuming the trappings of respectability, with a new, cofán mayor determined to clean things up, small businesses, restaurants, better lighting, cleaner streets, improved schools, honest cops, more churches, etc., so that lago agrio is less the wild Amazonian frontier outpost and more the ordinary thriving company town with all the unremarkable appurtenances—this is completely relative of course because driving into lago I am wide-eyed at the sight of prostitutes lounging in their sidewalk cubicles, the tiendas selling all manner of things, fruits, vegetables, plastic goods, clothing, tools, mechanical parts, the majority of course centered around the oil industry, the carnicerias with their hanging, fly-covered slabs of meat and pigs heads, the incredible, colorful mix of people crowding the streets, many of whom you know are from Colombia and other parts, all on the make in their modest but fevered ways because this is still a boom town, a wild town—here there is money to get, from very large to modest amounts, each pilgrim with his own goals and aspirations, illicit or otherwise, and with the reality of dollar bills, as it were, floating in the air, all eminently attainable—lago is a happening place, with everything and everybody in the mix, anxious, eager, energetic, sexy, dangerous, exotic—I love it immediately—and there's the rub, isn't it, because it's also about the things that I hate, violence, greed, corruption, hypocrisy, environmental destruction—in this way, at least for me, it embodies the paradox, or one of the many, at the bottom of the human condition—or maybe I insist on seeing the world as a graham greene novel—lago agrio reminds me of the R crumb sequence where a pristine natural environment in the US is transformed into a hopelessly tangled, developed, ruined modern urban landscape—in lago the landscape is transformed/despoiled with the discovery of a wildly valuable natural resource and over time mutates into something completely different, "respectable," middle class—conceivably in the not-so-distant future as the resource expires the town will be economically sustained by some other activity: the large scale cultivation and distribution of legal marijuana, the center of ecuador's burgeoning film industry, the manufacture of solar panels (happy ending), the jungle creeping back and taking over (happier ending), the violent and crazy past a thing of curiosity in history books or television dramas—I get off the bus and take a taxi to the hotel, less seedy than I imagined, in the middle of a busy intersection—the concierge, a friendly young woman, buzzes chris and he comes down to greet me—our room is on the second floor, two small beds, questionable bathroom, the ubiquitous television—we rest for a while, watch some television, then hit the streets to buy some food for our stay in dureno—I also need to buy a pair of cheap pants for our tour, which is likely to take us to some messy places—chris has brought rubber boots from rukullakta—the sidewalks are crowded with all manner of colorful, wild-looking characters, roughnecks, mechanics, indigenous women with children in tow, more blacks than I'm used to seeing in quito, sexy-looking women (colombianas!), hustlers of all stripe and persuasion—lago may be inching towards respectability but it's still a crazy scene with a restless, anarchic energy, and chris and I are both on our toes—people are aware of us but gringos are everywhere these days, the important thing to communicate in the usual manner, dress, attitude etc., what variety of gringo one is—there is a contingent of scruffy college-age gringos drinking batidos in a sidewalk café, most likely headed for an eco-tour in cuyabeno, and occasionally I see a westerner dressed in clean, casual clothes of the sort you would imagine a petroleum engineer might wear, an employee, perhaps, of mr. cheney's company—these types have an undeniable cachet and invite a certain curiosity and grudging respect, but my favorite character is an old one-legged mestizo carrying a machete, its blade, presumably newly-sharpened, wrapped in oily newspaper—he's leaning on his crutch intently staring at tools in an open-front hardware store—I imagine him an example of the stubborn indomitability of the species, a guy who came to lago decades ago, one of the original settlers or someone who came after the discovery of oil—lost his leg in an industrial accident, a piece of machinery, a knife wound that festered after a bar fight—this doesn't deter him, the lure of money, or something, keeping him in lago—probably there's nowhere else to go—he has a skill, a specialty, but what's the machete for?—i see him a half hour later in a dark, crowded indoor mercado where chris negotiates a pair of pants for me for ten dollars—the guy's face is intent, serious—younger than I thought at first—he's buying t-shirts—arms muscular and veiny—strong hands—he holds the machete with his crutch hand and fishes some crumpled bills from his pocket—he buys two red t-shirts—chris and I go back to the hotel with our supplies, rice, noodles, canned beans, drinks in plastic bottles, a few *paquetes* of powdered drinks—we shower and go back outside for some dinner, walking down the sidewalk in nighttime lago, passing stores and restaurants—not much activity—it doesn't feel too bad—some good-looking women—nobody pays us much mind—we find a restaurant that looks decent—it's a little late but there are a few people eating, a soccer game going on the television—we order the same thing, soup, a quarter of a roasted chicken, some rice, coca-cola's sweet lemon tea, *fuze*—coca-cola rules the world—we head back to the hotel and watch a bad movie, *knowing*, with Nicholas cage, dubbed in Spanish—chris falls asleep but I stay up late watching a gangster movie whose main interest, apart from some stunning females, is trying to figure out where the hell it was filmed—tomorrow we'll meet Martín and go to dureno—

Dureno

we meet Martín, a handsome, affable guy in his mid-thirties, around
10 o'clock after a good breakfast in a restaurant down the block
from the hotel—we shop for more supplies and then get on a rickety
bus filled with campesinos and indigenous people and travel to
dureno, which takes about 40 minutes—halfway to dureno there's
a problem and the bus is delayed for 15 minutes—no one seems
to know what's going on—in the front of the bus is a strikingly
beautiful mestizo woman with a small child who climbs all over
her—outside the landscape is cleared for the workings of oil, with
pipelines of different sizes running parallel to the road—beyond
is jungle—the small businesses and homes that appear here and
there are poor and shabby—much of the traffic is petroecuador, but
I see other vehicles related to the industry with company names,
mostly western, I don't recognize—I see one truck with the red and
white halliburton logo—at dureno an old, faded billboard advertising eco-tours stands at the head of the dirt road leading to the community—we get out and walk down the wet road, surrounded by
jungle, to the river, the aguarico—along the road are signs alerting
you to the pipes that run next to it—the aguarico is the biggest river
in sucumbios province and eventually empties into the napo—at
the river's edge is an open building where a relative of Martín's
makes long fiberglass canoes of the type that navigate the river—of

course in the past the canoes were wood, but Martín says the new ones are better—there's one half-built on a stand, looking like the carcass of a large reptile—Martín uses his cell phone to call someone from the other side to ferry us across to the community—a few scruffy chickens scratch the ground—a skinny dog appears from around the building, eyes us warily and starts to bark—eventually a canoe heads in our direction from the other side—the aguarico is a medium sized river, smaller than the napo, shimmering silver, its banks lined with thick foliage—the air is humid and warm—oddly, it reminds me a little of the rio grande in corrales, though much bigger—maybe in the past, when there was more water, the rio grande was as big—the canoe putters up powered by a small outboard engine, trailing blue smoke around the churning water—the gas that powers this engine was probably refined from sucumbios oil—Martín introduces us to a man and a woman, whom I take to be married, who shake our hands in the typical fashion—the man is middle aged and reserved, with a strong serious face—the woman has a broad, open, friendly face and smiles at us—we climb into the unsteady canoe with our packs and seat ourselves on either side for balance, Martín in front—the man starts up the engine after several pulls and the boat makes a circle and we head in the direction from which it has come, in the middle opening to full throttle—the skinny vessel speeds along into the current and from here the river seems larger than from the shore—the similarities with the rio grande though are still apparent—the aguarico does not have the feeling of a wild river—there are places along the shore that have been cleared for various purposes, no doubt related to oil—at one place a pipeline crosses high over the river—at another there's a high tension wire holding the large red plastic balls used to alert low flying aircraft—Martín says that several years ago, before the balls were installed, a helicopter from petroecuador hit the wire and crashed in the river—perhaps because I already know the history of this place I am filled with the dread and sadness I sometimes feel thinking about a world filling with poison and great things irrevocably lost—texaco discovered oil in 1968 and for decades the aguarico was polluted—communities that lived along its shores and whose life was sustained by its clean waters were devastated—for a time it was so bad people couldn't even bathe in the river, much less eat the fish that were such an important part of their diet—sickness and death—now the aguarico is a bit better—people swim and bathe but still don't eat the fish, and parents don't allow their small children to go in the river—the aguarico empties into the napo, the napo into the amazon—aguarico means rich water—on the other side we clamber out and commence the short climb to Martín's village—dureno has received some financial help from the government but it is a very poor community—the main evidence of governmental aid is an open gymnasium with a metal roof that stands more or less in the middle of the village and which serves as a meeting place as well as for recreation—when we arrive teenagers are playing a spirited game of Ecuadorian volleyball, "ecuavoley"—in Ecuadorian volleyball the nets are lower and the ball is propelled with more of a carrying motion than a striking one—the village houses are made of wood and in various states of dilapidation—there are many children, chickens and dogs—chris and I stick close to Martín as he leads us to his house, another wooden, crude affair, with two stories—the ground is muddy—though it is dry season here it is much wetter than quito and rains almost every day—it's about noon and the sky is clear, though likely the clouds will gather—Martín's house, all the houses, remind me of those I saw decades ago on a trip through the Mississippi delta, the same decaying, sagging structures, patched together, fending off heat, humidity and poverty—in front of Martín's house is a wide grassy field with rusty soccer goals at either end—other structures form a semi-circle around the field—none of the windows here has glass or screens—tilted wooden steps lead to the door of Martín's house—inside on the first floor is the "living room," dark and empty, with wide wooden planks for flooring, a wide window looking out onto the field—Martín's two adolescent daughters and young son, about five, come up and greet us shyly—they are all very beautiful—adjoining the living room is the kitchen—the family sleeps upstairs—we stash our stuff in a side room and the daughters cook some of the noodles and tuna we have brought— Martín puts together a makeshift table in the main room and we eat the tuna and noodles, with ketchup, which makes me think of Reagan—one of the girls has mixed a sweet powdery drink we've brought—chris and Martín talk about what we can see this afternoon and it's decided we'll head back across the river and hire a local cab to take us to the site where texaco first drilled for oil in cofán territory, in 1968—chris is using fullbright money to pay for expenses, staying at Martín's, the tour, food, etc., and I am chipping in—before leaving, Martín, who is a great talker and obviously highly intelligent, tells an involved cofán story (in Spanish, which he speaks fluently, the native tongue of the cofán is A'ingae) about a great adventure/quest with a lord of the rings flavor into the underworld, not too far from here, to do battle with strange godlike creatures—it occurs to me as he tells the story, which I more or less understand, that this has something to do with the oil that has now emerged from this underworld, a manifestation of these powerful forms, but this is more likely my overheated imagination taking me down another dead end—we cross the aguarico and pay the ferryman 75 cents—a taxi is waiting—the driver is mestizo and reminds me of a new york Italian—I can see him driving a cab in manhattan—cab drivers in the oriente are a trip—cab drivers all over the world are a trip—he used to work for petroecuador and knows all about the industry—we drive around and look at a few small wells, some active, yellow flames from the burn-off garishly illuminating the cloudy afternoon, incongruous midst the surrounding forest—after a bit we arrive at the infamous *dureno 1*, which was shut down by the cofán, after so many years disgusted and outraged by the ruination and poisoning of their land, in 1998—the old well is capped and there is a sign commemorating the action—the thick, dark, obdurate metal of the well pipe and cap stick more than four feet out of the ground, a symbol of arrogant

exploitation and subsequent small victory for the indigenous population, almost forgotten—but not quite—Martín informs us that
petroecuador is lobbying to reactivate the well, an exasperating bit
of information that just makes you shake your head—all around
dureno 1 are dozens of pools of toxic petroleum waste, covered with
dirt—texaco pledged to empty the pools and restore the land but
never did—the waste remains under a few feet of dirt, leaching
into the nearby tributaries to the aguarico and the aguarico itself—very little grows in these places compared with surrounding
areas—you'd see more vegetation in a vacant lot in the bronx—there
are thousands of these pits in sucumbios province, many unburied,
though buried or not they still present the same problem—petroleum wastes are among the most toxic that exist—the oil industry has a long shameful record of criminal irresponsibility in places
where environmental controls are weak—in places where environmental controls are "strong" there is fracking, the Alberta tar sands,
the coming keystone xl pipeline and the deepwater horizon spill,
among other things—back in the canoe we head to a small community where Martín's grandfather lives, taking a tributary of the
aguarico through dense forest, a typical Amazonian waterway full
of silence (except for the outboard motor) and mystery—reaching
our destination Martín ties up the canoe and we climb the em-
bankment—the community is no more than a few mean dwellings
surrounded by jungle—the usual mud, dogs, chickens, and barefoot
children—Martín's grandfather is resting in a hammock in an open
choza—he seems a content and peaceful fellow, very friendly, and
immediately tries to sell some things he's made, very nice little
combs and necklaces from natural materials, and I get the feeling
Martín has brought us here for this very reason—gringo equals
money and that's just the way it is—this is our purpose and distinction, and under the circumstances it is best to smile and accept
it—we buy some things, what the hell, for only a few dollars—we
bid the man farewell, our usefulness exhausted for the moment,
and head, somewhat sheepishly, back to the canoe—but if we feel

slightly diminished and used for the superficiality of this interaction, what must the indigenous feel after centuries of murder, pillage, arrogance and cultural and environmental destruction at the hands of the Europeans and their north American cousins?—we get a little rain and wind back on the aguarico, with enormous clouds on the horizon, restoring some wildness and drama to the river—back at the village Martín takes us on a little tour of the surrounding forest—we pass an animal pen holding ducks and geese and also a capybara, a somewhat startling sight—the capybara will be eaten of course but Martín says that it is not so tasty—he shows us the place where ayahuasca rituals are performed, an open choza in a clearing next to a stream—a beautiful place—I want to take ayahuasca with the cofán—later, before dark, we go to the house of the president of the community council and here the image of the "nice" cofán is unceremoniously obliterated in the presence of this man, a handsome, imposing guy in his mid-thirties, tussled black hair, bare-chested, thick and powerful, wearing a necklace of jaguar teeth—I immediately think of him as *el presidente* and adopt an attitude of attentive respect in the face of his physical power, authority, deep voice and sober suspicion of us bordering on hostility—though much of this is an act, peel a layer away and you have the real thing, in another time and circumstance two whites sitting in front of a cofán chief reading the riot act in A'ingae, explaining in graphic if indecipherable detail the charges and punishment to be meted out, a death penalty, slow and agonizing—and who can blame him for his act?—I do my best to conceal my discomfort, feeling a different sort of diminution in his presence than I felt earlier following the interaction with Martín's grandfather—both are disturbing and make me feel less than human, which, ultimately, is precisely the point, turnabout, after all, being fair play—*el presidente* goes on for a full hour as we listen, chris with his good Spanish able to have something of a dialogue, but not much—the man speaks rapid-fire in his deep forceful voice and I understand about a third of what he says—he speaks of the need to improve the situation of the cofán, mostly through eco-tourism, and speaks bitterly of the government's lack of help and concern—a couple of times he pointedly mentions the irrelevance and cultural arrogance of those from the outside who come to cofán territory thinking they can do good, or even worse, out of curiosity—Martín is in the back of the room and never says a word—finally *el presidente's* two small and very beautiful children are getting bored and hungry and are beseeching him to terminate the meeting—his countenance softens and he becomes more human, if not likable—abruptly it is finished—he gets to his feet and shakes our hands, actually thanking us for our interest in his community, and then, as if we are invisible, have never existed, he turns his attention completely to his children—we have been, in no uncertain terms, dismissed—Martín seems a little embarrassed, but I wonder what he really thinks—back in Martín's house we have another rudimentary and marginally nutritious meal and afterwards, Martín, who loves to tell stories, speaks for over an hour about his family history—it is rather an amazing story and I understand much of it—upheavals, craziness, alcoholism and violence—he talks about the circuitous path to becoming a teacher, his occupation in dureno—Martín is an exceptional guy and we are duly impressed—we sleep on the floor next to an exterior wall and in the middle of the night something sprays from the outside, as if a garden hose, coming through the cracks in the wall, and we are awakened in a puddle of liquid—everything is wet—it is impossible to comprehend what has happened—perhaps a monstrous jaguar, marking his territory—perhaps the totem animal of *el presidente*—but it has no smell, which only deepens the mystery—

Emergildo

chris has discussed expenses with Martín and, not surprisingly, they are more than we had anticipated—we can't afford Martín's services after today so this will be our last few hours in cofán territory—it is decided that we'll meet Martín's father, emergildo, and tour some of the oil fields around lago agrio—emergildo has been one of the leaders in the fight against Texaco/chevron for many years, a struggle that has consumed his life, and one to which he has given himself gladly—before we leave Martín shows us some of the community buildings in the village, including his school—Martín teaches A'ingae and Spanish to the children of the village—as one might expect the facilities are rudimentary but one can also imagine that the quality of the man and his passion for teaching more than compensate for the material shortcomings—we leave the village and once again cross the aguarico—the morning is warm with few clouds—we take the bus to emergildo's home in lago agrio—*el presidente* is also on the bus, going to work or a meeting, talking loudly on his cell phone the whole way—he doesn't acknowledge us—we get off on the outskirts of the city and walk down a dirt road to emergildo's house, where he is sitting outside—his face is painted in the traditional way and he is wearing a necklace of jaguar teeth—I wonder if this is usual or if he's prepared himself for our benefit—he greets us formally and we sit down at a table outside—emergildo has met many people like us and is obviously not easily impressed, but we have not met many people like emergildo—after a while I don't notice the face paint and jaguar necklace but rather the strong and passionate qualities of the person—he talks at length about the struggles of the cofán and other groups against Texaco/chevron/petroecuador, how he has been to the united states many times to testify before various groups and committees, how an allegiance has been formed among indigenous groups to fight this very difficult and, at least for the moment, losing battle—he describes the ways things used to be for the cofán, daily activities centered around the rivers, especially the aguarico, the rhythms and rituals of life, the relationship to a healthy and sustaining environment, and how, some time in the late 60s, Texaco came to their home—he tells the story of the first encounter with the oil company, of people in the village hearing explosions and other strange sounds coming from the forest and a contingent of elders going to investigate, finding white people with machines—the white people were friendly and gave them food, sandwiches, coke and chocolate—they explained that they were looking for oil and would soon be gone—the cofán knew about oil but had no experience with it and believed what the men told them—the men did go but returned a year later and began clearing the forest and making roads—this time the men were not so friendly—shortly thereafter they began drilling for oil—this was *dureno 1*—as time passed people began to be sick and they realized that something was wrong with the water—they developed rashes and began having headaches and intestinal problems—the old and very young were the most sick—the bright light from the flare shed its unnatural glow on the village, illuminating the night and frightening away the animals—the constant noise of the drilling, the heavy machinery, the trucks, the fabrication of the pipeline, the hammering, grinding and welding, changed a peaceful, quiet environment into something alien and disturbing—the Texaco people were indifferent to the complaints and entreaties of the villagers—then the company began to drill more wells around the area, more roads, trucks, machinery, noise, pipelines and, above all, more contamination of the environment, especially the aguarico and its tributaries—the company left its bubbling, tarry, toxic wastes in hundreds of open pools that emitted membrane-searing fumes—by this time there was no confusion about why the people were sick with skin diseases, birth defects, mental retardation, neurological disorders and cancer—the Ecuadorian government offered no help, instead taking the side of the company, petroecuador building the pipeline, the oleoducto, and working alongside its texas big brother—nueva loja became known as lago agrio—the oil frenzy grew and more outsiders came—the new economy not only created material conditions of poverty for indigenous people, with the destruction of the environment and traditional way of life, but also gave rise to a condition of psychological poverty and dependence—because of the dire economic conditions some of the indigenous people, including the cofán, began to work for Texaco/petroecuador—an old way of life was essentially destroyed—psychological problems, despair, alcoholism, violence, social dissolution, beset the people—in the 1980s the cofán and other indigenous groups, with help from international sympathizers, began fighting back, with protests and legal maneuvers—in 1990 petroecuador assumed all operations in the oriente, with Texaco lowering its profile, though the relationship between the two remained strong, Texaco providing technical help and equipment, still taking its share of the profits—texaco finally left the country in 1992, without cleaning its wastes, which it had promised to do—the Ecuadorian government had neither the resources nor the resolve to carry out texaco's cleanup work, leaving the environment and the people to sicken and die—in October, 2001, texaco was bought by chevron, creating a mega-company with billions in assets, but in a legal nicety the bolder, richer corporation has absolved itself of the responsibility for the toxic cesspools its swallowed fish created, the endearing partnership of lawyerly slime and deep pockets causing history once again to disappear—the Ecuadorian government ("no mea culpa!") has brazenly sued chevron and has been awarded nine billion dollars in damages by an Ecuadorian judge, a fine chevron will pay when lion and lamb at long last lie together—emergildo exhibits a stubborn will to continue the fight and no matter how bleak things seem gives the impression that some day justice, whatever form it takes, will prevail—his attitude, his faith, runs counter to my deep skepticism—I hope he is right—emergildo is a "traditional," probably more conservative than *el presidente* from the night before, a question of generational perspectives—both battle for the preservation of cofán culture, both intensely proud and serious—we call the same cab driver and go on a tour of more wells directly around lago agrio, including the first well ever drilled here, by Texaco, in 1967—it is preserved as a kind of museum piece, memorial, or testimony—it would be interesting to record people's associations upon first seeing it—for me it is a mixture of feelings, something like hopelessness after the fact, a symbol of lost cultural and environmental treasures, but also a tinge of optimism as the well is no longer functioning: this nightmare shall also some day pass—emergildo takes us to another place where there are large waste pits barely covered with dirt—the vegetation all around here is stunted and sparse—in one large area the tar is exposed—we scoop pieces with our fingers, the pure stuff, residue of the black gold, the smell of money—this also elicits different associations, not altogether unpleasant—I think of the tar balls on the beach when I was a child, cleaning my feet with turpentine after stepping on them, the smell of roads on hot summer days—but these pools of waste, vast and numerous, recall anything but childhood idylls for the people of the oriente—we return to emergildo's house and bid him goodbye, thanking him for his time and, of course, paying him—everything has its price—for the cofán the price has been very dear—at the hotel we say goodbye to Martín—we'll spend the night and return tomorrow, chris to rukullakta and I to quito—

Riverbend

6/21

I leave Ecuador in six weeks—julian assange has been informed by London cops that he will be arrested the moment he steps outside the embassy for supposedly violating the terms of his bail conditions—"realists" will smugly assert he gets what's coming to him because you just don't play with the big kids and expect to get away with telling their secrets, such as the July 12, 2007 Baghdad air strike by apache helicopters, code named crazyhorse 1/8 and crazyhorse 1/9—the death machine ingests the names of native Americans the same way warriors used to eat hearts for courage—the code name for bin laden was Geronimo, before that bit of puerility was good and properly squelched—our new Geronimo, assange, instead of holed up in the chiruchua mountains is in a little room in London, protected by diplomatic protocol, not that such a thing did much good for say, iraq, to name one victim of the empire's bloodlust—speaking of iraq, it amazes me, truly it does, how cavalierly most citizens of the US treat the total destruction of a country as of no more consequence than swatting a fly—down the memory hole—are we a civilized people?—where is the modicum of independent thought and empathy that true civilization requires?—do we have knowledge of other cultures and people?—do we understand and respect the humanity of others?—do we have the courage and moral force to speak against the dictates of a corrupt author-

284

ity?—I am reading *Baghdad Burning*, a book containing the blog posts of riverbend, the pseudonym of a young woman living in Baghdad during the invasion and occupation of iraq by the united states—riverbend is our anne frank, speaking to a contemporary conscience, if there is one, about the holocaust that has befallen her country at the hands of the US—one of the hallmarks of a civilized people is tolerance for the beliefs and customs of others, which was, broadly speaking, a characteristic of Iraqi society before the US invasion, the good relations between sunni and shia for example—riverbend writes about this and I have heard it from other sources—her own family is both sunni and shia—it was this way all across the country—after the invasion and virtual total destruction of iraq (already crippled after the first US invasion in 1990 and subsequent sanctions, according to unicef directly responsible for the deaths of 500,000 children under the age of five: "worth it," intoned secretary of state Albright), in the anarchic and violent conditions that followed, society fell almost completely apart, the most depraved and extremist elements in the country coming to the fore—various sects and groups began battling each other, old antagonisms rekindled, exacerbated by the horrifying conditions created by the US invasion and occupation—as usual, much of the conflict was rooted in long-standing economic injustices, suffered particularly by the shia—the same thing happened in Yugoslavia after tito and the imposition of the economic rules of the new world order, drawn up by the international monetary fund and world bank and enforced by the US military—there's your new world order, the mafia as template—iraq, a civilized and developed country, fell into a hobbesian state, of the sort survivalists imagine happening in the US should conditions sufficiently deteriorate—this is the world riverbend describes, and indeed it doesn't take much to imagine it happening in the US, a society armed to the teeth and riven with deep class and group animosities—three-quarters of it has to do with economic conditions—people with full stomachs and secure lives don't make war on their neighbors—no doubt saddam hussein was a sociopath, but the total destruction of a society to "take out" one person?—and of course the bush administration's propaganda campaign about weapons of mass destruction was a bunch of evil nonsense—obviously it was about oil, as it usually is—if Ecuador can decimate its own environment and trample its indigenous population in the mad pursuit of oil, maybe the big dog is capable of destroying a country to gain control of the third largest reserves in the world—do you think?—I joke with my students that if they see a tall white-haired man walking down ladron de guevara not to get too close to him—how do you suppose the cia will deal with assange in Ecuador?—curare?—

Carlos

6/30

carlos is a *vendedor de libros usados* and a good friend, whose tables full of used books on veintimilla I first came across back in august as I was walking to work, stopping of course, as I always do when there are books to see—spotting me he jumped out of his plastic chair at the back of the sidewalk in the shade to hustle a sale, a short compact man with an honest, agreeable mestizo face—I didn't buy anything but I promised to return, though I could hardly not as his business is on my way to work, and I soon found myself stopping by regularly to talk with this warm and friendly man, or talk as best I could with my bad spanish, another reason for befriending him, an opportunity to speak the language—carlos sells with equal enthusiasm highbrow literature, old copies of reader's digest, sex manuals, anthropological treatises on indigenous Amazonian tribes, maps, cook books, fashion magazines, school books, children's books, romantic novels and much more, in short, anything he can get his hands on that might be of interest to the generally middle-class, educated professionals that stream past his tables every day—the physical quality of the merchandise ranges from almost new to the respectably shabby, the majority tending toward the latter—99% are in Spanish but I did find a paperback copy of Norman mailer's *existential errands* in English (how many of the old pug's works have been translated into Spanish?) that I snatched immediately—carlos is a peaceful, gentle-mannered fellow, happily in his second marriage, which has produced a teenaged boy, Pablo, about whom he has the usual worries—his wife's name is maria de Lourdes—he has two other children from a previous marriage, shaking his head at the recollection, not the kids but the marriage—we often commiserate on failed marriages—we also share a love of beautiful women and conversations usually come to a discreet halt when a nice ecuatoriana walks by—once a particularly striking, large, dark and wild-looking female walked out of the drug store behind his tables—noticing my expression, carlos said under his breath, "*Colombiana*"—I wondered how he could tell, but I didn't doubt him—our conversations tend to run in the same groove because of my limited Spanish—I love to rail against the US and he loves to hear it—I have become very good at this but run the risk of repeating myself (those who know me will roll their eyes), though he doesn't seem to tire of my fulminations concerning the vacuity, violence, materialism, greed, ignorance, class divisions, exceptionalism, etc. of US culture—carlos is a philosophical sort, very wise, and tries to cheer me up if I seem down at the mouth—I try to do the same for him, and lately, because of health problems, his and maria de lourdes's, I've been more active in this department—carlos devotes a lot of time to his business, up every morning at six, after breakfast and so forth taking the bus from his town, la merced (the mercy), located in the great valley of los chillos, east of quito—the ride takes about an hour and he usually sleeps, setting up around nine at his usual spot—he rents a storage space in the building behind him—I have heard, by the way, that if Cotopaxi has a major eruption the inhabitants of los chillos, about one million, could be threatened by the mud flow, smoke and ash—quito of course could be decimated by an earthquake, in fact most assuredly will be some day—I usually see carlos two or three times a week, getting to his spot around 11, where he invariably greets me with enthusiasm and a big smile—there is something very wonderful about this—it is not false or manufactured—I, not always the most demonstrative of souls, find myself reciprocating—there is something about this country that loosens the spirit—I am often free of the heaviness I feel in the US—i have yet to determine if it is the novelty or something more profound—I sometimes think of moving here—for one thing it's nice to be in a country that's not literally and figuratively bombing the rest of the world—I am so tired of the moral burden, as a citizen of the US—I am so disgusted with the united states of America—carlos invited anita and me last Sunday for lunch at his home in la merced—we went by bus and managed to find his house, tucked behind a larger one that he and maria de Lourdes take care of when the owner is gone—it was in the larger house we had lunch, along with another of his foreign friends, a swedish woman, who brought her family with her, a stereotypical bunch, blond and phlegmatic—maria de Lourdes, whom I'd met once before, was sweet and shy with all the *extranjeros*—carlos looked almost shockingly different in casual attire, with his white shorts, red pullover sweater y *sin gorra*, exposing his shiny pate—he was the attentive and slightly anxious host, talking nonstop, offering snacks before lunch and playing latin music on an old record player—he'd suggested I bring my bathing suit to swim in the pool in the big house but when I saw the very small pool and its algae-green water, I demurred—none of the other guests seemed interested either—for lunch we had *una comida típica*, potato chicken soup with a side dish of *canguil* (popcorn) and a main course of chicken with rice and a salad—two huge plastic bottles of Ecuadorian coca-cola were passed around, precipitating a lively discussion about what happens to a tooth if left in a glass of coke overnight—of course I never tried this, preferring, to save mine (already damaged by the imperial beverage and wrigley's and bazooka bubble gum) for the tooth fairy—after lunch I went upstairs to the "playroom" where there was a ping pong table, a foosball table and a pool table, all in a challenged state of repair—before leaving we played late-afternoon soccer in a postage stamp-sized bit of yard outside until anita, who is remarkably athletic and strong, kicked the ball over the wall into the next yard where there were two rottweilers—we took the bus back to quito and after saying goodbye to anita in the north I arrived on ecovia at la marin—it was dark and as I walked home was approached by a sketchy-looking young couple aggressively asking for money—I was nervous, but nothing came of it—you always need to watch your step around these parts—the next day I had a nice talk with carlos at his bookstand and he was very happy about the lunch and anxious to know if we'd had a good time—I assured him that we had—carlos is a good friend and I'll miss him when I leave—

Fritada

I am a creature of habit, perhaps more so with food than anything else, and I have my favorites here, especially the wondrous fritada, una *combinacion* de chancho frito (fried pork), papas (potatoes), maduros (ripe bananas), choclo y mote (different types of corn), and there is a place, ah, what a place, another delightful hole in the wall on veintimilla owned by a young family that does a bustling fritada business all days but Sundays, a place I do my best to avoid four days out of five before going to work, not always success-fully—I love to eat good food and on one of my return visits to cor-poreal form i will be filthy rich and dedicate my life to terminal gourmandise, an Anthony Bourdain gone to slobbering seed, weigh-ing four hundred pounds, flying around the world in my specially-equipped private jet accompanied by the BYU women's volleyball team in loincloth employed to carry me via palanquin from one ex-otic gourmet eatery to another until at the ripe and overstuffed age of 27 keel over with a smile on my greasy porcine face—if it weren't for this irritating strain of Puritan, hair shirt adelle davisism in-habiting a small portion of my brain I would eat fritada every day and never tire of it—I'd probably live five years longer with a diet of whole grains, nuts and raw vegetables, but I doubt I'd be hap-pier—it's a terrible thing but sometimes i think poor adelle got the worst of both worlds—healthy hair shirt food and a shorter life—I

remember the shock when she died, an aquarian icon almost mock-
ingly toppled over—you could hear the bankers at the four seasons laughing into their chateaubriand—ah, but this fritada!—first
of all, the place—there are a million of these charming family es-
tablishments in quito and I suppose everyone has a favorite—typically lunch is cheap in quito and I decided long ago to eat in these
sorts of restaurants before going to work—after passing this place
several times, attracted by the smells, the energy, the latin music
videos on the television, I went in, bad Spanish and all, somehow
without calamity managing to procure a dollar-fifty bowl of fritada
and for another 50 cents a cold, genuine coca-cola—it was love at
first bite—I was smitten, in secret glee at being in such a place, "la
sarita" (actually, a chain, there are others about, all good), reveling
in the delicious food, the colors (tables covered in bright yellow oil-
cloth), the music, the inimitable latin atmosphere—customers understand the quality of this place—here there is a seriousness of
countenance, a sublimity of expression, a relaxed happiness that can
only come with the secure appreciation of the fulfillment of such a
basic (delicious) human need—most, as I am now, are regulars: there
is no surprise or uncertainty: this is good stuff: they know it: they
are happy—and I am happy watching them as I eat from my own
(Styrofoam, a downer, Ecuador, the world, is choking in plastic)
bowl, each with his or her own style, always content, purposeful, a
lunch crowd, professionals, students, chatting away in the beautiful
tongue, cumbia blaring from the television, a cheerful place where
tables are shared, as is the custom in ecuador—I ask a fritada lover,
intently eating, if I can sit, "perdon, esta bien?"—"si, claro"—"gracias, buen provecho"—"gracias"—the bowl of fritada arrives and I
get down to business—subdued, private ecstacy—some while ago i
switched from coke to *orangine de mora*, a blackberry soda made by
an Ecuadorian company—there is also the original *orangine*, which
is orange—*orangine de mora* is very good and goes perfectly with the
fritada—I will order coke if there is no *orangine de mora*—I prefer
not to give my money to the imperialist company but give the devil

his due—real coca-cola is damn good—concerns for teeth and arteries hover in the dim background of consciousness, a muffled scold
pointing its bony finger—worry about it later—I never miss an opportunity to communicate, if the occasion is right: "buena fritada,
eh?" invariably a smile in return, "si, si, muy sabrosa"—most people eat pretty fast—students and lovers will tarry—I tend to eat
slowly, drawing out the experience—every bit of it is good—I shovel
a different ingredient on my plastic spoon each time, husbanding
the pork, extra delicious—papa, maduro, choclo/mote, cerdo—re-
peat—ecuadorians love salt and I am astonished at the amount they
put on their already salty fritada—fanta is a big favorite—some
glance at the music videos as they eat and so do i—up front facing
the sidewalk the women and one man, one of the owners, prepare
the food in an unrelenting, hectic, steaming rush of practiced activity, placing the hot, juicy ingredients in the bowls with their
latex gloves, the two owners, the man and his wife, he mestizo,
she kichwa, their baby resting in a stroller in the back, calling out
to passers-by: "choclo/mote, fritada!–choclo/mote, fritada!"—these
two, the owners, are exceptionally sweet and always greet me with
a warm smile—they work very hard, all of them do—let it be noted
also that *la sarita* is a good place for meeting women—something
about fritada—every so often I'll buy a couple of bowls to take out
and carlos and I will have lunch together—he'll usually buy two bottles of *orangine de mora* from the store next to his tables—one day
as we ate together I lost a bit of tooth on some mote—i spat it out
and kept on eating—somewhere on carlos's sidewalk is a piece of
me—concerning fritada, such are the hazards—

Violence, home

yesterday the subject of why there is so much violence in the united states came up—most of what the students said about the causes of this violence was accurate and sensible, offering reasons that ranged from a heavily armed populace, to the breakdown of community and family structure, to the psychological toll resulting from the struggle for survival in difficult economic times, to the rampant use of drugs, pharmaceutical or otherwise—a few mentioned the wide popularity and cultural acceptance of violent video games and entertainment—this made some of the students uneasy because they admitted to playing these games and watching, and enjoying, violent movies—they allowed as how it might be possible that this sort of entertainment could influence unstable people to act in violent ways, although there is scant history, indeed, none that I know of, of the kind of mass shootings in Ecuador that occur with metronomic regularity in the US—following class, some five hours later, a little after midnight in the US, james holmes broke into a theater in aurora, colorado during a showing of *The Dark Night Rises*, an extremely violent film, and killed 12 people, wounding 58 others—obviously there was much to talk about today—surprisingly, in this age of hyper information, a number of students didn't know about the shooting—in fact, neither did carlos until I told him about it this morning—this had the interesting effect of making me a little envious, that there are still some people in the world who are not glued to their computers or televisions obsessively devouring the latest catastrophes and apocalyptic rumblings, as I am sad to admit is too much the case with me, to no salutary health benefit whatsoever unless you make the argument that to be forewarned is to be forearmed, which i think valid, if not conducive to peace of mind—addressing my role as bearer of hard reality and apocalyptic tidings (under the rubric of "critical thinking," one of contemporary education's great buzzwords, in practice assiduously and systematically discouraged) my students in the US would sometimes exasperatedly ask, "richard, why are you telling us these things?"—my standard reply was that while ignorance may sometimes be bliss, it is not necessarily good for one's well being—wouldn't you want to know about the rattlesnake in your closet?—but, unhappy coincidence, to have examined the topic the day before and now to be immersed again in the nightmare reality—not such a freakish roll of the dice either as the odds are quite reasonable now that the classroom discussion and the bloody deed occur very much in the same relative time frame—it is so fucking normal—the attitude of my students toward all this was one of a certain sympathy for me as a citizen of the US and towards the victims, but also a sort of breezy remove bordering on smugness that such a thing would be virtually inconceivable in Ecuador—whether or not this is actually true is a good question—for me the cause of "random violence," while there are a number contributing factors, boils down to one tragic and horrifying thing: the diminution of the individual's sense of self-worth and belonging in a world becoming more and more anomic, commodified and authoritarian day by day—since I see Ecuador following this path, aping the western model, I am less sanguine than my students—they see the US as a fascinating yet frightening place—most have no desire to go there—not only is there the fear of the society itself, but also the fear of the society in its actions towards others, outside itself—this of course is part of the bloody historical record, in latin America a very long and detailed one—with his permission, I leave you with a student's essay—this student is a physics major and very bright, with an uncommon thoughtfulness and poetic sensibility—he related the violence in the US to its aggressive, militaristic foreign policy, especially the invasion of iraq—this is interesting because it offers a glimpse of how others perceive the US, in this case as a dangerous bully intent on getting its own way by terrorizing the rest of the world—I present the essay uncorrected—if only I could do as good a job writing in Spanish:

The war with Iraq is an example of USA violence. That war is the tare of a plan to conquist the world. USA always wants to control other countries. There is many ways to do that: economicly, ther politolicaly or with militar power. The Iraq War started in 2003. A lot of inocent people died for that reason. It's effect in the world is very heavy, because all of the countries in the world are scared and quiet. The nuclear bombs, the guns, the toxic gas, all of this things could become in the devil for us. The war means the total destruction of Iraq. It means the lose of the oil too. It still affecting the world because USA will do the same thing in South America. USA doesn't have natural resources. It will need air, water, trees and wildlife. Actually, with a new war all of our Amazon region could be of they. That is the reason for our union. If all South America works together USA won't do something like the Iraq War with us.

Dogs

one week to go—winding down this account without describing the dogs of my neighborhood would be a serious omission—few people in the world pamper their dogs as those in the US, but dogs as pets no doubt exist everywhere, as they certainly do in Ecuador—witness tommy, the family dog here, who has grown into a magnificent creature, handsome, noble, intelligent—but I am angry with his family because they hardly ever take him out for so much as a sniff of the outside world—99% of the time he is locked in the compound with nothing but his own shit to play with, which sometimes he literally eats, as dogs will do when they are bored or malnourished—this disgusts me—when I see this I bang loudly on the window, which deters him, but only for a moment—a young buck of a dog like that, any dog, needs to be out and running every day—stupid family—they goo and fawn all over him when they venture outside, and the girl, when she feels like it, will throw a ball for him to chase within the confines of the compound, but that's it—it's a form of abuse—when I leave the compound I'm fearful of letting him out but I sometimes wish someone else would inadvertently leave the door open for his escape—outside he would meet the neighborhood dogs that run in the street—these dogs are different—they are independent, for the most part without owners—for them symbiosis is an irrelevant notion, a game for suckers—what possible use

are humans?—certainly they are of no use to humans in terms of
protection, early warning systems or affection—but the dogs know
about the garbage piled on street corners every evening because this
is where they get their food—by early evening the bags are ripped
apart, garbage strewn everywhere, dogs of all stripes and dubious
pedigree with their mugs buried deep in the edible stuff, happily
chomping away—in this sense they need humans, or at least their
garbage—they are like the wolves at the edge of our ancestors' en-
campments, waiting for scraps or foraging through waste pits—I
am always a little amazed at the mess caused by the dogs but every
morning the corners are clean, with no trace of the filth from the
night before—because the streets are narrow the trucks come at
night as not to cause traffic jams—there are a couple of older people employed to sweep the streets early in the morning—you see
them with their little civic uniforms, cleaning up the leftovers with
their brooms and long-handled dust pans—some are old and some
seem slightly addled—but it is a good job for them—at least they are
working and making a little money—perhaps this is part of correa's
economic program—if so, it's a good thing—during the day the dogs
run in pairs or threesomes, doing whatever they want, totally free,
ignoring the people—they are never bored, I doubt they ever eat
their own shit—at best, people seem like creatures to be tolerated,
of use only for their garbage at night—unless there's rabies about,
which rarely happens, the dogs are no threat to humans—they regard bipeds with sublime, if slightly wary, indifference—of course
I always give them a wide berth—if there's a gathering on the sidewalk ahead I'll go around them—there's a curmudgeonly old fart
who hangs out at the house next to mine—he startled me one night
by barking, a warning that I was a little close—I look out for him,
and get out on the street if he's there—I am of two minds about the
garbage—more and more big plastic garbage bins are popping up
around quito, and if they were in my neighborhood things would be
much cleaner, but then, what would happen to the dogs' food supply?—a real dilemma there, because even if they serve no purpose in

the normal sense of the human/canine partnership, they add something vital to the life and character of the neighborhood—they are its wild spirit—tommy would be much happier among them—free tommy!

A not-so-modest proposal

8/3

anita and I have seen each other often since our dreamlike, sub-aquatic time together in San Plácido—she is good company, full of spirit and strong opinions, *muy latina*, and, perhaps to be expected, very catholic—she is moving fast and has announced that she will remain faithful to me for one year, which is more or less when I am contemplating a return—I love Ecuador and this is a very real possibility—but it is also clear that I am envisioned as a potential Lou Gehrig to her deceased husband's Wally Pipp, a classic gringo/latina combo where *el gringuito* brings home the bacon and *la latina* serves *el postre dulce* and keeps house—I have no illusions—ecuador is a very poor country and these are the realities—I am a prospect here as I have never been in my home country, as I have always been relatively poor and whatever redeeming qualities I may possess have been, judged by ordinary cultural standards, vitiated by my lack of financial resources—to be fair to my troubled country however, this is a human universality when it comes to the female "choosing" her partner—to quote durante again, these are the conditions that prevail—I am not bitter as these prevailing conditions are the result of the choices I have made, not ever wanting to participate in the mad and maddening pursuit of material "success"—but, as always, there is a price to be paid—the way I see it everyone's a debtor in this go-round, rich and poor alike—anyway, anita, this day, likely our last together, takes me to a small chapel inside *la iglesia de san Francisco* and, after praying, surrounded by gilded saints and filled with piety and quiet solemnity, more or less proposes marriage, and I, much to my surprise, am not entirely opposed to the idea—it can't be, I tell myself, but could it?—it is a wild and impossible notion, but, for the moment, I nurture the fantasy and allow it to nuzzle my wayward soul—

Leaving

8/7

opening up to new experiences may yield good, even wonderful, results, but you always run the risk of getting your ass kicked—I knew this before leaving for Ecuador, and I did get my ass kicked a few times, in unexpected ways, as is usually the case, but in general I've been lucky—my greatest fortune has been the assistance, guidance and friendship of the kind and resourceful Susana Hidalgo, *mi ángel de quito*, without whom things would have been exponentially more difficult—ecuador is a beautiful country, not without serious problems, which are of course the world's problems—there is no escaping the mess we're in, which presents conscious people with a number of profound dilemmas, not the least of which, for me, is my relationship with my own country—ecuador has been a real eye-opener—to have lived for one year in a culture completely different from where I have lived most of my life has been a profound experience, one that will reverberate in my soul for a long time—sad to say, but for me, and I know I am not alone in feeling this, the US has become an empty, soul-destroying nightmare, a culture and system run off the cliff a long time ago, the seeds of the catastrophe planted in the very beginnings of European conquest, erected on the evil pillars of genocide and slavery and advanced by a vanguard of fevered mercantile adventurers who stopped at nothing to achieve as much material conquest as humanly possible, spurred by a religious faith bizarrely twisted from its original intent and buttressed with a genius for technological invention—these first mercantile adventurers have grown into something truly monstrous, far outstripping in power and influence the high-minded governing principles (at least for the white, male, propertied class) upon which the republic was founded, so that now such once-revered principles are treated as so much quaint, barely audible gurgling—this has been especially true since 9/11 and continues unabated, with the incredible spectacle of a self-empowered executive branch deciding for itself, without a hint of due process, whom to assassinate, including its own citizens, at a time and place of its choosing—about this there is hardly a peep from the electorate—in fact a majority of those who are even aware of these new powers approve—it used to be smugly asserted that we were a nation of laws, and if that were ever the case it is most emphatically not true now—as some fascist dimwit in the bush administration once remarked, the world is different now, reality is created by the powerful, by us, get used to it, exactly the prevailing sentiment of all tyrannies, including the third reich—those with the power, weapons, money, technology make the rules and decide what is reality, the rest of us meekly submitting—so I am ambivalent about returning—I have always felt something of a misfit in my own country, the only world I have known—intellectually it is easy to see the crass idiocy of popular culture, the materialism, the brute, competitive violence of the system, the endless wars, etc., but viscerally, in weaker moments, I have more often than not felt that the fault was not in the country (what could be wrong with the USA?) but with my aberrant, unhappy self—but acknowledging my own very clear faults, shortcomings, hostilities, insecurities, the whole train of personal baggage that mixes with healthier characteristics to form a personality, a different perspective of my *self* has emerged now that I have lived in another culture for a year—I am still the same person, with all the same imperfections, but now I consider the possibility that perhaps at least some of my unhappiness and dissatisfaction lies not with some grievous assortment of personal shortcomings, but rather with the beast itself, in whose gastric juices I have been stewing for so many turbulent years—it is impossible to separate the two, the self and the culture—we are very much a product of that which has molded us, and that which has molded us is a sick thing and getting sicker—its sickness is our sickness—the most obvious example of this is racism—racism is part of our cultural fabric—we are not born as racists but are damaged by this ugliness from the time we are exposed, as children, in some cases by the attitudes of our parents, and always by attitudes of the larger society—we whites, even the most pure-hearted among us, face a lifelong struggle trying to expunge the sickness of racism from our souls—this is only one of the most obvious examples—take a million other attitudes, presuppositions and values pressed into a mind at the beginning of those squalling breaths and what you have is a product of a culture—we are a product of culture before we are a product of family—it is also the case, thank goodness, that cultures are different, sometimes vastly different, and if you accept what seems to me the obvious proposition that all human beings are essentially the same, then you see what a powerful thing culture is—by culture I mean the Petri dish of physical environment into which an enormous mix of elements is thrown, not the least of which, history, resulting in a society with a distinctive dynamic and flavor, a "culture"—as for the US, I love the land, the physical environment, still beautiful but terribly wounded and under assault, the music, art and literature, which is glorious, and the many wonderful people here, including my dear friends—most else that has grown in this environment is odious and harmful, and I reject it with every ounce of my being—i know this rejection marks me as someone outside, or as a foreign object within, and I know that a body struggles mightily to eliminate all foreign objects—the occupy wall street movement consisted of a collection of foreign objects within, and the larger body, the state, violently rid itself of them—the most notable example of a foreign object now is Bradley manning, and we see how ruthlessly the state endeavors to destroy him—more and more we are all becoming foreign objects within the body of our own country—we are all Bradley manning, though most, myself included, lack his courage—what ecuador has taught me is that perhaps I am not so strange after all, not such a misfit in this world—there are other ways of looking at things, other values to embrace, a multiplicity of styles and flavors, a place for everyone—I return to my country—for how long?

Acknowledgements

Many thanks to my readers, Alegre Bussetti, Joan Cere, Kathleen Christison, Diana Coryat, Robin DeLapp, Eric Garretson, Chuck Gasparovic, Claire Lissance, Betti Sachs, Martha Somerville, and Michael Ward, with special thanks to my son, Eland, for his technical help.

Richard Ward's work has appeared in the Apple Valley Review, Bosque, the Concho River Review, the Gettysburg Review, and the Southern Humanities Review. He is a frequent contributor to Counterpunch.org. His short story, *A Persistence of Memory*, was nominated for a Pushcart Prize, and "Best of the Net" for 2020. He divides his time between Ecuador and New Mexico. He can be reached at r.ward47@gmail.com.

Front cover: from "La Fragua de Vulcano," Guayaquil, by Víctor Ochoa

Back cover: figure, la procesión de Jesús del Gran Poder, Quito